BECOMING JFK

John F. Kennedy's
Early Path to Leadership

bancroft
press

SCOTT BADLER

Copyright: © 2025 Scott Badler—All rights reserved.
This book is an original publication of Bancroft Press.

No part of this book may be reproduced in any form or by electronic means, including information storage and retrieval systems, without written permission from the publisher, except by a reviewer, who may quote passages in a review. To request permissions, contact Bancroft Press at bruceb@bancroftpress.com.

Cover, Interior & Photo spread design: TracyCopesCreative.com
All photographs courtesy of the John F. Kennedy Presidential Library and Museum.
Specific image citations available upon request.
Author Photo: Mario Glaviano, Frame Story Studios

978-1-61088-676-5 (HC)
978-1-61088-677-2 (PB)
978-1-61088-678-9 (ebook)
978-1-61088-679-6 (PDF ebook)
978-1-61088-680-2 (audiobook)

bancroft
press

Published by Bancroft Press
"Books that Enlighten"
(818) 275-3061
4527 Glenwood Avenue
La Crescenta CA 91214
www.bancroftpress.com

PRINTED IN THE UNITED STATES OF AMERICA

OTHER JFK BOOKS BY SCOTT BADLER

JFK & THE MUCKERS OF CHOATE

A compelling exploration of John F. Kennedy's formative years at Choate, where he defied expectations and began his journey toward greatness.

PUBLISHER'S NOTE:

This is a work of narrative non-fiction. Every effort has been made to ensure the accuracy of the historical events, locations, and figures described in this book. Some dialogue and specific interactions have been recreated or imagined for the purpose of dramatization and narrative flow. These reconstructed conversations are based on historical research, contextual evidence, and the author's interpretation of the characters' personalities and known behaviors. The author has attempted to stay true to the known facts and spirit of the time while providing a compelling and engaging narrative. Any errors or inaccuracies are unintentional and the responsibility of the author.

*To the memory of my father, Jerry,
and my mother, Claire*

TABLE OF CONTENTS

List of Characters

Allan J. Lichtman Foreword

Part One: Second Son

Chapter 1 3
Chapter 2 13
Chapter 3 27
Chapter 4 33
Chapter 5 41
Chapter 6 45
Chapter 7 53
Chapter 8 73

Part Two: Ambassador's Son

Chapter 9 85
Chapter 10 89
Chapter 11 95
Chapter 12 101
Chapter 13 109
Chapter 14 115
Chapter 15 121
Chapter 16 127
Chapter 17 141
Chapter 18 151

Photo Insert

Part Three: Lover Boy

Chapter 19 167
Chapter 20 173
Chapter 21 189
Chapter 22 199
Chapter 23 213

Part Four: Skipper

Chapter 24 221
Chapter 25 225
Chapter 26 233
Chapter 27 245
Chapter 28 255
Chapter 29 265
Chapter 30 273
Chapter 31 281
Chapter 32 289

Part Five : Writer/Editor

Chapter 33 299
Chapter 34 311
Chapter 35 317
Chapter 36 325
Chapter 37 333

Part Six : Candidate

Chapter 38 349
Chapter 39 363
Summing Up 367

List of Locations
Source Notes
Bibliography
Index
Acknowledgments
About the Author

LIST OF CHARACTERS

A

Albert, Ray: one of Jack's PT-109 crew; rubbed people the wrong way; complained a lot

Arvad, Inga: introduced to Jack by Kick; honey-blonde, blue-eyed, statuesque, with full lips; perfect complexion accentuated by high cheekbones; only minor flaw was a gap between her two front teeth, which Jack liked; studied at Columbia Graduate School of Journalism; fluent in four languages; former Miss Denmark; unhappily married to Paul Fejos; trained with the Danish Royal Ballet; interviewed Hitler

B

Bennett, Constance: blonde, delicate, and known for her glamorous style; well-known actress; set up to play tennis with Jack during his first trip to Hollywood

Billings, Lem: sometimes called Lemmer; Jack's best friend; Jack's roommate at Choate and Princeton; stocky with a high-pitched laugh

Billingsley, Sherman: owner of the Stork Club; friends with Joe Sr

Biuku: one of the two native men who found Jack and the 109 crew stranded on the island

Blok, Nils: Danish; student at Columbia with Inga Arvad; Inga's secret lover while she was seeing Jack

Bohlen, Charles: second secretary at the United States Embassy in Russia

Brantingham, Hank: commander of Group B squadron on Rendova mission to stop Japanese destroyers; skipper of PT-159

C

Cannon, Frances: JFK love interest

Christiansen, Glen: Chief Petty Officer on Jack's gunboat

Cluster, Alvin: Jack's squadron commander

Curley, James Michael: Massachusetts governor, Congressman, and four-time mayor of Boston

D

Dexter, Sheriff Thomas A: officer who arrested Jack and Joe when a regatta party got out of hand

Dietrich, Marlene: Both Joe Kennedy Sr and Jack were paramours with the famous German actress

E

Eroni: one of the two native men qho found Jack and the crew stranded on the island

Evans, Reginald: scout watcher on Komu Island

F

Fejos, Paul: married to Inga Arvad; Hungarian filmmaker

Fish, Bert: sixty-four-year-old minister to Egypt; used a cane

Forrestal, James: Secretary of the Navy; takes Jack on a trip to see post-war Germany

G

Greiser, Arthur: thick, bald-headed; the Nazi President of the Senate in the Free City of Danzig

H

Harlow, Dick: Jack's Harvard football coach; fat, bald, had high blood pressure and a prodigious appetite

Harris, Bucky: twenty years old; gunner's mate on Jack's first PT 109 crew

Haverty, Oklahoma Pete: one-legged cowboy who worked on the Arizona ranch and competed in the rodeo

Havilland, Olivia De: famous British and American actress; met Jack at a cocktail party; refuses a date with Jack to go out with a frumpy, middle-aged writer named Ludwig Bemelmans

Heine, Sonja: Olympic skater Jack meets at the Stork Club; married to Yankees owner Dan Topping; has an affair with Jack

Heinz: one two German soldiers Jack picks up during his tour of Italy

Hersey, John: friend of Jack's; *author of * A Bell for Adano; wrote a story about Jack and the destroyer crash for The New Yorker

Hopper, Bruce: professor at Harvard; Jack's thesis advisor there; former World War I aviator and newspaper reporter

Horton, Rip: friend of JFK from Choate; roomed with Jack at Princetin; serious-minded personality

I

Iles, Johnny: Jack's hut mate at Tulagi

Imhoff, Susan: Jack's first conquest at Stanford

J

James, Henry: grad student Jack met at Stanford; became friends and went to football games together

Johann: one of two German soldiers Jack picks up on his tour of Italy

K

Kennedy, Bobby: eight years old at the beginning of the book; painfully shy with strangers, but not at home

Kennedy, Eunice: thirteen years old at the beginning of the book; sister of Jack and Joe; wiry and resolute; looked out for Rosemary; skilled sailor and excellent tennis player

Kennedy, Jack: main character; aka JFK; reddish brown hair; six feet tall; suffered with health problems throughout his life; had many relationships, mostly short and focused on sex; skipper of the PT-109

Kennedy, Jean: seven years old at the start of the book; sister to Jack and Joe Jr

Kennedy, Joseph Jr: black hair; broader than Jack; oldest of the Kennedy sons; favored by Joe Sr; killed in action during WWII

Kennedy, Joseph Sr.: aka Joe Sr; called JP by Joe Jr and Jack; father of Joe and Jack and the rest of the Kennedy brood

Kennedy, Kathleen: fifteen years old at the beginning of the book; called Kick;

high-spirited, charming, and athletic; her rebellious personality matched Jack's

Kennedy, Patricia: eleven years old at the start of the book

Kennedy, Rose: married to Joe Sr; mother to Jack and Joe; never named in book, only addressed as Mother

Kennedy, Rosemary: oldest of the sisters; suffered from an unnamed mental disability; had a lobotomy at age 23

Kennedy, Teddy: three years old at the beginning of the book; ninth sibling of Jack and Joe

Kernell, Joe: one of the PT skippers

Kiley, Jean: crew member on rival boat at Edgartown Regatta

Kirk, Alex: American chargé d'affaires in Berlin

Kirksey, Andrew Jackson: Torpedoeman on Jack's PT-109 crew; protruding ears; deeply affected by the floatplane attacks on the 109

Krock, Arthur: New York Times Pulitzer-Prize-winning columnist; Joe Sr's ghostwrite; assisted Jack on book about why England didn't re-arm

L

Lani: young Melanesian boy who became friends with Jack, Johnny, Lennie; infectious and playful manner

Lannan, Pat: blue-eyed and solidly built; in Arizona recouping from a bronchial ailment; becomes friends with Jack

Larson, Bryant: skipper of PT-109 before JFK

Laski, Joseph: professor at the London School of Economics

Liebenow, Bud: twenty-three years old; youngest skipper in the fleet; distinguished himself in previous operations; roommates with Jack at Rendova; knew Jack from Melville

Lowrey, John: skipper of PT-162 ; one of the four boats on the Rendova destroyer mission

M

MacMurray, John: U.S. ambassador to Turkey

Maguire, John: radioman on Jack's PT-109 crew

Marie: pretty eighteen-year-old; hired to help Jack type his thesis

Marney, William: gunner's mate on the PT-109; died in the crash with the Japanese destroyer

Mauer, Edman: seaman on Jack's PT-109 crew

McDonald, Torbert: nickname Torby; Jack's friend from Harvard; also played football

McMahon, Pappy: oldest member of Jack's PT-109 crew

Mitford, Unity: part of the declining British aristocracy who fawned over Hitler

Moore, Eddie: assistant to the senior Kennedy

N

Niesen, Gertrude: sultry torch singer; age twenty-six when Jack persuaded her to perform for the Harvard freshman smoker

P

Patterson, Eleanor "Cissy": colorful publisher for the Washington Times-Herald; Jack met her through his sister Kick

Pell, Claiborne: an acquaintance of Jack from Princeton; heir to the Lorillard tobacco fortune; future U.S. senator

Powers, Dave: Democrat who helped Jack win his first political campaign for Congress

Price, Harriet: nickname was Flip; met Jack at Lake Lagunita; from Little Rock; one of few young women to refuse Jack's advances

Pritchett, Flo: attractive fashion editor of the New York Journal-American

R

Rosen, Fred: Jewish; friend of Jack's from the navy in Charleston

Ross, Barney: ensign; knew Jack from Melville; stationed together at Tulagi in the Solomon Islands; executive officer on PT-166; joined Jack on the Rendova destroyer mission

S

Shawn, William: assistant editor at The New Yorker

Skipper: appointed by Joe Sr to spy on Joe Jr and Jack; tall, slender guy who walked like he had a stick up his rear

Spalding, Chuck: friend of Jack's from Hyannis Port; author of Love at First Flight

Speiden, Jack: owner of the ranch in Arizona; dark-haired, brawny; fought in the Great War; former Wall Street stockbroker who had the foresight to invest in land during the Depression

Stack, Robert: twenty years old; actor Jack met on a trip to LA; an avid sportsman, owned two world records in skeet shooting, and had taken drama classes at Bridgewater State in Massachusetts

T

Taylor, Dr George: Jack's doctor at the Mayo Clinic

Thom, Leonard: Jack's hutmate at Tulagi; Jack called him Lennie

W

Warfield, Thomas: Lieutenant Commander; Jack's boss at Rendova; not liked by the men because they didn't agree with his war strategy

White, Byron: Rhodes scholar Jack met at the embassy in England; former all-American halfback who finished second in the balloting for the country's best college player; burly and lantern-jawed; nicknamed Whizzer because he whizzed by defenders; accompanied Jack and Torby on their trip to Europe

Wilde, Jim: nicknamed Smoky or Smoke; Jack's former Choate classmate who accompanied him to the ranch in Arizona

Wilson, Patricia: Joe's former mistress; sleeps with Jack after Joe's death

Z

Zinser, Gerard: motormac; only career navy man on the PT-109

FOREWORD

Why do we need another book about John F. Kennedy? This question is legitimate, and the answer lies in the wealth of insights and enjoyment that can be gleaned from an exploration of Kennedy's early life. That is how he became JFK. Scott Badler, the author of *Becoming JFK,* artfully intertwines historical facts with imaginative reconstructions of events and dialogue, illuminating the key experiences that shaped Kennedy's formative years.

His learning to navigate the unpredictable challenges of sailing taught him coolness under pressure. Kennedy's academic pursuits at Harvard, culminating in his senior thesis, *Appeasement at Munich: The Inevitable Result of the Slowness of Conversion of the British Democracy from a Disarmament to a Rearmament Policy*, later published as *Why England Slept*, deepened his understanding of the challenges and responsibilities of democratic leaders. His travels across Europe exposed him to diverse cultures and ideas. During World War II, his heroics showcased his dedication to those under his command, highlighting the gravity of his life-and-death decisions. His narrow escape from a wrecked PT boat and rescue of his crew during wartime contributed to his awareness of the fine line between life and death, success and failure.

Badler illustrates that Kennedy's journey was neither smooth nor untroubled. He faced the daunting task of overcoming an overbearing father and stepping out from the shadow of his older brother, Joe Jr., who was killed in action on August 12, 1944, while piloting a bombing mission. Kennedy grappled with self-doubt, insecurities, chronic health issues, and a penchant for womanizing that persisted throughout his presidency. Yet, Badler argues that these extraordinary talents and evident flaws made him "relatable to those around him, and later to a nation (p. 369). His early life experiences instilled in him, as Badler notes, the ability "to learn from his experiences and to grow in the face of adversity." (p. 370)

This blend of pragmatic courage and adaptability became a guiding force during his presidency. Kennedy took responsibility for the disastrous Bay of Pigs invasion in 1961, learning the hard way not to rely on the so-called experts, whose poor advice he later disregarded during the Cuban Missile Crisis of 1962. That crisis, which brought the world to the brink of conflict, prompted him to enhance efforts to reduce superpower tensions through arms control agreements. Repeatedly, he demonstrated an ability to evolve and adapt in his role.

Badler has a sharp eye for detail and a novelist's skill for dramatic, compelling narrative. His writing is crisp, clear, and readily accessible to a general audience. With license for his imaginative reconstructions, Badler provides an intimate and deeply human portrait of a flawed yet ultimately transformational president in just a thousand days of an incomplete term. He navigated some of the most perilous crises of the Cold War, committed the United States to arms control, and sought to ease international tensions. Furthermore, he set the nation on a path toward ending segregation and combating racial discrimination. To this day, many Americans believe that the latter years of the twentieth century would have unfolded more favorably for both the nation and the world had Kennedy survived.

Kennedy's story underscores an enduring truth about leadership: even those with profound flaws can grow into roles of immense responsibility. In an era of unprecedented public scrutiny of leaders' personal lives, *Becoming JFK* vivdly reminds us that imperfection does not preclude greatness and service to the people of America.

—Allan J. Lichtman, Distinguished Professor of History at American University, Presidential Historian, and Author of *The Keys to the White House*

PART ONE
SECOND SON

Chapter 1
July 1935

With his hands on his hips, Joe Kennedy Sr. loomed over his two oldest sons on the dock at the Hyannis Port Yacht Club. Joe Jr. and Jack were preparing their sloop for the Edgartown Regatta races held on Martha's Vineyard. "I'll treat you guys to a party after the races, but I won't pay for a bunch of waiters or extra help," said the father, the sun glinting off his tortoise shell glasses. "You get the food and drinks there on your own." He paused. "And behave yourselves. Don't do anything I wouldn't do."

The twenty-five-foot single-masted sloop was a family sailboat, but nobody had taken to her like Jack. With her hull of gold and sides painted blue, the *Victura* put Jack in mind of adventure on the open seas, of possibilities to come. Over his mother's objections, Jack kept her cotton sail in his bedroom at home. He'd named the sloop *Victura* because the term suggested victory—in Latin, it translated to "about to conquer." That's exactly what Joe Sr. demanded of all his children—winning.

Don't do anything I wouldn't do. Jack had seen his father with women who weren't Jack's mother and had heard gossip about potentially nefarious ways his father built the family fortune. He wondered where Joe Sr. would draw the line.

Joe Sr. clearly directed most of his attention at his oldest son. "It's Joseph's twentieth birthday! As of today, you're no longer a boy. You're a man—make sure to act like one. You're in charge over there."

For several minutes, their father extolled Joe Jr.'s promise and talent while Jack mindlessly tapped his fingers on the railing. Jack would have to wait his turn—if he was going to get consideration.

"I'm expecting a lot more from you from now on," the father

continued. "I know you won't let me down, Joseph."

"You can bet I won't, Dad," Joe Jr. replied, smiling.

Jack knew his father didn't have the same faith in him. Only a few months earlier, he'd warned Jack, "Don't make me lose confidence in you again because you'll find it nearly impossible to restore it." It had felt like his father was about to set him adrift like a boat without sails or a rudder.

Joe Sr. turned to his younger son, hesitating as though unsure of what to say. "Congratulations to Jack for graduating and winning the 'Most Likely to Succeed' award. Good way to leave Choate. I hope that is a sign of good things to come. Before that, we both knew you weren't doing a goddamn thing at school."

Joe snickered.

Pointing his finger at Jack, his father added, "Now it's up to you to succeed."

Jack had decided to campaign for that particular class award with no idea what he might succeed in, how, or when. And his father was right. He hadn't achieved much in his four years at Choate, aside from forming the Muckers Club and spearheading the upheaval that led to his temporary expulsion and that of his friends. Jack wanted to leave the school having accomplished something. He'd considered vying for other awards like "Most Influential" or "Most Respected" and even thought about a gag award—"Class Caveman"—but made his final selection for one reason: He wanted to prove to the headmaster and his housemaster that he wasn't a total screw-up. That he might do something with his life. Campaigning hard, Jack had enlisted his school friends to help. They agreed to vote for a candidate seeking a different award, on the condition that the guy on the other side of the deal would vote for Jack. Jack ended up winning easily.

"Have fun before school starts . . . at Harvard," his father had told him.

Although he'd gotten his acceptance letter from the school a few days before, Jack still hadn't decided whether to join his Choate friends, Lem Billings and Rip Horton, at Princeton or succumb to pressure and follow his father and Joe to Harvard.

Joe Sr. began to walk away, but after a few steps, he stopped and turned around to face his sons. He fixed a stare at them. "One more thing: Make sure you win."

That was the Kennedy creed—second place was for losers. Whether it was a touch football game, a sailboat race, or a school election, winning was the only option. And Jack bought in—only a month prior, he'd ordered a heavy-set crewman into chilly waters because his onboard weight was slowing them down. But when he didn't win, his father tore into him. "What happened out there?" he snarled after Jack lost the local race. He didn't wait for an answer. "Do better next time. Win."

The Kennedy patriarch's competitiveness was borne of an us-against-them mentality. He had suffered the indignities of anti-Catholic prejudice at Harvard, where they'd ignored his efforts to win entry into the school's version of fraternity clubs. Those slights, and others, spurred his drive for success. He'd become the youngest bank president in Massachusetts history and competed successfully to amass a fortune. There were rumors he had been a bootlegger during Prohibition, but the accusation was unfounded. Actually, he'd invested wisely in stocks, commodities, real estate, and movie studios. Still, after he bought a summer home south of Boston, he was denied entry to the Cohasset Golf Club, based not on those reasons, but on his religion.

"Got our orders." Joe Jr. laughed, took the helm, and placed his hand on the tiller. "Let's get going," he said, directing Jack to cast off.

After Jack hauled the docking line in, they embarked on the sixteen-and-a-half nautical mile trip from Hyannis Port across Nantucket Sound

BECOMING JFK

to Martha's Vineyard. As they pushed off, Jack inhaled the salty air and felt a familiar warmth radiating through his body. Rejoicing in a period of good health and freedom from the shackles of Choate, he hadn't felt so liberated in a long time.

The Regatta was both the high point of the Cape Cod sailing season and the premier social event of the area's sailing season. Thousands of spectators invaded the island to watch nearly two hundred boats compete. They also enjoy the local beaches and nightlife.

Jack snatched a glance at his brother, his black hair a contrast to Jack's reddish brown. No doubt Joe was the family favorite and the apple of his father's eye, but perhaps events of the last several months had changed the dynamic a half turn. Much broader than Jack, Joe had always dwarfed Jack physically, and only a year before, Joe had towered over him. But when they'd stood for a family picture, Jack was pleasantly surprised to discover he was now a half-inch taller at six feet.

Jack and his brother were friendly but fierce competitors with each other. Preparing for a typically intense Kennedy touch football game, Jack waited for Joe to choose his team—then he stepped over to the other side. Once the game began, the brothers sought any chance to body-slam the other, even wrestling each other to the ground between plays. They were egged on by their father, who wanted to bring out the best in them. Jack smiled at the recent memory of beating Joe in a sailing race. He'd had to overcome a broken tiller and mainsail malfunction to nip Joe at the finish line.

Now, Jack viewed Joe from a different angle. He wondered if Joe saw him with a different perspective. Still, Jack understood that, for now, Joe was in charge.

"Hop to it," Joe ordered, pointing to the sail.

Jack let out sail and the sloop surged. Joe maneuvered the *Victura* into the open sea, and the hair on Jack's neck tingled. That always happened during the first few moments of the sloop's initial rush forward. There was no place Jack would rather be than the open water. He exulted in the sport's freedom and physical challenge, and the mental acuity required to adjust to changing conditions.

The Edgartown Harbor was packed with ships and sails of all sizes. They ranged from the smaller Cape Cod Knockabouts and Wianno Seniors like their own, to the larger dories, ketches, yawls, and schooners. Past the boats, the Edgartown Yacht Club's slanted thatched roof jutted out thirty feet from land to wharf.

The brothers gave each other a smile of appreciation at the sight. But the good feeling ended as they approached the dock. Jack spied a familiar and unwelcome figure sporting a worn captain's hat. *Skipper.* "Oh no," said Jack. "Not him."

"What the hell is he doing here?" said Joe, shaking his head. "JP says I'm a man, but he sends this guy to spy on me." The brothers typically used their father's initials when talking among themselves.

Their father had hired the man to oversee the younger kids during the summer in Hyannis Port, but Jack never expected to see him here. A regular Cape Codder, Jack had taken an immediate dislike to the tall, slender guy who walked like he had a stick up his rear.

"I'll be watching you this weekend," Skipper warned the boys after they docked. "Especially you," he said, pointing at Jack. "Not going to let you get away with anything." He spat into the water.

"Ah, why don't you stand in front of a mirror and watch yourself?" Jack said, scowling.

"C'mon, Jack," said Joe. "Let's go."

Brushing past Skipper, they walked the short distance to their lodging and checked in at the expansive, multi-level, Old English-style hotel.

BECOMING JFK

Jack surveyed the competition while preparing the *Victura* for their 1:55 p.m. start. They were entered in two Wianno Senior Second Division events, each one a circular race of six and three-eighths miles.

The harbor was alive with activity as eighteen crews selected sails, ran lines, and stowed gear in preparation for the day's first race. Crowds of people packed the wharf, ready to make a day of the races. Sailing conditions were good. Winds were steady but not overbearing.

Jack and Joe had done well over the years at the local races around Cape Cod. In fact, they'd won so often people complained. But this was their first time competing at the Edgartown Regatta, which drew more serious, expert sailors. The competition was stiffer here, sometimes for reasons that weren't entirely fair. For example, some of the contestants hired skippers and professionals—sailing instructors and others in the maritime trade—to provide expert tactical advice during the races. Often, they did everything but touch the helm. And a few did that as well, skirting the rules. Jack watched with disgust as the skippers set the sails and cast off the mooring.

"Will you look at this?" Jack said, as launches delivered the owners to their sloops. He was close enough to see several dressed in silk frocks as they climbed aboard and set themselves down on canvas-covered camp chairs. They placed their white gloves—not their bare hands—on the tillers. After the race, they'd step back into the waiting launches and be taken back to shore. Bunch of crumbs, thought Jack.

"That's all right," said Joe. "More fun for us when we beat them."

Jack was feeling supremely confident. In the last couple of months, he'd tasted success. He'd graduated—even if it was sixty-fourth in a class of 112—won a school election, and his health was good. Jack had spent the better part of the prior summer at the Mayo Clinic in a vain attempt to determine the source of his gut pain, and he'd been told he set the record for most days in the infirmary at Choate. We're going to win, he said to himself. He was sure of it.

Boom! went the gun, and the *Victura* got off to a quick start, flying with the wind. Jack and Joe worked smoothly together, exchanging brief physical gestures and oral commands as they made tactical adjustments. Jack felt the familiar joy and exhilaration of commanding the sloop. Sailing windward, he had the *Victura* neck and neck with five others fighting for the lead.

Suddenly, they were battling a strong headwind. A wave hit the side and splashed over the edge, causing salt water to slap Jack in the face. "Hard alee!" he shouted. "We're flapping!"

Joe responded quickly to move the sail to the protected side, and the *Victura* regained momentum.

Leads were exchanged as the race entered the final downwind stage. The *Victura* fell back to third, then surged to first, heading for the final marker. But the Kiley family's *El Cid* had stolen the *Victura*'s wind and was within several boat lengths. The elder Kiley was at the helm, his daughter Jean crewing.

Trying to defend his lead from the *El Cid*'s attempt to go below and get the inside overlap, Jack yelled, "Pull in the mainsail!" But Joe was slow to act. The *El Cid* was about to secure the inside track—and the right of way. Jack decided he wouldn't budge. The *Victura* smacked the *El Cid* as the boats rounded the marker. The *Victura* was thrown off course and cradled. The *El Cid* surged ahead, but the *Cave Canum* took advantage of the collision and swept to the lead. Adding to Jack and Joe's frustration, the *El Cid* finished ahead of the *Victura* by one second at 3:20:54.

After the race, the elder Kiley stormed over. "I'll be lodging a protest for what you did. You deliberately threw us off and cost us the race."

"You got it all wrong," retorted Joe, shaking his fist. Joe was quick to anger and a poor loser.

Jack wondered if Joe was going to duke it out with Kiley. As he stood behind his brother, he could see Joe's neck turning red. Jack had often felt the physical brunt of his brother's temper.

"You were in *our* way!" Joe screamed.

"We'll be giving the race committee the facts about what happened and let them decide," said Kiley. "But tomorrow the *El Cid* comes in first." He laughed scornfully. "Don't expect you Kennedys to be within shouting distance of us then, so I'll say goodbye now."

If second place was for losers, according to their father, then finishing third was a complete waste of time.

Joe said, "Pappy ain't going to be happy. Can't let that happen again, Jack."

Was Joe hinting that he was to blame for the third-place finish? Joe had a habit of blaming others for his failures. Silently, Jack took in the rigging and Joe packed things away. Jack was disappointed with the results, especially since a victory had been in their grasp.

On Saturday, the final day of the regatta, Joe again took the helm. The winds were fierce, and the *Victura* struggled against the choppy seas. When they crossed the finish line, Jack and Joe exchanged disconsolate expressions. Never in contention, the *Victura* finished eighth, two places behind the *El Cid*.

Jack's shoulders drooped as he shuffled off the boat. Not only had he not met his own expectations—winning at least one of the races—but Jack knew he and Joe would soon feel the wrath of their father. They had lost. That was unacceptable. JP didn't accept excuses. Well, at least they had some time before they faced his disgruntlement. The upcoming party would help them forget what lay ahead when they got back.

Jack's mood lifted when, on the landing, he saw a captivating brunette he'd met at a pre-regatta social. She waved and broke away from her friends to greet Joe and then Jack with warm embraces as they exited the dock area. She greeted Jack with a friendly kiss on the cheek and added in a whisper, "Looking forward to seeing you later at the party."

Chapter 2

People came to the Vineyard to get away from their everyday lives, and a party provided the perfect escape. Having shed their beach and sailing clothes, women arrived in floral, cape sleeve dresses, and men in herringbone linen and striped gabardine suits. Some donned commodore hats. Jack wore a seersucker suit and sported a white and black captain's hat as he greeted the party's arriving guests.

He danced confidently with several women, using moves from the Lindy Hop—steps he'd only recently learned. After a few dances, Jack went to grab a bite. He and Joe had spent the afternoon hauling massive quantities of food and hooch to the banquet room. As he reached for a chicken liver in a bacon blanket, Jack bumped into somebody.

"Nice party, Jack."

"Thanks," he said, not recognizing the speaker. He glanced up from the spread and did a double-take. It was Jean Kiley. In grubby sailing clothes, Kiley wasn't worth a second look. But now, in a flowered dress and lipstick, she was one of the more attractive women in the room.

"Was just about to stuff my face," said Jack. "You Kileys are always in the way."

"Yeah," Jean retorted, "and you Kennedys always think you have the right of way!"

"And I have it now!" Jack said, leading her to the dance floor. "C'mon, let's see what kind of moves you have on land."

They fox-trotted and Lindy-hopped to "Honeysuckle Rose" and "We're in the Money." Jack made his move—since he hadn't beaten her out on the water, a tryst would soften the defeat. He draped his arm around her waist, letting it linger and pulling her closer.

BECOMING JFK

"Better luck next year, Jack," Jean said, excusing herself.

Jack shrugged and snacked on a piece of mushroom toast. He surveyed the room and was pleased to see the dance floor packed. Others, drinks in hand, engaged in lively, energetic conversations. Jack bounced on his toes, elated that the party was a rousing success. Best of all, nobody was going to put a damper on his spirits. Earlier that day, Jack and Joe, hoping to avoid interference, had declared within Skipper's earshot their plans to go to the movies that night. Their father had housed them in a cheap hotel.

Jack spotted his brother and walked over. "Helluva party!" he shouted above the roar.

"Yeah, nobody can say the Kennedy boys don't throw a great bash," Joe said.

Smash.

Behind them, a wine glass hit the floor. Joe shrugged, kicked the glass into a corner, and walked away.

Jack's attention was diverted by the sight of a beautiful brunette coming straight for him, her hips thrust forward. She was striking in a floral cinched dress. At the dock earlier in the day, she wore nondescript beachwear; now she was glammed up, her hair in a French twist accented by a flower pinned behind her ear.

"You made it," Jack said.

"Not yet," the young woman said, winking.

"Let's get you out on the dance floor." Jack took her hand, anxious to feel her body.

She was quite the dancer, though not as smooth as Olive, his first steady at Choate, but more physical. She leaned into his caress so that her breasts were pressed against his chest. Very unlike Olive, who always backed away from his advances.

Emboldened after a few dances, Jack said, "Would you like to see my trophy? It's upstairs in my room."

"But I don't remember you winning any races here," she bantered.

"Who said anything about sailing trophies?"

Jack grabbed the young woman's hand and led her out of the room. The party had expanded to the lobby, which was now jammed with exuberant partygoers shouting and singing. Jack glimpsed people outside, drinks in hand, crowded together on the front door landing. Below them, more guests packed the steps.

Jack led his new companion up the stairs to his room. Closing the door, he turned to face her.

"Where's the trophy, Jack?" she teased, stroking her hair. "Don't tell me you brought me up here under false pretenses."

"For the time being, consider me your trophy," he said, putting his hands on her waist and leaning her against the door as they kissed.

Enveloped in her embrace, Jack felt a surge of desire, his body responding instinctively to her warmth. The thought crept into his mind—could this night offer more than companionship? He was growing weary of the transactional nature of his recent encounters, craving something deeper, more meaningful.

While still kissing her, Jack became vaguely aware of the mounting noise level downstairs. Especially loud voices and an unusual commotion from the party seemed closer than the banquet room they'd left moments ago. Then was heard another crash of some kind. Did something else break? Trouble? Somebody was playing the piano, and the crowd was joining in on the chorus. What was that song? Could it really be "On the Good Ship Lollipop?" Were they really singing that Shirley Temple tune?

Jack cocked his head toward the door. Several more instances of glass smashing. He pulled away from his new friend.

BECOMING JFK

"Sorry," he said, reluctantly removing his hands from her waist. "I should probably see what all the ruckus is about."

He walked to the top of the steps. The sun had nearly set. From the windows, a dark glow washed over the dim lobby. He was shocked to see the crowd had doubled, and with it the noise. New people had joined in the revelry—most of them Jack didn't recognize. Dressed in work shirts and dungarees, they were clearly party-crashers.

The sudden drop in the outdoor night temperature had sent everybody scurrying inside. The lobby had become impossibly full. Atop the piano, two women, stripped to their girdles, flanked a guy conducting partygoers in song. Broken glass and empty bottles littered the floor. Discarded plates were strewn on tables, couches, and the floor, and chairs were overturned. In just a few minutes, the lobby had become a pulsing mob.

Jack saw the hotel owner plant himself in Joe's face, gesturing wildly with his hands, but Joe just smirked.

Then Jack's attention was diverted to a man waving his hands wildly, his belly spilling out from his unbuttoned shirt.

"Somebody bring me a drink!" the man shouted, knocking over a lamp, which shattered on the floor. He locked eyes with Jack. "Hey, buddy! Catch!"

He tossed his empty glass in Jack's direction. Jack caught it, priding himself on his quick reflexes.

"Hey," Jack said, steering the man to a corner of the room, "might be a good idea to tone things down." The man's eyes were bloodshot and glassy, his face sopping with sweat. "The owner has a bug up his ass. Warned me he'll call the police if things don't calm down. We don't want that, right?"

The guy sneered and pushed Jack away. "Asshole got a bug up his arse . . . and probly shumething more," he slurred. "All right, no problem." He put his hands on Jack's shoulders in an attempt to steady himself. "I'll behave." He winked at Jack and marched back to the center of the party.

Jack spied Joe holding court with two women. Then Joe stumbled, spilling his drink. Joe was obviously drunk. Jack had never seen him inebriated, but Joe had told him he frequented the Harvard Square pubs by campus. Not acting very presidential, Jack thought.

"Joe," Jack said, grabbing his arm, "what did the owner say to you?"

"Relax," Joe said, putting his hand on Jack's shoulder. "Don't worry about him. Said something about calling the cops. Bluffing. I can tell." He turned away.

Jack didn't think the owner was bluffing, but it was Joe's call, wasn't it? Their father had put him in charge. Anyway, they'd been given permission to throw an all-out party. JP had said to have a blowout on his dime. Well, this was definitely a blowout. And Jack didn't want to shut down the party. He was making time with a very attractive young woman and was willing to take the chance that nothing serious would happen at the party. Take the risk. Even if the police came, they'd probably just quiet things down.

Jack was headed back toward the staircase when he heard, "Look out!" He turned to see a table lamp tip, then crash to the floor in an explosion of shards scattering in a wide arc.

Someone nudged him from behind, and he came face-to-face with an irritated, bleary-eyed man. "Whose party is this anyway?"

"I don't know," Jack replied. It didn't seem to be their party anymore.

Two party-crashers engaged themselves in a shoving match. A heavy-set guy sat on a chair, which collapsed under his weight.

The din was pierced by the sound of a siren.

Cops.

BECOMING JFK

A blue-uniformed, mustachioed policeman who looked to be about their father's age entered the lobby.

Oblivious, the drunk kept his back to the cop and to the hotel owner. When the lawman tapped him on the back, everyone in the lobby fell silent.

"Why's everbody so goddamn quiet? Sing!" When he turned around to see the policeman, he mocked, "Nice costume, Officer."

"Party's over," the officer said. "Go home."

"I want to press charges." the hotel owner said, waving his hand at the damage. "Look at all this. Look what they did to my hotel!"

"Who's responsible for this party?" the cop demanded.

"They are," the hotel owner said, pointing at Jack and Joe. "Those guys."

"How old are you?" the cop said, staring at Joe.

"My birthday was Thursday," Joe said, grinning. "I'm twenty."

"Happy birthday. What about you?" The cop pointed his finger at Jack.

Why was the cop asking their ages? It made Jack uneasy. "I'm eighteen."

"That makes it simple. You're both of age and you're both liable. What that means is this is all your fault. Public disturbance. Vandalism. You're coming with me."

Jack's thoughts became jumbled. *Liable for what? How come Joe and I are getting the blame for what others did? That's nuts. Where are they taking us? Police station? Probably just write us a ticket.*

But then the lawman took out his cuffs and ordered the Kennedy boys to put their hands behind their backs. He shackled them both. First Joe, and then Jack.

The cuffs were heavy and the metal cold. How could this be

happening to him?

Jack felt the eyes of the crowd on him. He stared at his shoes. A common lawbreaker. Only a few minutes earlier, he had been their charming host.

The cop pushed the two of them outside.

"But we didn't do anything," Jack protested. Other people had made all the noise, broken hotel items, damaged furniture. Not them.

The cop shoved them into the back seat and gunned the cruiser. As they pulled away, Jack caught a glimpse of Skipper, sneering happily. Jack glanced at Joe, who was smirking behind a curled lip. It was just a joke to him.

The ride lasted all of a minute. One right turn and they had arrived.

Oh. This place. Jack had passed it several times. It was on Main Street, just a few blocks from the Edgartown Yacht Club. The police headquarters was in a fine-looking, two-level clapboard house encircled by a white picket fence.

Once inside, the cop directed the boys to an office. A name plate on the desk read: "Sheriff Thomas A. Dexter."

"Sit down," the sheriff said, pointing to two chairs. "Give me your full name and address." The sheriff snorted as he jotted down the information on two separate cards.

Now what? Jack expected a stern warning, some sort of promise to pay for the damages, and then to be released.

"My father is Joseph P. Kennedy," mumbled Joe. "He's chairman of the Exchange and Insecurity Commission." Hearing no response, Joe continued, falteringly. "You know, the SEC. In Roosevelt's administration."

"I could care less. Welcome to Martha's Vineyard. And the Dukes County Jail."

Sheriff Dexter removed their handcuffs and guided them to a door

BECOMING JFK

that led to a hallway lined with cells. Looking to his left, Jack caught a whiff of urine and glimpsed an old man staring vacantly at him from his bed. On the right was a young guy about Jack's age. He had no front teeth and dried blood spotted his face. The smell of vomit made Jack want to vomit too. He covered his nose.

"If our accommodations aren't what you rich Kennedys are used to, I apologize," said Dexter. "You got your own room. Can't leave, though. Hope you enjoy your stay."

The sheriff guided them to separate cells. "Get in there," he said to Joe, pushing him inside, then locking him in. Joe gave Jack a disingenuous wave.

"Here's your cell," said Dexter.

When Dexter shoved him, Jack said, "Hey, you don't need to do that."

The cell door clanged shut. Dexter turned the keys. "I know. But I like to. Especially to you Kennedys. You think you're better than the rest of us."

The sheriff whistled mindlessly as he clattered down the corridor.

The cell block went dark, except for a dim bulb in the hallway.

Alone with his thoughts, Jack pondered how he had wound up here. Most of all, he had relied on Joe. Joe had said everything was going to be fine, that the hotel manager was bluffing, and Jack had gone along with it. But he didn't think he could rely on Joe anymore. Better to rely on his own judgment and instincts. This time, he hadn't, and now he was a criminal. No, that wasn't true. He hadn't been convicted of anything. A rebel? Or a Mucker? Maybe he still was.

It also bothered Jack that he had no idea that they were legally responsible. He had been ignorant. Had he known, this debacle never would have happened. He and Joe would have talked about making sure the party didn't get out of hand. Jack resolved to educate himself on the basics of law.

Feeling like a lion in a cage, Jack paced in the cramped, confined space. The floor was seasoned with dirty sand. A jail cell was something he'd seen in Westerns starring his boyhood hero Tom Mix. The lockup didn't seem so bad in the movies, but when it was you behind bars, it was a different story. The cell reeked of human suffering—an oppressive mix of sweat, filth, and despair that clung to the air. Yellow spots decorated the bedding. Hardened excrement stuck to the cracked toilet, which was attached to a smudged, rusty sink.

How long would he be held captive? A day? A week? Jack didn't know how the legal system worked. Would he have to get a lawyer? Appear before a judge?

Putting his hands on the inch-thick iron bars, Jack peered ahead to the nothingness of white granite stone walls. The units were arranged so he couldn't see the other inmates. Not that he wanted to.

He sat on the steel-framed cot. It made his butt sore. Jack put his face in his hands. Worst day of his life… and preventable. In the first place, they could have stopped the party-crashers from coming in. Should have announced that the party was going to be shut down if people didn't quiet down. Removed the liquor.

Gloomily, he remembered scribbling a joke on Rip's photograph at graduation about rooming with him at the infamous Sing Sing prison.

Jack convinced himself that he and Joe would only be here for a couple hours at most. Dad was well-known and had an important position in President Roosevelt's administration.

A flash of light. Jack bolted from his bed like he'd found a spider crawling up his shorts.

Sheriff Dexter entered the corridor. "Hey, you Kennedy boys. Got news for you." He paused. "You ain't getting out. You'll be spending the night with us. Maybe longer. Order of a guy calls himself the Skipper. Says staying here might teach you a lesson. He thinks it'll do you good. You know something? I think he's right." Dexter grinned. "I'd say 'sleep well,' but you won't."

Jack slapped the wall. *God damn Skipper.* Remembering the pleased expression on his face as they were led to the police car, Jack contemplated payback. He turned to see a blob in the corner of the cell. A closer look revealed a colony of ants feasting on a rat.

"Hey, Sheriff! There's a dead rat in here!" shouted Jack, as the cell block went dark.

It was going to be a long, angry night. He was mad. Mad at the guy who'd called the cops. Mad at the cop. And mad at both Skipper, brother Joe, and his father. *Why hadn't Father arranged for their release?*

Something else bothered him. The hotel owner said he was going to press charges. They might have to go to court. They'd probably be written up in the island's paper and then *The Boston Globe*. Their father would let them have it, rage at his sons for the disgraceful publicity that would befall the family.

A few hours later, Jack began having crazy thoughts. Would they rot in here? Did his family know where they were? He remembered seeing *20,000 Years in Sing Sing*. It hadn't ended well for Spencer Tracy. He got the electric chair.

A jangle of keys interrupted his fitful slumber. Then lights.

Dexter shoved a tray under the cell door—a tin of oatmeal porridge and a cup of milk.

"Here's your breakfast. Enjoy your Sunday morning."

"When are we getting out of here, Sheriff?"

"What's your hurry, Sonny? Not liking your accommodations?

Don't see why not. Got all the amenities. Bed, toilet, sink. Food is on the house. Don't like our home cooking? Sorry. Let us know when you're coming next time, and we'll make sure you have a nice side of Sunday roast with all the fixin's."

Jack kicked the tray into a corner of the cell and lay back down on his cot.

A few hours later, Sheriff Dexter returned. "Got news for ya. Lucky for you the hotel owner isn't pressing charges, but is holding you responsible for the damages. Got it?"

Relief washed over Jack like a cool shower after a hot day. "Yes." Anything to get out of here.

Sheriff Dexter unlocked the cell and led him to the rear of the cell block. Joe was flat on his back, snoring like a banshee. The clanging of keys in the lock brought him to life.

"Where am I?" Joe said as he sat up. "What happened?" He was sweaty and his hair was matted.

"A bad dream," said Jack. "That's all. Let's go. Tell you about it later." It was the first time Jack could remember taking care of his older brother.

Outside, Skipper was waiting for them. "I told you guys to stay out of trouble." He spat at their feet. "You didn't listen. And another thing—"

"Screw off," said Jack, turning away.

"Yeah," agreed Joe.

They walked south on Main Street toward the harbor. The races were over, and the town had cleared out.

"Let's get breakfast before we head home," Joe said.

From one side of the Edgartown Yacht Club came the faint scent of salt and fish. Crews unloaded their glistening catch of swordfish. On the other side of the club, a coffee shop on Dock Street offered a view of Edgartown Harbor. The town was quiet, but the harbor was a hive of activity as crews made preparations for the return voyage home.

Jack bought a newspaper. After ordering orange juice, poached eggs on toast, crisp broiled bacon, marmalade, milk, and coffee, Jack read the *Vineyard Gazette*. The paper covered the entire table. Dated July 26, 1935, the edition had come out before the Regatta. It didn't have the results, only notices of the participants and an upcoming race schedule.

"Here we are, Joe," Jack said, pointing to their names under Wianno Senior Second Class.

"How did we do?" Joe asked.

Jack stared at his still-addled brother. Had he forgotten?

"Just okay. Could have done better. We will next year. Guess we should be getting back. Not looking forward to facing JP, though."

Joe wobbled as he stood up. "Haven't got my sea legs yet."

As he climbed aboard the *Victura*, Joe grabbed his stomach and immediately crawled into the cabin below. Jack prepared the sloop for departure back to Hyannis Port. When it was ready, he swung the *Victura* out, sailing northeast into Nantucket Sound past the Edgartown Lighthouse on the port side.

Joe was out of sight but not out of mind. The weekend and recent events had further altered Jack's view of his older brother. Perhaps that shift had begun during therapeutic sessions with a Columbia University psychology professor after the Muckers episode at Choate. When he entered Choate, Jack began to opt out of any comparison with his brother, who had been popular and successful academically and athletically. Believing he couldn't measure up to Joe's success, Jack had stopped trying. But since then, he'd made adjustments and hadn't shied away from competing with Joe. He'd taken him on, whether the competition was racing, debating the issues of the day, or engaging attractive girls.

Jack was content at the helm. Martha's Vineyard and last night's confinement were behind him. Ahead, he knew there'd be a reckoning back on the mainland, but for now he was liberated.

Jack suddenly realized something important. He wasn't going to follow Joe to Harvard. That hadn't worked out when they both attended Choate, or here on the Vineyard. He needed a break from Joe. He'd tell his father he was going to Princeton.

The *Victura* caught a breeze and surged, and Jack swung her into the North Atlantic. Nothing but the vast ocean as far as he could see.

Chapter 3

Conditions were perfect for the sail home. The winds were gentle at under eight knots, producing small wavelets and glassy crests. Jack welcomed the warmth of the sun after the night in the dank jail, but his reverie was interrupted by a creaking on the wooden steps.

Joe emerged from the hold. Shielding his eyes with his hand, he said, "How long was I out?"

"About an hour."

Joe sat, his head down.

Jack had something to ask his brother. "So you think I'm a smoothie."

Joe rubbed his eyes and looked up. "What?"

"What you wrote in my scrapbook. That I'm a smoothie."

"Oh, that. Kind of."

"What did you mean by that?" Jack had been surprised when he saw it. He hadn't been sure how Joe meant it.

Joe sighed. "You got a way about you. Getting along with people. Making them like you. Without even trying."

Joe was revered by the family, especially their father. When the elder Kennedy was away, Joe was the de facto head of the family, sitting at the head of the table, carving the Sunday roast, and giving orders to his brothers and sisters. Jack couldn't recall his brother ever expressing any envy of him.

After docking in Hyannis Port, they walked the path lined with scrubby beach pine trees to the Kennedys' expansive summer home. Jack brightened as the white, triple-turreted clapboard house came into view. He had never been so glad to see this place, with its majestic view of the water. In front, a circular driveway wrapped around a plot of greenery. To the right of the driveway was a large lawn used for touch football games. The property also included a tennis court, a pool, and a motion-picture theater.

"It's good to be back," said Joe.

"It's good to be anywhere other than that goddamn jail," said Jack.

Their much younger brothers and sisters came screaming down the steps, running between Joe and Jack. "I'm first!" eight-year-old Bobby yelled. Painfully shy with strangers, Bobby had no problem speaking up at home. He was followed out the door by seven-year-old Jean and eleven-year-old Patricia.

Jack and Joe had barely set foot in the house when they were intercepted by their father, who was waiting for them in the vestibule. He pointed to his office and said sternly, "I need to have a talk with you two."

Jack and Joe dutifully entered the office, and their father shut the door behind them. With his lip twitching from a rage barely under control, he stomped his foot, removed his glasses, and put them on the desk. He towered over them. "Sit down," he began. "I can't tell you how disappointed I am with what happened. I allow you to throw a party and it turns into a disaster—not just for yourselves but for our whole family. You embarrassed us. Do you realize that?" He didn't want or expect an answer.

"Mostly, I'm upset with you," he said, pointing at Joe. "You're supposed to set a good example for the oithers, but you get yourself and your brother thrown in jail. And before you do, you get rip-roaring drunk. You know how I feel about the association people make between the Irish and booze. They think we're all drunks. We've got enough to battle against without that."

Jack had never seen his father so upset. He winced and drew into himself.

Normally, Joe Sr. hid his anger behind a tight smile, but this time it was on display for all to see. Acknowledging the other time Joe had been in lockup, he said, "How are you going to be president if you keep screwing up?"

Joe looked down at his shoes.

"You might as well know," said the elder Kennedy: "Skipper and I talked after you were taken to jail. I could have had you released." He paused. "But I didn't do it. I wanted you boys to spend a night behind bars. I trust it wasn't pleasant."

Jack's mouth gaped open. He'd assumed it had been Skipper's decision not to have them released right away.

"How could you let everything get so out of control that the police had to be called? It was your party. You were responsible. Do you have anything to say for yourself, Joseph?" Joe Sr. fumed, extending his right arm, hand open, demanding an answer.

Joe shifted his weight. "No, I-I guess I don't."

Joe Sr. now turned his attention to Jack. "You had better learn from your brother's mistakes."

Jack nodded. Sometimes it was better to be the younger brother, he thought. He didn't have the weight of expectations that his father had placed on Joe. That was a lot to live up to.

Their father walked back to his desk and put his glasses back on. "This is important, so listen carefully: I want what happened on Martha's Vineyard to be forgotten. There's no more record of your stay in the jail. I've taken care of that. I haven't told your mother. Skipper will keep his mouth shut. You two will do the same. I want your word that you won't ever tell anybody about this. That means your friends and your sisters and brothers. I've got enough to deal with. Agreed?"

Jack and Joe nodded.

"One more thing. You didn't win. Why the hell not?" He opened the door. "Go say hello to your mother."

Relieved to escape his father's indignation, Jack walked with his brother down the hallway and entered the kitchen. Their mother's back was turned. She hadn't heard them come in. "We need more corn syrup and—"

"Good afternoon, Mother," Joe said.

They stood at opposite ends of the room. No attempt was made at affection. That wasn't her way. Jack had long ago given up hope of any tenderness.

"Oh, Joe and Jack," she said matter-of-factly. "It's good to see you."

Their mother was tiny, already dwarfed by four of her young daughters. Small squares of paper were pinned to her blouse and skirt. Written on each were reminder notes: *Shoes, Bobby. Sweep basement. Milk.* To Jack, his mother seemed more interested in managing the household than caring for her children emotionally. She sometimes went away for weeks at a time. As she left for a trip to Europe when he was five, Jack had shouted tearfully, "You're a great mother to go away and leave your children!"

A maid pinned with additional tasks entered the kitchen. Behind her, three-year-old Teddy, the ninth sibling, waddled in.

"Did you have a good time?" their mother asked.

"Yes, Mother," Jack said. "We had such a wonderful time I thought the cops were going to arrest us for having too much fun."

She looked at Jack and then Joe, but they offered only blank faces. "Arrested for having too much fun. I've never heard of such a thing. Nice to have you back. Well, I have a lot to do," she said, turning away to look in a cupboard.

In the living room, alone on the couch, sat their striking oldest sister, Rosemary. She needed special attention, but her condition wasn't discussed among the family or in public. Eunice—wiry and resolute—came in and joined Rosemary on the couch. Eunice was thirteen but already a skilled sailor and excellent tennis player. She looked out for Rosemary.

"Hey, Rose, want to take a walk?" Eunice said.

"Sure, let's go," Rosemary said, jumping to her feet.

Down the stairs came fifteen-year-old Kathleen, or Kick as most everybody called her. Kick was high-spirited, charming, and athletic, and her rebellious personality matched Jack's. Unlike Joe, Kick could take a joke.

"Did you win?" she said hopefully, clutching her hands to her chest.

"No," Jack said. "But we had a wonderful party. And we got a tour of police headquarters!"

"What?" said Kick, stopping her descent on the stairs.

"If you happen to be on the island," added Jack, "don't bother going on the tour. There's nothing much to see."

"Bless me Father for I have sinned," said Jack. He was at St. Francis Xavier Church in Hyannis, whose religious services his family regularly attended. Confession offered him little comfort, and he considered whether to continue. But after the events of the weekend, he felt a yearning to do so—he had truly committed a mortal sin. "I have been in jail for a night. It was a truly awful thing. I let a party get out of hand, and I did not do enough to stop it. I am truly sorry for the shame it has caused my family."

When Jack paused, the priest said, "Go on, my son."

"I have also felt angry about certain people. I have felt anger in my heart for a man who is supposed to help us but only desires the worst for us. This man, the Skipper, whom my father hired to watch over us, told my father that it would be for the best if my brother and I spent the night in jail. My father agreed. I have bad feelings toward this man and wish him harm."

After a recitation of a few venial sins and receiving absolution, Jack exited confession, only somewhat relieved. Jack's attendance at church was part routine and part obligation. Sometimes, he went just to get his mother off his back.

Chapter 4

Jack joined his friends Lem and Rip at Princeton in late October, cramming a cot into Room 9 of South Reunion Hall. Stocky and possessed of a high-pitched laugh, Lem had roomed with Jack at Choate, and they had become best friends. Rip was the serious sort, a bookend to Lem's boisterousness.

Jack had arrived after a short, unsuccessful stay in London. His father had sent him to study, as Joe had, under Professor Joseph Laski at the London School of Economics. But after Jack became ill and realized how much he missed his friends, he'd legged it back to Princeton just as he had planned.

At Princeton that first semester, Jack posted mediocre grades in military science, history, English, and mathematics. But it wasn't long before his skin yellowed, and he was dispatched to Peter Bent Brigham Hospital in Boston. He stole a look at his chart and breathed a sigh of relief—the Wasserman test revealed no sign of syphilis. After weeks of tests, invasive examinations, and consultations, the doctors initially believed he had leukemia, but they had backed off. His illness had defied diagnosis once again.

While he recovered, Jack contemplated whether to continue at Princeton. Outside of attending classes, there wasn't much else to do in the small, rural New Jersey town. He detected a provincialism that rubbed him the wrong way. Princeton was an enclave that felt apart from everything, yet secure in its separateness. And nightlife was nonexistent.

In contrast, when he visited Joe, he found Harvard and Cambridge appealing. When he and Joe strolled the campus and Harvard Square, Jack was pleased to see that bookstores, restaurants, and nightlife were only steps away from campus. Adjacent to Harvard was Radcliffe Women's College, and other women's colleges were nearby as well.

"I've enjoyed it here," Joe had said. "My first year I was the chairman of the freshman smoker. Big success."

"Freshman smoker? What's that?"

"It's a big party in the spring for freshmen to meet each other. It's a long-standing tradition. And there's a lot of smoking."

"Sounds interesting."

Jack realized he no longer needed to go someplace Joe wasn't or go against his father's wishes just for spite. His decision would be based on what he wanted—not what others wanted him to do. No longer would he be compared to his older brother, as he had been at Choate. Joe may have been a big fish at the prep school, but at Harvard he was just another student.

Jack's illness was also a factor. If he was going to be infirm, he decided, he preferred to be at Harvard. He didn't want to squander time at a place he didn't want to be. Jack formally withdrew from Princeton on December 12, 1935.

Jack stepped out of the pool and grabbed a towel. He was at the family's winter estate in Palm Beach, Florida. His father got up from his chair and stared at his son's wasting physique.

"We've got to do something, Jack. Add some pounds. Some muscle to your arms and legs," Joe Sr. said.

What did his father have in mind?

"I think a few months on a ranch out west would do you good. You'd get fresh air and dry heat, and the work will do you good. Build you up."

Jack was intrigued by the idea because he was planning on going out for the Harvard football team. "I suppose it could help my chances to score a few more touchdowns."

Because of his fragile health, Jack had been banned from all athletic competition in his final years at Choate. Jack desperately wanted to prove himself a college football player.

"That's the spirit, my boy. I've lined up a stay for you at a ranch in Arizona. There won't be much to do out there but work your behind off. But I'm positive you'll be a lot stronger by the time you leave."

"Okay. I'll be sure to watch some cowboy movies before I go," Jack said with a wide grin. "Learn the tricks of the trade."

"Smoke, here we are," Jack said to Jim Wilde, using his own version of a nickname to address the former Choate classmate who'd accompanied him to Arizona. Wilde was four inches shorter than Jack, but they weighed about the same. The dry desert wind blew their hair in all directions. Jack wiped his brow. It had to be a hundred degrees. And it was only early spring.

They grabbed their trunks from the car and looked at each other quizzically. They hadn't seen anything but desert since they got off the train in the small town of Benson and arrived at the ranch ten miles later. The dusty acreage of the 40,000-acre Jay Six Ranch, consisting of a main lodge, mess hall, and bunk house, was slightly less than fifty miles away from Tucson. Mexico was about the same distance going south. Scrub brush surrounded the property, which was populated by about a thousand Hereford cows hemmed in by barbed wire. A mountain range loomed in the distance, but there was nothing else in sight.

A ranch hand came out of the main house and led them down a path to the shared bunk house. They each put on boots, jeans, and a cowboy hat.

BECOMING JFK

"I always wanted to be a cowboy," Smoky said, admiring his outfit.

"Haven't we all, Buffalo Bill," Jack said to Smoky, as he clomped around trying to get used to the cowboy boots.

"You boys look like ranch hands now," said a dark-haired, brawny man standing in the doorway. Jack Speiden had fought in the Great War and was a former Wall Street stockbroker who had the foresight to invest in land during the Depression. "Now, let's see what you can do. I need an office, and you boys are going to build it for me."

The next day, after Speiden gave them a brief tutorial on how to make adobe bricks, they were left on their own. The heat was so onerous that Jack stripped to his underwear. For several hours, he and Smoky mixed soil and water into a thick mud. Sand and pine needles were added, and the mixture was poured into molds and baked in the hot sun for five days. At a dollar a day, it was Jack's first paid job.

They made bricks, rounded up cattle, and fixed fences six days a week. Jack grew to appreciate the contrast between his privileged upbringing and this new environment. He worked alongside people from vastly different circumstances than his own. That included Mexican immigrants, who laughed at the boys' early mistakes making bricks, and a hardworking Scotsman, who hit the bottle hard when the sun went down. There was also Oklahoma Pete Haverty.

"Boss has ordered me to take you along to the rodeo," said Haverty, while they ate in the mess hall. They sat at a long communal table with the other ranch hands. "I'll be taking part." Haverty wiped the remains of beef stew from his mouth with his sleeve. A one-legged cowboy, Haverty did every job on the ranch—and more.

Jack and Smoky exchanged expressions of interest, eager to see a rodeo and curious to see how Haverty would do in the tie-down roping competition.

"You boys git in the back," Haverty said, pointing to the truck's open cab. He drove skillfully despite his missing limb.

When they arrived at the rodeo, Haverty said, "I'll see you boys later."

Jack and Smoky took seats in the stands. "Pete's up next," Smoky said.

Haverty sat atop his horse, pigging string in his mouth. After the calf got a head start, Haverty gave chase. He was on the calf in seconds and lassoed the animal with dead-on aim. After an awkward dismount, he wrapped three of the calf's legs and threw his hands in the air. *Time!*

"That was pretty damn impressive," said Jack, making a mental note of Haverty's independence, skill, and fortitude. Haverty didn't let his missing limb stop him from working or pursuing his goals. The performance only reinforced Jack's belief that he couldn't allow his health issues to get in the way of what he wanted to do in life.

"Another day, another dollar," Jack said to Smoky, as he crashed onto his cot in the bunk house. Both were exhausted at the end of another backbreaking, tedious day. Jack's hands were muddy, and he had developed a few bruises and scrapes after a fall from his horse.

"What shall we do with our savings?" said Smoky. "Buy a cow?"

"Got a better idea. Use it for a road trip to Mexico," Jack offered with a mischievous smile. "See what goes on down there." He was curious to see what lay south of the border. That's where the good times might be. There were no available women at the ranch.

"What do you think goes on down there?" Smoky said.

"Only one way to find out."

Overhearing their conversation, the Scotsman told them the best way in Mexico to find women was at a bar. "Things will take care of themselves after that," he said with a wink.

BECOMING JFK

On a subsequent Saturday night, Jack and Smoky bumped their way in a ranch truck to the border town of Nogales, seventy-five miles away.

"I know you haven't forgotten that you were voted the first to get married back at Choate," said Jack, "but don't feel like you have to bring one of these girls back so you can achieve your goal."

They entered the dilapidated saloon with caution, its air of neglect and shadowy corners adding to their unease. The Scotsman's recommendation had come with a grin that now felt more like a warning. Inside, there were no tables or stools, just a row of well-worn booths that had seen better days. They had barely settled into their seats when two heavily made-up Mexican women emerged from a back room, sliding in beside them with practiced ease.

The woman next to Jack was curvaceous, her dark, curly hair framing a face lined with experiences he couldn't guess. She looked to be in her thirties.

"They don't waste any time," Jack muttered under his breath as he felt her hand glide suggestively up his thigh.

"You gringos want sexo?" she asked with a smile that didn't quite reach her eyes. Jack nodded after a brief pause.

A price was quickly agreed upon, and with a wordless understanding, the women led Jack and Smoky through a narrow hallway to the back rooms, each of which was dimly lit and sparse, its atmosphere as transactional as the exchange that had brought them there.

Later, back at the ranch, Jack retrieved his pen and began crafting a letter to Lem. He scrawled a title at the top: "Travels in a Mexican Whorehouse with Your Roomie."

I've just had an escapade. Got a go-round in a Mexican bordello for sixty-five cents and am feeling strangely fit and cleansed by the absurdity of it all. Smoky and I stumbled into this two-bit establishment where they say only one guy in five years has escaped without a healthy dose of the clap. True to form, your roommate is upholding the motto of 'always finding the most unlikely place to get your piece.' Nine South style lives on, my friend.

After producing a pile of bricks several feet high, the two began construction of the office. Even though most of the work tested his boredom threshold, Jack was pleased with what it had done for his physique. In a few weeks, he'd added a layer of muscle and a healthy tan.

"I think I'm ready for football," he said to Smoky while they took a break. He pretended to throw a pass with a brick. "I just hope Harvard football is ready for me."

Several weeks later, Jack and Smoky appraised their now finished work—a slanted-roof office. To Jack, building the addition was significant since his father hired people to take care of manual work. To see the structure rise from nothing was gratifying. Jack surveyed the finished product with his chest thrust out and a gleam in his eye.

"You did a pretty good job," said Speiden. "I'll call it the house that Jack and Smoky built."

Their ranching days were coming to an end. Jack's father had invited him to come to California to celebrate his nineteenth birthday on May 29. Joe Sr. had been a consequential player in the movie business, including arranging the financing of several Gloria Swanson films. He was in Los Angeles now, consulting for Paramount.

Their bags packed, he and Smoky walked outside. Jack took out his knife and carved his initials in the fence like he'd done on a chair at graduation.

Jack Kennedy had been here.

"Okay, Smoke. Now we can go."

Chapter 5

Jack had high hopes for his holiday in Hollywood—movie stars, celebrities, bright lights, and parties. He wanted to dig into the lifestyle and have an adventure to celebrate his birthday. Other than a return visit to Nogales, the ranch sojourn had been a staid existence—rise early in the morning, work all day, eat, sleep, and do it all over again the following day.

As the train pulled out of the dusty station bound for Los Angeles, Jack imagined what Hollywood would be like. He pictured endless orange groves, movie stars walking the streets, and California girls, their wondrous physiques enhanced by the California sunshine and endless days at the beach. But when he arrived, he was mildly disappointed to see palm trees and women dressed similarly to Florida—but no familiar faces from the silver screen.

"Jack, my boy," his father said, greeting him on his arrival at the train station. He surveyed Jack's lean, toned frame. "I think working on the ranch did you good. Toughened you up."

"Thanks." Jack laughed and posed bodybuilder style a la Jack LaLanne. "Nothing else to do."

"Learn anything out there?"

"Learned I never want to see another mud brick for as long as I live."

His father chuckled. "Understandable, but I think it was worthwhile. You're in great shape."

When they arrived at the hotel, Joe Sr. said, "You deserve some fun. Would you like to join a set of tennis doubles? Your partner would be Constance Bennett."

Jack's eyes widened at the thought of partnering with the well-known actress. She was blonde, delicate, and known for her glamorous style. Jack wondered how well Bennett was acquainted with his father. He recalled Gloria Swanson staying a few days in Hyannis Port. He was a twelve-year-old at the time. He'd caught Ms. Swanson and his father in an intimate moment and filed away a lesson. Women outside of marriage were fair game—and the highest level of female attainment would be Hollywood actresses.

Jack tossed the ball up. Hoping to impress Bennett, he served as hard as he could. The ball nearly hit the back fence on the fly. He played terribly.

"Sonny," said one of the players to Jack during a break, "get us a cold drink."

Constance gestured for Jack to pick up balls only a few feet from her reach. Jack clenched his jaw. When the match ended, he had hoped to join them for lunch, but they strode off without goodbyes.

One of the next things Jack did in Los Angeles was get a preventative shot. He'd read worrying news reports about outbreaks of gonorrhea. "I don't know why it is that every time I've had my fun, I end up reading some article about the risks people take," he confided to Smoky on the train. Jack had little patience for precautions, even though he knew he was flirting with danger. After his encounters in Mexico, he found himself anxious about the possibility of contracting syphilis.

Since his time in Los Angeles was limited, Jack didn't wait long before looking for available women. His father suggested he hang around the back lots of Paramount movie sets because it was the perfect place to find attractive women without watchful parents. Jack wandered over to a set that was a Western town. It had facades for a saloon, a bank, and a jail. He noticed a cute young woman waiting outside the studio gate. Along with a hundred others, she was hoping to be called as an extra for a crowd scene. Jack asked the guard to let him out.

Sidling up to her, Jack said, "I'm sure you'll get picked."

She looked curiously at him but smiled appreciatively. "Oh yeah, what makes you say that?"

"Nobody's *making* me say it," he kidded. "I know when a gal has the goods. You'll definitely be called. And I don't think you'll be an extra for long." Jack asked where she came from, about her family, and how her career was progressing.

When her name was called, Jack said, "See. I knew it. Will you tell me later how it went?" They made plans to meet later. Maybe Joe's right, he thought. Maybe I do have a way with people, and some of them are women.

Jack spent time with the extra and later wrote to Lem, noting how stunning she was and how effortlessly she seemed to command attention. "She could easily be the lead in her own story," he quipped, even suggesting that Olive, his old flame from Choate, could "take a ship by herself because I've met this extra in Hollywood. She's the best-looking thing I have ever seen."

It was about the conquest for Jack, and in that way of thinking, he took after his father and mirrored his brother in the pursuit of young actresses. He recalled Joe Jr. going out on dates with starlets. Jack found excitement in the pursuit, relishing the dynamic interplay of charm and attention. It struck him that, in a way, he shared more similarities with these women than he had realized—both he and them navigating a world where appearances often held the most power. In addition, Jack often saw his social interactions as a lively dance, where wit and charm held the lead roles.

Jack left California resolved to return, drawn by the allure of its freedom and its warmth.

Chapter 6

Jack removed his football helmet and shouted to his Harvard friend and teammate Torbert McDonald: "Let's go, Torby. Ann is waiting for us." Jack had enrolled at Harvard in the fall, roomed by himself in Weld Hall in the freshman dormitory, and joined the football team.

It was late Friday night, and Jack and Torby's destination was Boston's rowdy Scollay Square and the Howard Athenaeum, or Old Howard as everyone called it. The century-old Athenaeum's three large stained-glass windows gave it a church-like appearance, but the gothic style building composed of Quincy granite was famous for burlesque.

The slogan at the Old Howard was "Always Something Doing from 9 a.m. to 11 p.m." But tonight, there'd be something to do after eleven because of a special Friday late-night show. That would be when the Harvard contingent showed up.

Their favorite was the statuesque burlesque stripper Ann Corio, who'd been a star in New York at Minsky's Burlesque. She loved the Harvard boys, and they loved her back. It was said that when an astronomy professor had asked his Cambridge class to name a heavenly body, a student quipped, "Ann Corio."

Jack and Torby bought their tickets, then raced up the long stairway to the auditorium and sat in the side upper boxes. A few minutes after the opening act, there was a commotion. Staffers were setting up chairs in the aisle space up front. What was going on?

"Hey, it's Curley!" Jack shouted, pointing to the current Massachusetts governor and four-time mayor of Boston, the flamboyant and cunning James Michael Curley. He and his entourage were making their way up the aisle.

BECOMING JFK

"Wants everybody to see him," Jack said. "Maybe he'll run for president."

Jack's father had referred to Curley in less than glowing terms. Curley and the Kennedys had a long-standing rift dating back to the time Curley had floated a rumor that Jack's mother's father, Boston Mayor John Fitzgerald, had an affair with a cigarette girl. Fitzgerald was forced to withdraw from the mayor's race. Curley had ruled the town for many years, effectively combining equal parts arrogance and corruption.

"Figures. It's in his best interest to be in the public eye." Jack recounted some of Curley's memorable acts of ostentation. "That's part of the reason he's won so many elections."

After the opening acts, the ravishing Corio made her entrance. She didn't do the bump and grind like other strippers. Instead, accompanied by a drummer pounding on his toms, she performed with a sweet innocence. While the crowd cheered, Corio stripped down to her bra and a two-panel front and back dress. One panel came off and then the other. Soon, all that was left were pasties adorned with tassels covering her nipples. A G-string covered up her private parts.

Shimmying and sashaying, Corio neared the boxes where all the Harvard boys. including Jack and Torby, sat. "Here she comes," Jack said, as Corio waved to the college students. The boys moved to the edge of their seats, hopeful for a closer look at her bosom. But suddenly the spotlight switched from the stripper to the attendees. The crowd roared as the Harvard boys were bathed in the spotlight. After a moment, the spotlight returned to Corio.

Later, Torby, who lived at home, dropped Jack off at his dorm.

Jack crowed, "Tonight was an important part of a Harvard education. I learned how great politicians make an entrance—and we saw a great show. See you at practice."

Jack ladled water from the bucket and gulped it eagerly while Torby waited his turn. Sweat pooled on Jack's chin, and his muscles ached. It was the end of the week, and they had been drilling for an additional hour after practice ended.

"That's enough, Torby," said Jack, clapping him on the back. "I've got to save some energy for the books and my weekend at the Cape."

Eddie Moore, assistant to the senior Kennedy, had arranged for several gals to join Jack and five members of the freshman football team at a hotel. No doubt his father was aware of the plan or had proposed it.

Back in his room, Jack wrote Lem a quick note before beginning to study.

> *Exam tomorrow so have to open my book to see what the fucking course is about.*

Jack was so tired he merely glanced at his book before nodding off. He'd catch up at the end of the semester, he told himself. Happy with mediocrity, Jack figured he could balance his carousing with enough studying to pass. He garnered Cs except for a surprising B in Economics. He wasn't ready to buckle down. After the strict discipline at Choate and the social quarantine of Princeton, he craved fun and pleasure.

Jack dropped to his knee, taking an extra minute to gather himself after slamming into the tackling dummy. The week before, he'd gotten a liver injection that doctors hoped would diminish a variety of his ailments, but he didn't feel any different. It was Monday, and Jack had returned late the previous night from the Cape. He was worn out from the weekend, but it had been worth it. The days away had been the wildest of his life, a full-blown debauchery even. Four girls had joined them at the hotel. It had been non-stop partying with plenty of drinking, dancing, and sex.

"Kennedy, get over here!" Coach Dick Harlow bellowed, crooking his finger at Jack. Harlow was fat and bald, and known to suffer from high blood pressure.

Jack was surprised that Harlow even knew his name since he coached the varsity, leaving the freshman team to assistants. Jack trotted over to Harlow, wondering what he wanted with him.

Harlow got in his face, his large belly pushing against Jack. "Kennedy, what the hell were you doing this weekend? You look like a bag of bones out there."

Warily, Jack replied, "Just relaxed."

Harlow got in his face again. "Really? My understanding is you and several of your teammates were misbehaving. I won't have that in my football program. I won't have a playboy on my team, somebody who will lead the others down the wrong path. I want football players. You were the ringleader, weren't you?"

"I invited a few of the guys to come down—"

"And do what? Lead your team members into depravity. You got anything to say about that?"

"I don't see what having a little fun has to do with playing football. I'm doing my best out here."

"That's not good enough. Harvard has principles, and I am charged with maintaining standards of propriety on my football team."

Jack shrugged. "Yes, sir."

"As of now, you are demoted."

"Demoted?"

"You'll practice with the third team until, or if, I deem it time to put you back on the second team. Now get over there," he said, pointing to several players on the far side of the field. One of them tripped over his feet and another had an easy pass clank off his hands. "Those are your new teammates." At that, Harlow turned his back on Jack and walked over to the varsity players.

Jack trudged over with his head down. He fumed at the thought of Harlow's tentacles reaching into his private life. What did it matter what he did in his spare time? He hadn't done anything illegal, unless having a good time was illegal. He was tempted to quit—chuck his helmet and pads and walk off the field. If this was going to be the price that had to be paid to play football, then it wasn't worth it. How would he ever letter in varsity from the third team?

Jack guessed one of the five had blabbed to a graduate coach who had relayed it to Harlow. He turned around to see the other partygoers participating in drills. They hadn't been demoted. Apparently, he was taking the fall.

"Happy to have you join us, Kennedy," the graduate coach said, pointing to the ground. "Now drop and give me twenty push-ups Wait. Make that thirty."

His football career might have been in the dumpster, but Jack had something else to be excited about. He picked up the May 4, 1937 edition of the *Harvard Crimson* and smiled.

"John F. Kennedy, chairman of the Freshman Smoker, will present his heterogeneous conglomeration from the sports and theatrical world at 7:45 o'clock tonight," the article read.

Jack had decided to try his hand at the event Joe had chaired—but do it bigger and better. The guest list for the event at Harvard's Memorial Hall ran more than a thousand names. Jack had arranged for a host of entertainers, including legendary baseball players Dizzy Dean and Frankie Frisch, as well as Neal O'Hara, the well-known humorist for the *Boston Traveler*, and two jazz orchestras. There'd be free ice cream, donuts, the traditional corncob pipes, cigarettes, and ginger ale.

Jack was especially excited that he'd booked one of the top entertainers of the day, sultry torch singer Gertrude Niesen. At twenty-six, she had already added comedienne and star of stage and screen to her many credits. She'd been the first to record "When Smoke Gets in Your Eyes."

The acrid scent of smoke hovered over Jack as he stepped to the microphone. He looked out over the standing-room-only crowd, suddenly realizing this was the largest audience he had ever addressed. Jack welcomed everyone to the event and introduced the sultry, sassy Niesen. "Here's a gal who can do it all. Miss Niesen, you sing, you act, you write songs, and you were named the greatest torch singer of 1935. What can't you do?"

"There's a lot more I can do, but you'll never find out," she teased.

"I guess that means I won't get to taste your pigs in a blanket," Jack deadpanned to laughter. "Will you do us all the pleasure of singing 'When Smoke Gets in Your Eyes?'"

"Sure, but before I do, I'd like to ask our master of ceremonies whether he's ever had smoke get in *his* eyes?"

Jack thought about Olive. Maybe a wisp. "There might be smoke in my eyes right now, but I don't know if that's because of you or all of this," he said, waving at the thick cloud of gray.

After drawing out the final note of "Start Cheering," Niesen turned to Jack, who was rejoining her from the wings. "Jack, what do you do for fun at Harvard? You can't study all the time."

"Did I say I study all the time? I play end on the freshman football team."

"Really," she said, surveying his scrawny frame. "What end do they put you on? The end of the bench?"

Jack laughed at himself. "Somebody's got to keep it warm."

In between songs, Jack and Niesen traded soft balls, light roasting, and kidding. The crowd loved it.

At the end of the evening, Niesen said, "It's been a wonderful night, and we owe a lot to Jack Kennedy as our master of ceremonies and the organizer of the whole event. Let's sing 'Happy Birthday' to him, even though his birthday is a couple of weeks away." With that, Niesen, throwing out her hips, went into a breathy rendition. "Happy birthday, Mr. Master of Ceremonies. Happy birthday to you." She blew him a kiss, then sashayed off stage to wild cheering.

When the crowd finally quieted down, Jack said dryly, "After that, my birthday might be a disappointment."

Following the show, the bestselling writer John O'Hara tapped him on the back. "You were pretty good up there, Jack. I think they liked you better than me."

"Torby," Jack said, as they walked through Harvard Yard, "have you heard of King Francis?"

"No, but I have a feeling I will soon."

"This guy was quite the man." As the essay topic for his freshman French class, Jack selected King Francis I, the sixteenth century French ruler. "He becomes king at twenty and then hits the road looking for conquests. This guy was quite the ladies' man. He had a wife, but that was simply for reasons of state. Nothing to do with passion."

"No? What for, then?"

"He kept his first wife busy producing children while continuing with a variety of other women. Listen to this." Jack stopped and took out a page from his essay.

"Ambitious, spoiled, possessed of an unbounded vitality and a physique capable of tremendous physical activity, he was the pride and personification of his age. His lusty interest in life took many forms—the chase, war, and women."

"Sounds like you've got a new idol, Jack."

"Maybe I have. I wouldn't mind having a life like that."

Chapter 7

During Christmas break, Jack's father advised him to visit Europe "before the shooting started."

After completing his freshman year in June 1937, he and Lem boarded the SS *Washington* along with Jack's black, white-walled Ford convertible. He couldn't think of a better traveling companion than the easygoing Lem, who was also his best friend. Packed in his trunk were six tailor-made suits, fourteen shirts, and three pairs of monogrammed silk pajamas. Besides a letter of introduction from U.S. Secretary of State Cordell Hull, he brought a leather-bound travel diary, titled "My Trip Abroad," a gift from Kick.

"Let's go, Lemmer," Jack said, when the ship arrived in Le Havre, France. The car's top down, Jack gunned the Ford toward Paris. "We've got a lot to see. And we've got to see it before all hell breaks loose."

"All right," Lem said, "but that doesn't mean you have to drive a hundred miles an hour." Jack had a penchant for speeding.

Whisking by the tidal flats of the Seine, Jack thought about the trip ahead. Though he planned to enjoy the journey, and engage with the local women, he also wanted to learn about the different cultures and make up his own mind if war was truly on the horizon. To do that, he would need to speak with a wide variety of people—on both sides of the potential conflict.

They stopped for the day in Beauvais. Because of the vast difference in family wealth between his and Lem's, Jack agreed to stay in cheap rooms during their trip.

"Let's hide the car around the corner and appear poverty-stricken so we can get a good rate," Lem suggested.

BECOMING JFK

"Now you're thinking." Jack had become incensed with what he saw as the French habit of fleecing American tourists. They'd already been charged an exorbitant rate for having a headlight changed. After parking the car, they put on dirty clothes and mussed their hair.

"It worked," Lem said triumphantly, entering their quarters after they'd paid up. "Eighty cents for the both of us. I think we've got a plan for the rest of the trip."

A few minutes later, Jack spied two French military officers looking for a ride. "Make room for the Frenchies. We are about to get a strong whiff of that lovely French breath," Jack chuckled. "Let's see what the boys in the army have to say." Using his most basic French, Jack turned the talk to the political situation after a few minutes.

"No. There is nothing to worry about," said one of the French soldiers. "We'll not need your help this time."

The more confident the French came across, the more Jack doubted them. He wondered if France and other countries in Europe were prepared, or in the process of preparing, for conflict. And if there was a war, would America become involved again?

When they arrived in Paris, Jack immediately began conversing with strangers.

"We are much too well prepared for Germany," said one impeccably dressed French businessman seated next to them at a Paris café on Boulevard Saint-Germain. He told them he owned several men's clothing stores.

When Jack asked him if Germany posed a threat to France, he said, "We have now the Maginot Line in the northeast. It is invincible." He put a Gauloises cigarette in his mouth and drew walls in the air with his hands. A white-coated waiter served him an espresso. "And many weapons," he continued. "The Germans will never try to break through. We would chew them up."

Was it wishful thinking?

After dropping the soldiers off, Lem said, "Let's find a nice place on our first night in Paris."

As the pair entered their hotel room, Jack shouted, *"Vive la France!"* The expansive room was lavishly appointed with a sitting room, fancy drapes, and their own bathroom.

The next day, they attended the International Exposition in Paris and visited the German pavilion. "That's really something," Jack said, staring at the powerful symbols of the Third Reich. A Nazi swastika and eagle illuminated the pavilion's tower. Several German soldiers in full dress uniforms were patrolling the building. "The Germans are making quite a statement here."

They walked over to the Soviet exhibit. "And so are the Soviets," Lem said, pointing to the grand building topped by a large exhibit of a male worker and a female peasant, their hands intertwined, thrusting a hammer and a sickle together.

"I wouldn't be surprised if these two countries go to war," Jack said, shaking his head. The Communists and Nazis had very different views of the world, but Jack had no doubt both were intent on acquiring new territory and spreading their ideologies.

The Germans were already on the move in Spain, which was the boys' next stop. Jack knew of a bombing attack by the German Luftwaffe which destroyed the Spanish town of Guernica and killed more than a hundred civilians. Those who tried to flee the horror were machine-gunned by forces waiting for them in the fields. If the French were confident of staving off any German advance, the situation in Spain was much different. There, the Fascist Nationalists, led by Generalissimo Franco, were attempting to topple the democratically elected government.

BECOMING JFK

On the way to Spain, the boys stayed in Saint-Jean-de-Luz, close to France's border with Spain.

"What shall we do?" asked Jack as they drove west. They'd been told by the American Embassy that they would be denied entry to Spain. Their passports even read "Not Good for Travel to Spain."

"No way we can get in," Lem said, "although I do recall your talent for getting into places where you don't belong."

In Paris, Jack had used the VIP entrance to enter Notre Dame and sat five seats away from the French president on Bastille Day.

Jack smiled. "Worth a try, Lemmer."

They were turned back. The closest they came was a view of the border, where they saw the bombed-out Spanish town of Irun. Both Italian and German planes had assaulted the city.

"In the mood for a bullfight?" said Jack, looking for something else to do. Because of the Spanish civil war, the bullfight was to be held in Biarritz, France, instead of Spain.

Jack and Lem took seats in the middle of the circular arena. A band played a spirited bullring march. The late afternoon event attracted a curious mix of enthusiastic Spaniards and more subdued French. In the first stage, a bullfighter on horseback thrust a lance into the bull's neck, but the horse was gored and had to be dragged away, its guts spilling out.

Jack nudged Lem, nodding at a French woman and her child sitting beside them and laughing at the horse's plight. After the bull was killed, Jack said, "This is not my kind of sport. The bull doesn't have a chance."

It was one thing to read about a bullfight and another to witness one. They walked silently out of the arena. Jack spat, something he rarely did. Then he stroked his throat and grimaced, consumed by disgust at what he had just seen. "Can you believe that, LeMoyne?" he raged. "These southerners—these French and Spanish—are happiest at scenes of cruelty.

They thought the funniest sight was when the horse ran out of the ring with his guts trailing. How can anybody find that entertaining?"

"I certainly didn't," agreed Lem.

The night before they left for Cannes and before visiting Fascist Italy, Jack stated his beliefs about the situation in Spain. He realized he'd been swayed by the sentiment for Franco in Saint-Jean-de-Luz, thinking Franco would surely topple the government. But after talking with people closer to the border, he wasn't so sure.

He took out his pen, filled it with ink, and wrote:

> *Not quite as positive now about Franco victory. Shows that you can be easily influenced by people around you if you know nothing and how easy it is for you to believe what you want to believe, as the people of St. Jean do.*

"We've got a long day of driving ahead," Jack said, after filling the Ford's gas tank in the morning. "But at least we've got something to look forward to—Cannes."

"Should be fun, and I'm ready for the beach," agreed Lem.

After a few days at the shore and a couple of hours at a Monaco casino, where Jack came out $1.20 ahead, they motored to Italy.

"Don't they always say to leave while you're ahead?" Lem said.

"Yes, they do," said Jack "I'll take my winnings with me to Italy."

"Interested to see what Mussolini has got going on here," Jack said. They had just crossed the border into Italy on their way to Genoa.

Once they reached Genoa, they stopped for supplies, and Lem said, "He's everywhere," pointing to the ubiquitous pictures and murals of

BECOMING JFK

the fiery Italian dictator Benito Mussolini. "Can't miss him even if you wanted to."

In Milan, Jack became friendly with the hotel owner, who spoke passable English. Noticing Jack looking at a picture of him in military uniform, the manager told him that he had served in Italy's recent conquest of Ethiopia. "It was very easy to control. The Ethiopians were no match for us, but I was glad to leave. Very uncomfortable place." He paused and frowned. "I am not happy about the things we did there."

"Like what?" asked Jack.

"In February, there was a terrible event. After I returned home, I was told by several of our soldiers that we executed thousands upon thousands of people from Addis Ababa."

"Why?"

"There was an assassination attempt on Governor-General Rodolfo Graziani. He rules the territory for Il Duce. Lined them up and shot them all day. Maybe twenty thousand people. And that's not all."

Jack leaned closer.

"We dropped bombs on them. And not ordinary bombs."

"What do you mean?"

"Bombs with chemicals. Can't breathe." The manager wrapped two hands around his neck.

Jack shook his head. He was learning more than he wanted to during this phase of the trip.

When they arrived in Rome, they were alerted to a rally where Mussolini would be speaking. "We can't miss this," said Jack.

They hung back on the outskirts of the plaza, packed with wildly cheering Italians. Chanting *"Duce! Duce! Duce!"* the Italians awaited the appearance of their leader. The moment Mussolini strutted into view on the balcony, the crowd erupted in a roar and a Roman salute of outstretched arms. Resplendent in gray military garb, Mussolini drank in the adulation, nodding and jutting out his chin. Jack and Lem exchanged dubious glances.

"Black shirts of revolution, men and women of all Italy, Italians all over the world, beyond the mountains, beyond the seas, listen," Mussolini bellowed.

Mussolini spoke in Latin, a language Jack had been forced to take at Choate—and had done poorly in—but it was helpful now.

For the next twenty minutes, Mussolini punctuated his speech with theatrical gestures. While praising the virtues of Fascism and warning its enemies, Mussolini thrust his fist in the air, strutting to different sides of the balcony, leading with his chin.

"Whatever you might think about his politics, you have to admit, he's something else," Lem said after the rally.

"There's no doubt the Italians have bought in," said Jack, admitting he had never seen one person grab and retain such a psychological hold on people. Whatever Mussolini asked, they would do. If he asked them to walk off a cliff for the good of Italy, they'd probably do it.

With the Fascists gaining ground in Spain, and the fascist Mussolini in full control here in Italy, Jack considered the fate of Europe. They still hadn't been to Nazi Germany. That was next.

"Let's have a little fun before we visit Hitler. Might be kind of grim there," said Jack.

They snuck into the Colosseum and visited the city of Pisa a few days later. Standing in front of the famous leaning tower and bending slightly to approximate the building's angle, Jack said, "Lem, take a picture of old man Pisa doing an impression of me."

BECOMING JFK

They had company for the ride to Germany. Ever curious to chat with the locals, Jack picked up two young men wearing Bavarian shorts and sandals.

"*Guten Tag*," said Jack, as the men clambered into the back. They were German soldiers on leave in Italy.

"Germany is great once again," the one called Heinz said, after Jack asked him about Germany's resurgence. "We owe it to Hitler, though I am worried that he will take things too far."

"Europe needs a strong Germany," said the other, who was named Johann. "It is best for all the people. Only Germany can bring a strong will. And Hitler is doing it."

They continued driving north. After a brief stop in Milan, Jack saw a nice-looking hitchhiker as they crossed into Switzerland, and he offered her a ride. Lem moved to the back seat to join the soldiers.

The young woman was blonde and green-eyed. Jack guessed she was a few years older than him.

She said hello to the Germans, but after learning they were soldiers, she answered their questions with one-word answers. When Heinz flirted, she ignored him. Jack puzzled over why she was so curt with her countrymen. Maybe she didn't like soldiers.

The young woman said she lived in Berlin and had been vacationing in Switzerland. Now she was going to Cologne, which was on their way. Jack decided not to ask if she was a Hitler-loving gal; it might ruin his chances with her. The five of them spent the night at a youth hostel in Innsbruck.

The barebones accommodations weren't to the woman's liking. "Her Ladyship," Jack wrote in his diary, "complained of not sleeping well. It was none too good as there were about forty guys in a room the size of a closet, and it is considered a disgrace to take a bath."

The weather turned sour the next day, rainy and cold. Jack's excitement and curiosity about Germany was tempered with wariness. Motoring through Brenner Pass to Austria, they dropped off the soldiers in Innsbruck.

"Perhaps we'll meet again someday," said Heinz. "I have always wanted to visit America."

They continued on to Munich, now a threesome. The mood of their female companion improved immediately.

"Tell me about America, Jack. Is your Roosevelt a good man?"

"I suppose. Most people seem to think so. They made him president for another four years. He is trying his best to improve the lives of people. But many are struggling. It's a very difficult situation that will take some time to fix."

"Germany no longer has elections. Hitler has seen to that."

After entering a small grocery store, Jack asked a question of the proprietor in basic German.

The owner, a large man wearing suspenders over his distended belly, snarled. "American?"

"Yes," said Jack.

"American, British. All the same. Enemies of the Reich. I don't like having you in my store. Get what you need and get out," he said, pointing to the door.

Without the cover of the soldiers, they faced the wrath of Germans who saw them as potential adversaries.

"Better yet, we'll get out before wasting our money," retorted Jack.

Based on Johann's remark about Europe needing a strong Germany and the shopkeeper's vitriol, Jack worried that the rest of their visit might turn out to be unpleasant. Hoping to offset the pall, Jack directed his charm at his female friend, asking questions about her life. Though she answered in vague terms, Jack could feel her warming to him. But as they neared Munich, her mood became darker, and she slunk into her seat as though she didn't want to be seen. She avoided any attempt by Jack to engage in conversation about politics.

"Please," she said, "I don't want to talk about such things. I just want to have fun while I can."

Almost every building in Munich was decorated with banners—chiefly the black swastika in a circle of white surrounded by blood-red. From a distance, they heard a marching band and the roar of a crowd. Enthusiastic people filled both sides of the street awaiting their heroes. They had run into a Nazi military parade. As the stern-looking soldiers passed by, the adoring crowd gave the Nazi salute. Several women ran out into the street to give flowers to the soldiers.

Jack couldn't stop himself from mocking the spectacle. He gave a limp wave, and Lem followed suit while mouthing, "Hi ya, Hitler," and "Hell to Hitler." When the Germans' arms went up, Jack and Lem's went down and vice versa.

"You can't do that here!" warned the woman, grabbing Jack's shoulder.

"But we're American," said Jack.

"It doesn't matter to them," she said. "I have seen it. People beaten for turning their backs on him. They will come after you!"

Now beginning to draw angry stares, Jack said, "Time to get out of here."

They bolted down a side street. Excited to taste the local cuisine, they went to the multi-level German beer hall, the Hofbräuhaus. It was a favorite among Nazi soldiers, but also a fair number of Europeans looking for a good time.

On their companion's suggestion, the boys ordered the pig knuckle with sauerkraut. "This is really good," said Jack. "You can order for me anytime."

Jack sat close to her, his leg touching hers. He could feel her respond, and she gave him a vivacious smile. When Lem left to go to the bathroom, Jack put his arm around her and gave her a quick kiss.

"I had a feeling you were going to do something like that," she said, batting her eyelashes.

"I may do something more later."

From across the communal table, a soldier clad in a black SS uniform said, "*Guten Abend.*" Speaking crisp Oxford English, he smiled and said he had been educated in England. He introduced his fellow soldiers. The conversation was light—no political discussion at all. Jack was thoroughly enjoying himself, and it seemed like everybody else was too. The pleasant smell of beer and roast pork permeated the large, boisterous hall.

Caught up in the lively atmosphere and of Germans, Brits, Americans, and others joyfully participating, Jack momentarily dismissed the idea that war was inevitable. If people of many nationalities were getting along here, couldn't there be a path to avoid hostilities? Perhaps his father was being overly pessimistic about war being inevitable. Still, Jack couldn't stop looking at the symbol on German's cap—a skull and crossbones representing death.

"You may be interested to know that this is where the Führer gave his first speech to the Nazi party in 1920," the soldier said.

"That is interesting," said Jack diplomatically.

When the soldier saw Lem admiring the large beer stein, he smiled and said, "You should take a couple as a souvenir. I can help. I know the best way for you to do it without getting caught." He nodded to one of his friends. "You can sneak out there," he said, pointing to a door. He clinked glasses with them. When Jack and Lem finished their beer, he said, "Go," and gave Lem a push.

After their female traveler said she'd meet them outside, they casually strolled toward the exit. But as they neared the door, their departure was suddenly blocked, and they were surrounded by several large waiters. Snatching back the mugs, the waiters jostled and shoved Jack and Lem. One slapped Lem. Others hurled incomprehensible threats. Out of the corner of his eye, Jack saw the soldier and his friends on their way over.

"You come to Germany and steal from the Reich?" the soldier asked with a sneer.

Jack felt the sting of the soldier's slap on his face. He was inches from Jack, his putrid breath insufferable.

"Get out of here," he said, pushing Jack with both hands and putting his boot behind Jack's leg. Jack tumbled backward, falling to the ground. Another soldier kicked Lem in the shin. "Stupid Americans!"

When Jack got to his feet, the soldiers propelled them out the door.

"That was pretty damn unpleasant," Jack said, breathing heavily.

"Never trust a Nazi," Lem said, holding his shin.

Yes, they planned on lifting souvenirs, and Jack had been a prankster himself at Choate—but he didn't like being set up by that damn Nazi.

After they reconnected with the woman at the entrance and told her what had happened, she put her hand on Jack's arm. "Are you all right? You must be more careful." She whispered in his ear, "Come to my room when we get back."

When they got back to the inn, Jack said to Lem, "I'll see you a little later. I've got some important matters I need to discuss with her."

In her room, Jack greeted her with a full-on kiss. Soon, they were together in her bed, trying to keep quiet so as not to alarm the proprietor. After a short but lively session, Jack returned to his room. While Lem snored, Jack took out his diary and wrote, "I went to sleep tired, but happy."

The next day, the young woman sidled up to Jack while Lem was packing.

"I need to get away from these Nazis," said Jack. "Let's go see a movie."

They decided on *Swing High, Swing Low*, a romantic comedy starring Carole Lombard and Fred MacMurray, even though Jack had already seen it. Jack sat between the young woman and Lem. Still, they couldn't get away from Hitler and the Nazis. Before the movie, there was a ten-minute newsreel, mostly of Hitler exhorting the masses and other propaganda. While her eyes remained closed, the crowd cheered throughout and offered lusty "Heil Hitlers" at its conclusion.

"The movie wasn't great," said Lem, as they walked out, "but at least it had a happy ending."

"Yeah, but I don't know if Europe is going to have a happy ending," remarked Jack, flipping a German coin. "What do you think?"

"I don't have much hope," the young woman said

Later that night, Jack again slipped into her room. Their tryst this time was interrupted by the hotel manager pounding on the door. "*Verboten!* No men in ladies' rooms! You must leave tomorrow!"

No doubt their conversation about politics had changed the dynamic. As Americans, they were no longer welcome.

In the morning, Jack took out his traveler's checks. The manager grabbed the checks and treated him to a cursing session. "You Americans are *der shit*. Stay where you are in your own country. Don't come over here. If you do, there will be bad trouble for you!"

Happy to get out of Munich and to see what else the country might offer, the threesome hit the road towards Nuremberg.

"One thing you have to like about this country," Lem said from the back seat, "is the quality of the roads."

"Yeah, maybe the only thing," Jack said.

They were speeding along one of the new autobahns, the world's first interstate highway. It was a pleasure to drive without having to deal with intersections, pedestrians, bicycles, or animal-powered vehicles.

"More importantly, you can drive fast," Jack said, giving the Ford a jolt of gas.

Driving took his mind off the single-minded Nazi way of thinking. And now he had an errand of joy. Although they hadn't been intimate together, he and Olive remained friends. When he was with her, she'd stop to pet or adore dogs. Jack had decided to bring her back a surprise.

"This one is so cute," said the German woman when they stopped at a kennel on the way to Nuremberg. Jack agreed and purchased the adorable black dachshund for eight dollars. Jack named him Offie, because he resembled the American ambassador's secretary he'd met in Paris. His soft eyes, almost always trained on Jack, constant wiggling, and frequent tail wagging captivated Jack emotionally as nothing had before. He held and petted Offie almost continuously, even talking to him like he was an old friend.

"Offie, how would you like to live in the U.S.? Get away from these awful Germans and Hitler? I think you'll enjoy your new home. We've got dachshunds there too."

Jack rarely let the dog stray from his arms. While he drove, Offie sat between his legs, and when Lem drove, Jack took the dog and cradled him on his lap.

"I'm starting to think you find that dog better company than me," Lem said, feeling left out.

"Well, he's a lot better looking, and his bark is a lot more inviting to my ears than your screeching voice," Jack cackled.

Jack's unconditional love for the dog was a complete revelation. His mother's lack of physical affection had convinced him that it was normal to be standoffish, but he craved touch, even though he found it uncomfortable. He shied away from touching women unless it might lead to an amorous encounter; he didn't really know how to relate to women physically. Usually, it was sex or nothing. But Offie allowed him to give and receive affection without conditions. So enamored was he of the dog, he tried to get a dachshund for himself but had no luck.

Suddenly, Jack began sneezing, and his breathing became labored. "Is it you?" he said to Offie's soulful face.

They arrived in Nuremberg, the chief commercial and manufacturing center of southern Bavaria. But now its primary industry was National Socialism, Hitler's Totalitarian political ideology. Nuremberg was a beautiful walled city featuring an Imperial castle, cobblestone streets, and half-timbered houses, but it was marred by symbols of the ever-present Nazi propaganda.

The Nazi fury in Nuremberg was intensifying. It seemed as if every few hours there was a military parade like they'd seen in Munich. The city was preparing for a week of rallies held every September. A hundred thousand people would cram into Zeppelin Field to wave their flags and cheer the Fuhrer. Already the city was swelling with people. After learning the events would begin in several days, they considered extending their stay.

Seeking accommodations, Jack asked a stern-looking woman for directions. The woman wore a Nazi lapel pin. "Are you American?" she asked. When they nodded, the woman spat on Jack's coat.

"I guess they still don't like us for joining the fight against them in the last war," Jack said, wiping himself off. "They know we'd side with Britain again."

BECOMING JFK

After a short stay in Nuremberg, they'd had enough of the Nazi frenzy and decided to skip the rally and drive on to Cologne. Jack's allergies worsened, but he refused to believe it was Offie. Maybe it would go away.

Jack had tried to be alone with his woman friend several times since Munich but hadn't been successful. When they arrived, she said, "Jack, I've enjoyed our . . . shall we say . . . encounter, and traveling with you and LeMoyne. But now I must go. Perhaps we'll meet again."

After exchanging information, they bid goodbye. "Keep me informed of the situation here," Jack said. "You'll be my spy."

Amsterdam was the final stop on their European tour before returning to London and then the United States. After the political upheaval they had witnessed elsewhere, Amsterdam was a pleasure. It was a lively city full of coffee shops, bars, and a thriving red-light district. It was a balm to their spirits after Germany. The first night, they dined on traditional Dutch food—herring, deep-fried cod fish, and cheese—and strolled the old city as darkness settled.

"What do you want to do?" asked Jack.

But Lem wasn't listening. He was staring at people entering a bar. A sign jutted out: The Empire. The door flew open for a few seconds, revealing a crowd of men. Two of them were kissing. The door closed. A man outside the door smiled at Lem, and he nodded back.

Jack thought back to his doubts about Lem after their visit to the Harlem brothel when they were students at Choate. Afterwards, Jack had never seen Lem so distraught. And then there was the sexual favor he offered Jack while he was at the Mayo Clinic. The hospital sequestration had inspired Jack to pen a letter of sexual frustration, and Lem had written back on toilet paper—so the evidence could be flushed away—suggesting a sex act when he returned. Jack rejected the offer but didn't think too much of it. He knew other boys at Choate experimented.

Lem had dated, both at Choate and after graduation, but now Jack wondered if it was a cover.

The two best friends looked briefly, but deeply, into each other's eyes. They had become close while at Choate, but the last couple of months traveling throughout Europe had been a bonding experience for them both. Lem grimaced and turned away. It was obvious to Jack that Lem yearned to go into the bar, but if he did, he'd be giving himself away. Homosexuality was illegal in the United States.

Still congested and sneezing, Jack took a test confirming his allergic reaction to the dog. "Looks like the odds are about eight to one against Offie getting to America," Jack said.

After he sold the dog in The Hague for five guilders, Lem said, "That's a loss of a few dollars for you."

"It's a bigger loss than that," Jack said, his head down.

Before he gave the dog away, he had the new owner take several pictures of him and Lem cradling Offie while sitting on the bumper of his car. Jack hugged and petted Offie for several moments. Finally, Jack gave him a final kiss on the head. "Bye, Offie," he said tearfully, as he handed the dog to its new owner. "Have a good life."

They headed for Calais and the Channel boat, but due to a misunderstanding involving Lem's passport, they missed the scheduled sail-away time. Jack went ahead and took the mail boat from Boulogne, and Lem stayed with the car, expecting to arrive later. They met in England and stayed in a private room in London's Talbot Square. Jack was happy to be back in this country, considering it his home away from home—familiar but different.

Jack joined Joe Jr. for breakfast one morning. "Want to come with me to say hello to Professor Laski? I'm going to be meeting with him today."

"I've got plans to go shopping with Kick," Jack said. "But say hello to him for me."

"Are you sure? Might learn something about what's going on in the world."

"I might, but I did a lot of learning on my own the past few months. Come to think of it, do you feel the same way now about Germany that you did a few years ago? You seemed to think then that they had a good thing going," Jack said.

"I do, but as JP says, we've got to stay out of whatever happens over here. It's none of our business. Let them fight it out if that's what they want to do." Joe Jr. regularly pawned his father's views off as his own.

"Some of these countries may not have any choice, Joe. They could be in Hitler's line of fire. Britain and France have been our friends for many years."

"Then best of luck to them."

"They'll appreciate that."

Jack and Lem spent a few more days traversing England, going grouse hunting, and exploring Edinburgh before boarding the SS *Washington* on September 10, bound for New York.

Sitting on the deck, Jack took out his diary and wrote about what seemed to be an inevitable conflict. As he jotted down ideas, he was coming to the conclusion that England might hold the key to keeping the peace in Europe. The UK could serve as a bulwark to prevent the Germans,

French, Italians, and Soviets from facing off. Would the chances of an all-out war be lessened if Britain re-armed? As Jack saw the situation, somebody needed to deter Germany.

Chapter 8

With the top down to catch the fall breeze, Jack whizzed down Memorial Drive in his convertible, a cute Boston waitress riding along in the passenger seat. He put his hand on her leg and gave her a killer smile. Jack pursued available co-eds with the same competitive spirit as he displayed for sports. He asked out anybody he found attractive. Many of those were Radcliffe, Wellesley, or Mount Holyoke co-eds. He tried to have sex with almost all of them. Charlotte and Frances and Margaret . . . the list went on. Jack's goal was to have sex with as many of them as possible. It happened quite often, but once it did, Jack lost interest quickly. On to the next gal, or back for occasional seconds—depending on the circumstances.

This term he'd set his sights on getting into a Harvard finals club, the university's version of a fraternity. He targeted the Spee Club, believing membership would open doors, convey status, as well as provide a comfortable retreat. But getting in wouldn't be easy. His father and brother had both been rejected, and it still rankled them. The word was Joe had been denied because he was thought too brash, which didn't bode well for Jack's chances. But he thought he might have a leg up. His successful freshman smoker was still being talked about six months later. Maybe he'd earned enough goodwill to get in. Jack hoped Torby, now his roommate, might also get in, but the scuttlebutt on him wasn't good—he drank too much and was considered rough around the edges.

"If Torby can't get in, that's his problem," Jack said. "I'm going for it." He was with common friends of theirs at the Waldorf Cafeteria in Harvard Square. A sign outside advertised "Whale Steak. 60 cents." Everybody got the whale steak, which had a curious gray-brown color. It didn't look much different from a sirloin, except there wasn't any bone. Jack took a big bite of the oily, salty steak.

"Best whale I ever had," said Jack with a chuckle.

A few weeks later, Jack was invited to vie for Spee membership. He survived the rude treatment bestowed on new recruits—a harrowing time of bowing down to the members and running foolish errands for them, but soon it would be over. Final rites were tonight.

Jack and a friend arrived at the Spee Club, the well-appointed, spacious Georgian-style building at the corner of Mt. Auburn and Holyoke. He and his fellow plebes were blindfolded and given a goblet.

"Drink up," said the Spee president. "You'll enjoy it once you get used to it. But it's an acquired taste."

Jack took a breath, closed his eyes, and gulped down the drink. Unbeknownst to him or the other applicants, it had been concocted from a bull's balls—the club's mascot was a bull—augmented with a special sauce that tasted like rotten eggs. Tearing off his blindfold, Jack bolted for the bathroom and upchucked his stomach's contents into the toilet.

He walked back to his room after they'd been inducted, the sickly aftertaste of vomit still in his mouth. "This is going to be terrific," Jack said to a friend. "It's not everything we wanted, but I think it's going to be good for us."

The Spee offered conveniences, and Jack began taking his meals there. He used the quiet in-house library to write letters to family and friends using Spee stationery. It also offered a welcome refuge when he wanted time away from Torby and the dorm. Although Jack ignored the evidence that he could be difficult to live with, there was the continuing problem of a messy room. Once, while preparing to go out, Jack heaped everything onto the floor.

"It's looking like a goddamn rummage sale, Jack," Torby complained, looking at the pile.

"Don't get too sanctimonious, Torb. Whose stuff do you think I'm throwing mine on top of?" Jack said and walked out the door.

Jack fiddled with his football helmet. Now a mere substitute on the junior varsity squad, he nonetheless expected to get in the game for at least a few plays. Since Joe hoped to play for the Harvard varsity later that day, their father had his driver take him to the games at Harvard Stadium, just across the Charles River.

The JV game began, but Jack languished on the bench. Disconsolate, he looked down at his jersey and the four thick horizontal stripes that ran across his chest. He fingered the same stripe pattern on his right arm. At every time-out, he got up and tried to make eye contact with Harlow, who ignored him.

With only a quarter left in the game, Jack stood up and walked up to the coach. "Think I could help here, Coach. How about giving me a try?"

Harlow looked at him with light contempt. "I'll let you know, Kennedy," he said and turned away.

Jack never got in.

Now in his street clothes, head down and feeling like he'd let his father down, Jack walked sullenly across the field. He looked up to see his father's chauffeur running towards him.

"Take me out, Jack!" shouted the driver, hoping to pull Jack out of his funk.

Jack thought he'd stop, but the driver plowed right into him, knocking Jack flat on his back. A painful twinge shot up Jack's spine, but he saw his father watching and didn't want to show weakness. Gathering himself, Jack forced a tight smile and winced. "Hi, Dad."

BECOMING JFK

What a day! he thought. The only football action I get is my father's driver smashing into me when I'm not ready and hurting my back.

The back pain—akin to being prodded with a dull knife—didn't go away. Jack stuck it out and got in a few plays against Dartmouth. He was proud to get his "minor H" but wondered if he'd had enough tackle football. I spend a lot of time practicing, but I rarely play, Jack thought. And it was hard on his body. He'd often come back to his room tired and sore. Touch football on their Hyannis Port lawn was more fun anyway. And he could still compete in other sports at Harvard, like swimming and sailing, without the risk of bodily harm.

"No more football for me, Torby," Jack said the day after the season ended. "See if you can get on without me." Torby was a star player on the varsity.

"We'll do the best we can. Probably do better without you." Torby laughed good-naturedly.

"I still intend to kick your ass when you come down to Hyannis," Jack retorted. It was a different game there, one not so reliant on brute strength, and Jack often outmaneuvered the bigger, brawnier guys like Torby and Joe.

Lem and Rip were waiting for him outside the Stork Club, New York's famed night spot. Jack was late as usual, but his two friends were used to it.

"Hi, boys," said Jack cheerily. He'd come up from Florida immediately after the new year to meet his friends at *the* place to be in New York. Anybody who was anybody came to the Stork. They passed under the green awning and the fourteen-karat gold chain and were ushered into the main room. The club's mascot, a stork with a monocle and top hat, was everywhere—on swizzle sticks, water pitchers, matchbooks, and ashtrays.

"Change is afoot for the Kennedys," Jack said once they were seated. "Looks like Dad is going to be ambassador to the Court of St. James. That's where Roosevelt wants him. So, I may be due for a return visit."

"Cheers," Rip said, offering his glass for Jack and Lem to toast. "Soon you'll be talking with a British accent."

"Joe's going to serve as Dad's secretary, and I'll help out too in a capacity yet to be determined."

Jack's attention was diverted by a blonde who looked familiar. She was sitting at a booth almost directly across from them.

Nodding in the direction of the pixieish young woman, her glowing face outlined by golden curls, Jack said, "Hey, isn't that Sonja Heine? The Norwegian skater who won all those Olympic gold medals?"

"Could be," Rip said.

"Do I remember a picture of her giving the *heil* to Hitler after one of her wins?" Lem said. "I think she even went to his box. Flirted with the Fuhrer. Might be best to stay away from Nazi-loving gals."

"You're right, Lem. Your advice is always appreciated, but it can't hurt to say hello. Maybe get some skating tips. Besides, she's with another guy, although she doesn't look very tight with him from what I can see."

After making eye contact with Sonja, Jack got up and approached her table. "My name is Jack Kennedy. I was just talking with my friends about the awful time I've been having with my lutz."

Heine smiled. "Jack, this is my brother Lief. I don't know if this is the time or place for a skating lesson, but perhaps you'd like to show me your moves on the dance floor?"

"With pleasure," Jack said, offering his hand and leading the way. Jack felt especially light on his feet and pleased that his back pain had receded.

Heine moved with grace, fluidity, and strength. At the conclusion of the song, Jack said, "I'd give you a gold medal for dancing, but I left it at home."

"Nice to meet you, Jack," said Sonja. "Maybe we'll meet again. If we do, I'll give you a skating lesson."

Jack went back to the table.

"Any luck?" said Rip.

"For her. She got to dance with me. That guy was her brother. Hope to see her again."

After Lem and Rip left, Jack headed for the inner sanctum of the Stork's Cub Room. Here, celebrities and power brokers were in abundant supply. So was the head waiter, known as Saint Peter, because he determined who got in. And Jack gained a nod and immediate access. His father and the owner, Sherman Billingsley, had been friendly acquaintances in the liquor trade.

The windowless, wood-paneled room was decorated with portraits of beautiful women. Present in real life were celebrities of considerable stature. Off to the right was a mustachioed Ernest Hemingway in deep discussion with a gorgeous lady. At another table was FBI Director J. Edgar Hoover with a male companion. On the other side of the room was a guy on the opposite side of law enforcement. Frank Costello was a mobster and reputed to be a part owner of the club.

At Table 50, known as the royal box, sat Walter Winchell, the powerful writer whose newspaper column was syndicated across the country. Fedora cocked to the side, a cigarette in his mouth, Winchell pounded away at the typewriter on the table-turned-desk.

Why not say hello? "Jack Kennedy, Mr. Winchell."

"Oh, the new ambassador's son." So, Winchell already knew of his father's impending appointment. Probably before Jack did.

"What are you doing here, kid?" He didn't wait for an answer. "Don't think your Pa is going to be popular there if he doesn't want to help the Brits out."

Winchell had been one of the first to attack the Nazis. He was at odds with the elder Kennedy's insistence that the United States keep its distance from the troubles in Europe and refrain from arming Great Britain.

"They'll take to him," defended Jack. He wasn't sure if he believed what he was saying.

"Yeah, sure," retorted Winchell. "By then, it might be too late. See ya, kid." He returned to pecking away at his typewriter.

There were different ways to wield power. Nobody was more influential than Winchell when it came to making or breaking careers.

In the wee hours, Jack went out to wait in his car for one of the Stork Club waitresses he'd been seeing. Among other things, she cooked him steak dinners—his favorite.

Billingsley also had come outside. Seeing Jack in his car, he shouted, "Having steak tonight, Jack?!"

"Yeah," said Jack, licking his lips, "and that's not all."

With his football career over, Jack set his sights on earning a varsity letter in swimming. He swam the 100-meter breaststroke and 300-meter relay his first two years and was primed to be a major team contributor his final season. He was in the best condition of his life, and his times continued to improve. He was on a roll, excited to finish the school year with this important athletic achievement. Joe had never earned a varsity letter in football, so Jack would be a Kennedy first. But in the third week of February, he was overcome by chills, fever, and fatigue.

BECOMING JFK

In his sick bed at the infirmary, he was melancholy, worried that he'd never be completely healthy. What kind of life would he have if, every few months, he'd be laid up in a hospital, bedridden, and unable to do much of anything. Tired of reading, Jack took out a pen and paper and wrote Lem:

> *Well, once more my athletic career has been blighted. Have the grippe—been in the infirmary for four days now and it looks like I shall be here another few days. The Yale meet is two weeks from Saturday so I don't see how I can ever get back in shape by then.*

"Thanks," he said to Torby in their quarters as he cut his meat. Torby had smuggled in steaks and extra food, trying to get Jack to gain weight. Jack got back in the pool briefly, but in March, he developed an intestinal infection and was hospitalized at New England Baptist Hospital.

After his discharge, he decided to try once more, but today he huddled in the locker room. Representatives from the local papers were waiting outside, wanting to take pictures of the ambassador's son on the swim team.

"I'm not going out there," said Jack to his swimming coach. "Look at me." Jack pulled up his shirt to reveal ribs that were sticking out. "I'm all skin and bones. Tell them I'm not here." There was no way he'd allow his emaciated body to be pictured in the papers.

At the ensuing meet, Jack did his best to compete, but his stamina was severely diminished. He'd start off strong, then fall behind at the end of a race. A letter in swimming was not to be. Jack was left off the team.

It was the summer of 1938, and Jack's father had stayed in town to attend Joe's graduation. He was also expected to be awarded an honorary degree that would be conferred on contributors to the film industry. Instead, the award went to Walt Disney. Embarrassed at being passed over and the negative press, Joe Sr. was ready to return to a country where the press fawned over him and his family. With school out, the family would regroup for the summer.

"Boys," he said to Jack and Joe, as they prepared to board the SS *Normandy*, "I never thought I'd say this, but I'm looking forward to returning to England."

PART TWO
Ambassador's Son

Chapter 9
July 1938

From the beginning, the idea of a large, lively Irish-American family descending on London fascinated the British. Ambassador Kennedy, with most of his family, had arrived by March, and the initial press coverage was glowing.

The Kennedys, welcomed with open arms, began socializing with British aristocrats and royalty. In April, the family were guests of King George VI and Queen Elizabeth.

In July, Joe Sr. returned to England with Joe and Jack and the family's presence was complete.

"I told the press you were both coming," said Joe Sr. of his two oldest sons. He'd ordered them to put on suits, carry their hats, and flank him on the ship's railing as they arrived. A large contingent of press crowded the dock, anxious to see the ambassador and his sons.

The Kennedys headquartered at the expansive but rundown fifty-two-room residence at 14 Prince's Gate, close by Hyde Park. It was a half-hour walk to the American Embassy.

"Tomorrow," Joe Sr. said to his sons privately that evening after dinner, "you'll get a chance to see how the British go about governing. You'll be joining me to attend a meeting of Prime Minister Chamberlain and his cabinet."

When Joe Jr. excused himself, his father said, "Speaking of money, Jack, there's one other thing for you to know. Now that you are twenty-one, you are a millionaire. The money has been transferred to your account."

"Okay. Thanks, I guess." Jack didn't feel any different now that he was a millionaire, although he wondered if his new status would change his relationship with his father. Perhaps it would give him more independence—he wouldn't have to ask his father for money. Not that he'd ever worried about money. He was also good at not spending it. It wasn't uncommon for Jack to ask others to cover his expenses at events because he didn't carry cash. He didn't think being rich would change the way he did things. And having a pile of cash certainly wouldn't affect adversely his drive for success.

At the House of Commons meeting, to Jack's eye, Chamberlain appeared overwhelmed. The prime minister wearily addressed his ministers and agreed to Hitler's demands for allowing German occupation of Czechoslovakia's Sudetenland.

"JP is in a bit of a tough spot," Jack said to Joe as they filed out. "The Brits are going to want our help, but that's the last thing he wants. It's not up to him, though. We have a long history with this country. Including the last war."

"Dad knows what he's doing. Maybe it's Roosevelt who doesn't." Joe always offered fierce support for his father, but Jack was learning to tread the fine line between voicing his own views and not abandoning his father politically.

"We'll see," Jack said.

Jack spent most of August vacationing with his family in the south of France. At a summer ball held at the legendary Hotel Du Cap, he donned a white tuxedo and danced with the daughter of Marlene Dietrich, the renowned German actress known for her outspoken disdain for the Nazis. Later, Dietrich herself approached him for a dance.

Jack had noticed his father spending time with Dietrich earlier in the summer, and now, face-to-face, he couldn't help but admire her striking cat-shaped eyes and elegant high cheekbones. As they moved to the slow rhythm of "Begin the Beguine," Dietrich leaned in closer, her smile both mysterious and playful.

Their brief exchange left Jack with mixed feelings. He was intrigued by the encounter but also unsettled, suspecting his father might have orchestrated it. Though he appreciated the attention, Jack resented the notion that his father might be meddling in his personal affairs. After all, he was doing just fine on his own.

"Looks to me like you and Marlene were dancing pretty close," his father said to Jack the next day. With a gloating smile, he added, "I sent her over to give you a thrill."

"Thanks, Dad. I did. But, if you don't mind, you don't need to do anything more like that. I'm doing pretty good on my own."

His father offered a close-lipped smile. Then he said, "Sure, Jack. If that's the way you want it."

In September, Jack boarded the SS *Bremen* for the voyage back to the states to begin his junior year at Harvard. Lem was waiting for him when he arrived, his hulking figure animatedly waving as Jack came down the ramp.

After handshakes and a hearty exchange of shoulder claps, Lem asked, "How was your trip? Something different about you. You're looking a lot more English. Do I detect a hint of a British accent? Even looks like you've grown a stiff upper lip."

Jack laughed and touched his lips. "Soft as ever. At least the British women thought so." It was good to see Lem.

Several reporters and photographers swarmed around him, peppering him with questions about his father's views on the increasingly dangerous situation in Europe. How did the press know he'd be arriving?

He was surprised that they cared what the twenty-one-year-old son of the ambassador thought.

A reporter for the *Boston Herald* asked, "Jack, what does your father say about the European situation? Does he think there's going to be a war?"

"It is my father's view," said Jack, "that there is no immediate possibility of war and therefore no need to evacuate American citizens. The fact is the rest of my family will be staying in Europe for the next year. So, at this time, I don't think he sees any need for alarm."

Jack parried a few more questions, then he and Lem grabbed lunch at a diner. After they ordered from their counter seats, Lem said, "Nice job there, Ken. With the press I mean. Handled it well. Your father would have been proud."

"Thanks."

The next night, he and Lem attended a Cole Porter hit musical called *Leave it to Me*! Its subject was a diplomat called home after pleading for enemy countries to put aside their differences and get along.

"I bet the Kennedys are boiling," one actor said during the show.

The crowd roared. Jack and Lem looked at each other. As they walked out, Jack said, "It was pretty funny, and jokes about us get by far the biggest laughs—whatever that signifies."

Chapter 10

After enjoying Mardi Gras in New Orleans, Jack gazed out the window of the plane taking him back to New York. An idea for his senior thesis had begun to take shape. He wanted to write about the events in Europe. Perhaps something to do with diplomatic history and international law. And he wanted to combine it with travel. There was so much more he wanted to see of Europe and the world.

Harvard granted him permission to forgo the second half of his junior year to do research abroad. His father whole-heartedly approved of the idea and agreed to supply him with credentials that would give him access to key players who'd help him gather material.

Jack was scheduled to depart New York February 24, 1939 on the *Queen Mary*, but his health took a turn for the worse, resulting in intense intestinal pain and weight loss. Once again, he found himself at the Mayo Clinic.

It was near midnight and a snowstorm had blanketed the small town of Rochester, Minnesota. Jack put down his book and stared at the wall, unhappy about being back at the clinic for a third stint. His gloom was interrupted by a knock at the door.

Dr. George Taylor entered, carrying a medical file. Taylor was a tall, bent man with only a small covering of black hair atop his head.

"Hi, Jack. How are you feeling?"

"As good as can be expected," Jack said dourly. He wondered why Taylor had stopped by so late. It certainly wasn't to say good night.

The doctor pulled up a chair. "It's about your plans to travel overseas. How long do you plan to be on the road?"

"Several months. Give or take."

"That's a long time. I wouldn't recommend it."

"No? Why not? Think war is going to break out?"

"No, I think it wouldn't be a good idea based on what's going on with you. It could be disastrous to your health. Traveling for that long would be quite strenuous."

"I can handle it," Jack said defensively.

"I'm going to put the facts in front of you." Dr. Taylor read from a chart. "Your white blood count is very low. At intake, it was six thousand. Now it's dropped to thirty-five hundred. If it drops much more, you'll be in serious trouble. And you've dropped twelve pounds in six days."

"What did you expect would happen when I'm fed nothing but rice and potatoes and a steady diet of enemas."

"I don't think that's the reason."

Jack wasn't going to give in. Short of a catastrophic illness, nothing was going to stop him from his overseas assignment. "The *Queen Mary* is expecting me. It's bad manners to keep the queen waiting."

Taylor chuckled. "I suppose it is."

Jack had heard the possible diagnoses before. Acute colitis. Spastic colon. Agranulocytosis, which he could barely pronounce. That was a disease of the bone marrow. The doctor said that might be a reason for his susceptibility to colds, infections, and the hives that appeared with maddening regularity.

"Have you thought about what might happen if you take ill while sailing the Atlantic or gallivanting through Europe?"

"Plenty of doctors in London. Europe too. I'll take my chances."

Taylor stood up and put his hand under his chin. "I have an idea. But it might not be a good one." He sighed, as if resigned to the fact that his patient was going to leave, and thus even an experimental solution was in order.

"Can't wait to hear it."

"Perhaps we can do something about your colon, which could give you relief. Bring down the inflammation. It's called DOCA. That stands for Desoxycorticosterone acetate. It's an adrenal extract. A steroid. If it works, you might be able to eat semi-normally, add weight, and your blood count will rise."

Jack didn't hesitate. "Let's do it."

"Before you say yes, I must advise you that this treatment hasn't been fully tested. There could be significant side effects. Perhaps even long term."

"I don't care. As long as it doesn't kill me. Worth the risk. When do we start the treatment?"

"Now. I'll be right back."

When he returned, the doctor was holding a white pellet in one hand and a scalpel in the other. "I'm going to make a small incision, tuck the pellet in, and cover it with a bandage. It will dissolve in your system."

While on his trip, Jack would have to administer the adrenal extract himself. "Since I'll be the one operating on myself," Jack said, "I might as well do the dirty work now."

"I guess you're right," Dr. Taylor said, handing over the scalpel and pellet.

With Taylor's guidance, Jack made the incision a few minutes later, placed the pellet inside, and bandaged up the wound.

"Nice job," said Taylor. "Have you thought of a career in medicine? You might make a good surgeon. We'll be needing more if war breaks out."

"No, I spend too much time in hospitals as it is."

"Understandable. Let's see how things go for a few days, and if there are no complications, you and the queen have a date." If he had any problems, Taylor said a doctor could handle the procedure, or inject him, and complete a quick check-up on his health.

In the next few days, Jack's energy surged. Maybe this pill was the answer to his health problems. Or at least some of them.

Before embarking on his European research, Jack spent a few weeks working for his father at the embassy in London. The embassy was situated in four newly renovated brick townhouses. He manned the phones, ran errands, and handled incoming cables. I'm a glorified office boy, Jack thought, but the job has advantages—he was privy to diplomatic documents that increased his understanding of the evolving European situation.

He also secured introductions to English royalty. Jack wore the required white tie and tails for a formal introduction to King George and Queen Elizabeth, and had tea with their princess daughter, then called Lilibet. As the time for his departure to the continent drew near, he felt ready.

Late one evening, Jack decided he wanted some ice cream. He took out a carton from the freezer and scooped it directly into his mouth. The freezer had been shipped from New York to the ambassador's residence because English freezers didn't handle ice cream well. It was a treat only a few in the UK had access to.

His father walked through the kitchen door. "Good idea, Jack. I'm in the mood for some ice cream too. Scoop me a bowl. Then let's talk about your trip."

After listening to Jack's itinerary, Joe Sr. leaned closer and swallowed his ice cream. "Jack, I know your primary purpose is to gather material for your thesis—and to have a good time. But I'd like you to do something else."

"What's that?" Jack put down his spoon.

"I also want you to be my eyes and ears. You'll be meeting some interesting people, many of them in high places. And you'll be on the streets with the common people. Talk with as many of them as you can. You have a way of drawing out people. They want to talk with you. Use that talent. Perhaps you might learn something that could help keep our country out of war—or at least delay it."

"I'll do my best."

"I'm also sending Joe out into the field. He'll start in Spain and go on from there."

Jack wondered if this was another competition their father had initiated between his sons to see who'd secure the most valuable intelligence for him.

Before Jack departed, he wanted to see what his father's position was on the plight of the Jews. He needed to ask one more question of his father. "What about the people the Nazis are persecuting?"

Joe Sr. shrugged. "The Jews. What about them?"

"I've heard, as you have too, that Hitler is making life difficult for them."

"Jack, that's none of our business. I don't want you, as my representative, to get yourself mixed up in that. We can't get involved in German affairs if we're to stay out of any conflict."

Before beginning his journey, Jack, along with his family, attended the investiture of Pope Pius XII, then skied for a week in Switzerland. He stayed a few days in Paris, where he attended a luncheon at which the famed pilot Charles Lindbergh was a guest. Jack was ten at the time Lindbergh made his first transatlantic flight in 1927, but he remembered how it had made Lindy an American hero. Jack walked up to the tall, serious man after lunch and introduced himself.

"It's a pleasure to meet you, Jack," said Lindbergh. "Your father and I have much in common—which is keeping our great country out of Europe's business. I'm glad to hear your brother shares that same view also."

"They have their opinions and I have mine," replied Jack. "And I don't think England shares their view that we shouldn't help them. The Brits are worried that Hitler might visit them."

"I don't think so. Hitler wants peace. I have been told that the Germans have a deal to sell their airplane engines and parts to France. Why would a warring country do something of this nature? Hitler would make an excellent trading partner with the U.S. He has no quarrel with us."

"Not yet."

"Good to talk with you," said Lindbergh, turning away to speak to a line of admirers.

Chapter 11

Jack drove the small, blue, rented Citroen to Warsaw and checked into the Polonia Palace Hotel. It was May 1939. The city's preeminent accommodation, a favorite of diplomats, was a Parisian-style building with a mansard roof, situated across from Warsaw Central Station. In his hotel room, Jack reached into his trunk and took out his new bible—John Gunther's *Inside Europe*. The first edition had come out in 1933, and Gunther had revised it every year since. This indispensable guide had sections on every country and special chapters devoted to Hitler, Mussolini, and Stalin. Poland, wrote Gunther, was positioned as the "nut in the nutcrackers." Germany desired to recover the Polish Corridor it had lost after the first world war.

Jack was ready to begin researching his senior thesis. As he wandered outside, he saw many Germans about town, some in uniform and others in civilian suits. It seemed as if they all wore a small swastika pin.

That night after dinner, Jack took a walk around the city, then returned to the hotel. He ventured into its nightclub, where cocktail tables surrounded the dance floor and a band played to a mixed crowd of Europeans. But it was the uniformed German officers who stood out. When Jack noticed a young, blonde Polish woman enter the club, he raced over and asked her to dance before he had competition. She had on a chiffon blouse and calf-length skirt that flared out at the hemline. While dancing a Viennese waltz, Jack told her he was an American on holiday.

"Everybody is coming to Poland these days," she said. "The Americans, the British, the Russians, and of course, the Germans." She nodded in the direction of a German officer lingering nearby.

"And whom do you prefer?" Jack asked.

"That depends. But it seems the Germans may be the best for our future. They are very confident, and Hitler is very strong. The British are doing their best to avoid war. It may not be possible, no? As for you Americans, you are happy to see what happens. By then, it might be too late."

"Too late for what?"

"You may think me a simple dance hall girl, but after a few drinks, even the tightest diplomats loosen up." She took a sip.

"Oh, what do they say?"

"That the Munich Agreement was *oszustwo*. It means nothing. It gave Hitler part of Czechoslovakia, but that won't be enough to satisfy his appetite. Herr Hitler will soon be on the march. If you go to Danzig, you will think you are in Germany."

The Free (Polish) City of Danzig had its own parliament, currency, anthem, and flag. Most importantly, it had profitable shipyards and access to the sea.

"Might be worth a visit," Jack said.

"By the way," she asked, "what brings you here?"

After Jack told her he was gathering material for his thesis and that his father was the ambassador to England, she said scornfully, "What can an ambassador do? It is in the hands of the generals now."

"And whose side are you on?"

She smiled cunningly. "I want to be on the winning side. Don't we all? Will you excuse me?" she said, nodding at the German officer, crooking his finger in her direction. "My presence is being requested."

After a few more dances, Jack headed for his room. He passed his former dancing partner and the German officer in the lobby. They were leaving the hotel, her arm linked in his.

Jack took a few days to explore Old Town, the medieval center of

Warsaw. Only a short distance from the Vistula River, Old Town was dominated by the immense Royal Castle where the Polish monarch resided. Outside, guards in crisp uniforms patrolled the entrance. The flag was raised, signifying the monarch was in. Jack wondered how much longer that would be.

The town square was busy. The early summer brought out the residents and others to buy goods at the market stalls, many of which sold beets and potatoes.

At night, Jack ducked into a number of small clubs playing what he considered stilted jazz.

Using his father's connections, he had made an appointment to meet with two Polish diplomats at the hotel. As they lunched on stuffed dumplings, one of the diplomats said, "It is a very bad situation for us. Hitler might try to put Poland in the position of being the aggressor. Make up a story about Poland attacking Germany and use it as an excuse to invade."

"Will you be able to defend yourself if they do?" asked Jack.

The other diplomat looked down for a moment, then said quietly, "We have an army of four million. But we are not ready for war."

"Why not?"

"Our military equipment is outdated. We are a farming country. Not an industrial one. We haven't kept up."

Jack digested this admission. It seemed that nobody was ready for war. Except Germany.

The next day, Jack gunned the Citroen toward Danzig's port city of Gdańsk. After checking into the Kasino-Hotel, he roamed the port city's narrow, cobbled streets, entranced by the medieval halls, red-tiled roofs, and the varied languages being spoken. He heard the voices of Scots, Russians, and the Dutch, but mostly what he heard was German. The Polish attaché in Warsaw told him that ninety percent of Gdańsk's population considered themselves German. And no wonder. German soldiers in field gray uniforms were everywhere..

Jack later stopped at a kiosk and bought a few pierogies. He decided to strike up a conversation with a German soldier standing nearby who was scanning the streets. "Things seem to be heating up here," Jack said.

"Why is it you ask?"

"Just an interested observer."

"It will become much more interesting once the Reich consolidates this area. It is German in most ways. Soon it will be German in all."

"How soon do you think that will be?"

"Won't be long. *Auf Wiedersehen* [Until we meet again.]"

Jack next visited the Senate of the Free City of Danzig in Gdańsk.

"You have come at a very interesting time," said Arthur Greiser, a thick, bald-headed man who was the Nazi president of the Senate. "Your father has taken the correct position of staying out of European affairs. We only want what the people of Danzig want," he said, responding to Jack's question concerning the future of the Free City. "It is all but German anyway, so it is only right that it be returned to Germany. For many years, it was proud to be a part of the German Empire."

Greiser plucked an errant thread from the armband of his swastika and flicked it away. "The biggest problem here is the Jews. They are increasing tensions between Poland and Danzig. It will be best not to have these Jews behaving in this way. It only brings trouble to everybody. I'm sure you agree."

Jack didn't reply.

Seeking a different view, Jack paid a visit to the British Consul General Gerald Shepherd, hoping for encouraging news. Shepherd had the look of a man who'd endured many sleepless nights recently.

"Jack," he said, making a motion to usher Jack into his office, "I have great respect for your father, and as ambassadors we have a lot in common. But we are on opposite sides of the fence when it comes to dealing with this madman Hitler."

"I understand," Jack said. "But don't you both want to stop a war?"

"Yes, but we have different ways of going about it. He would prefer to placate Hitler, and I don't think that's possible. Give Hitler a little and he'll want more. He controls Czechoslovakia and right now is eyeing Poland and Danzig."

"Really?" Jack didn't think the war, if it came, would arrive that soon.

"I've already taken measures to help those in the most danger," said the British Consul. "And those, of course, are the Jews. I've arranged for many to emigrate to England and others to Palestine. It's legal now, but soon it won't be. Then they'll be trapped here and probably killed. The Germans are after Jews everywhere."

"The situation seems more desperate than I thought," Jack said. "Is it too late to stop Hitler?"

"I think so. But it didn't have to be. I'm ashamed that, after the war, we didn't re-arm. Instead, we disarmed. We are at a great disadvantage now, and I don't see much hope. Chamberlain is trying, but in the wrong way. Acquiescing. And we, the British press, people, business, labor, politicians, and well, everybody, want to avoid another Great War." Shepherd sighed. "Seems like it only ended yesterday, but it's been twenty years."

Jack left the consul general's office curious about Britain's unwillingness to defend itself. He made a mental note to explore the issue further, thinking it could be a key piece of his thesis. He'd have the advantage of being able to obtain correspondence, cables, and interviews of key British players to document their viewpoints. But he didn't want to decide just yet. He had plenty of other places still to visit. And more people from all walks of life to talk with.

That night he read a chapter on Stalin in *Inside Europe*. Gunther called him "probably the most powerful single human being in the world . . . and different from other dictators because he is not only the undisputed leader of a national state but of a movement which has roots in all countries."

Before he went to sleep, Jack wrote Lem, teasing:

> *Leave tomorrow for Russia. This last bit is confidential, but I have a divorced Romanian princess with whom—however, on second thought, will save this tidbit till I see you.*

Chapter 12

Jack shuddered as the ancient Russian Aeroflot aircraft rumbled its way to Moscow. He sat on the floor, a loose strap around his arm. He'd decided to visit the Soviet Union, intrigued by what he'd learned last semester after taking a Russian history class.

After endless lines and bureaucratic hold-ups at the airport, Jack checked in at the famed Metropol Hotel, the art nouveau-style hotel close by the Kremlin and the Bolshoi Ballet. It had been built before the Communists had taken over in 1917.

Attendants in gold-braided uniforms, a lobby featuring ornate brass carvings, and plush, red and gilded furniture stood in stark contrast to what he had seen on the ride to the hotel. Moscow appeared drab and colorless. But the Communists, having kicked out the local apparatchiks, had gussied up the hotel so foreign visitors might report favorably on their time in Russia.

Waiting for him when he stepped out of the elevator was a floor lady, or *dezhurnaya*. Jack showed his hotel card to the thick, unsmiling woman sitting at a table. She handed over his room keys without any attempt at pleasantries. During his stay, she or somebody else would glower at him from the table whenever he arrived or departed—twenty-four hours a day.

"Try the caviar," said Charles Bohlen, the second secretary at the United States Embassy, during dinner in the Metropol's grand dining room.

"Would you fill me in?" Jack asked. "This is my first visit to a Communist country. What should I expect?"

"Expect a lot of delays, red tape, and grimness," Bohlen said. "You may already have noticed the way things are done here."

"Yes," Jack said, remembering the interminable delays at the airport. "Where does Stalin figure in all this?"

"He's a wily character—and ruthless."

"Tell me about him."

"When farmers resisted his efforts to collectivize, he ordered troops to confiscate the wheat. Millions starved to death. A famine the world doesn't know much about. He also jailed and executed Ukrainians and others."

Jack shook his head at what Stalin had wrought. Behind that avuncular smile was a mass murderer. "And to think we may have him as our ally."

"That's right, although you may be interested to know that the Germans and Russians have been working together since the end of the Great War."

"Doing what?"

"The Treaty of Versailles prevented Germany from re-arming, so the Germans have been quietly working on weapons in Russia. Until a few years ago, they had secret laboratories, workshops, and testing grounds in Russia in which they developed major weapons systems. Once the inspectors left Germany and declared it unarmed and in compliance with the treaty, they moved the operation to German soil and saved themselves a ton of money. This all happened before Hitler came to power. You can bet they'll put that to good use—perhaps even against Russia."

This bit of information stunned Jack. He was shocked that Germany was clandestinely building up its military before Hitler came to power. They had been playing an international game of chess while no one was looking. An enlightening, if sobering thought.

"I don't think the Russian-German friendliness will last," Bohlen continued. "Hitler hates Communism. I bet he already has Russia in his sights."

"Invade Russia?" Jack said incredulously.

"Wouldn't surprise me in the least. Nor surprise the Russians."

Jack asked Bohlen for nightlife recommendations.

"They keep a tight control on everything here," Bohlen said. "You won't find any Soviet citizens in the hotel. They aren't allowed. I'd say enjoy yourself right here at the Metropol. It has a nightclub, and the Shalyapin Bar is quite wonderful. There's an extraordinary variety of people coming through here from all over the world, more so now that things are heating up." Bohlen held up his hand. "But a word of caution."

"Yes?"

Bohlen leaned closer. "Be careful what you say and how you talk to people. The hotel is thick with spies from every country, all looking to get an edge if and when the shit hits the fan."

After dinner, they strolled past the hotel's ornate fountain stocked with fish. Two men, one of them a guest, approached the fountain. The uniformed hotel employee had a net. When the guest pointed to the water, the employee netted the thrashing fish and took it away.

Bohlen laughed at Jack's shocked reaction. "It happens quite often. Somebody will pick out their dinner from the fountain and take it to the chef. The chef promptly throws it away and prepares a suitable filet. Nobody knows the difference."

"I'm starting to understand that it's hard to tell what's real here. Even when it comes to what's on your plate. But how can you tell who's a spy?"

"You can't—until it's too late. Some play both sides."

Later, at the Shalyapin Bar, Jack met the Romanian princess. The dark-haired princess was as beautiful as she was somber. She wore her brown, shoulder-length hair parted in the middle with a multi-colored braided headband across her forehead, secured in the back. Her dress was a series of draped layers of red, dark brown, and blue. An altogether charming picture.

"You're the first Romanian princess I've had the pleasure of meeting. And the most beautiful. Not that I have other Romanian princesses to compare you to."

"*Spasibo.*" Her smile seemed forced. "Tell me, what brings you to Moscow?"

The hair on the back of Jack's neck tingled. "I'm gathering material for my senior thesis. I haven't yet determined what it's going to be about."

"Any other reason?"

"No. Why?"

"Perhaps Ambassador Kennedy's son might also be gathering information."

"How do you know who I am?"

"Let's just say it is in the best interests of the Soviet Union to know who comes and goes here. You understand. It is a dangerous time. It is very possible the country of which your father is an ambassador, and the Soviet Union, may someday find themselves allied—or enemies. Who knows? Like everybody else, we are holding our cards … how do you say?... close to the vest. But perhaps I can help you." She lit a cigarette and inhaled deeply. Stroking her hair, she held Jack's gaze, offering the barest hint of warmth.

What did she mean? Was she suggesting she could provide information? The otherness of the Romanian princess was enticing. She reminded him of the starlets he'd encountered in Hollywood and on the beaches of

France. He had a thing for those kinds of attractive, shimmery women.

"In what way?" Jack said, fighting the obvious conflict between the chance for a romantic encounter and his own safety. The ever-present determination of risk versus reward. The Russians might want to use his activities as leverage.

"With knowledge. Intelligence. We are on the same side, are we not? I don't think either of us likes the Nazis."

"True."

"Or whatever way you wish," she replied with a knowing smile. "I like Americans. And I like you." She placed a hand on his leg, her touch lingering for a moment.

Jack felt a flicker of tension but quickly reminded himself to remain composed. He considered steering the conversation away from anything too complex. Perhaps it would be best to keep things light and uncomplicated. Still, a part of him wondered if she could be trusted or if her intentions might be less than sincere.

"I just arrived," he said with a casual smile. "Maybe we can discuss political matters another time. For now, I'd just like to unwind."

The princess frowned. "I'm sure your father would be quite happy to know about certain things that could help him. As of now, he is not in the best position. Don't you want to help him?" The princess raised her eyebrows.

"Since you put it that way, perhaps you could tell me what you know. Then we can go on to other matters." This was becoming quite the negotiation. What could she know that could help his father?

"No," she resisted. "It's best we go someplace private where we can be alone—your room—before there is any exchange of information." Her hand inched forward on his leg.

So, he would not get information unless they were alone. That wasn't a good deal. Maybe the information was no good. In that case, he could relay it to his father but let him know it might be bogus. Then it would be up to his father to do what he wanted with the intelligence.

The princess nodded at the bartender, who brought over shot glasses—a larger one for Jack—and filled them with vodka. "*Za zdorovie*," said the princess. "To your health." She downed hers but frowned when Jack took only a sip.

Was she trying to get him drunk? Perhaps there'd be no rendezvous in his room. Some foreign country might want to kidnap the son of the ambassador and hold him for ransom. Or something else. It wasn't worth it. By walking away, he could avoid any possible problems. But that wouldn't be easy, not with the alluring princess in front of him.

He removed her hand from his leg and stood up. "Thank you for the offer, but I have a very busy schedule. Perhaps another time."

"What I can offer is quite valuable. And enjoyable. Sit down," she said, pointing to his seat.

Jack composed himself and continued to walk away. Sex and politics had become indistinguishable. Likewise, blackmail and foreign intrigue, unless he was imagining everything. Still, he had to be careful, at least once in a while.

While taking a stroll with Bohlen the next day, they ran into a festival held in honor of factory and plant workers. A parade began with accompanying tubas and marchers shouting triumphantly.

"They're saying 'Workers of the World Unite,'" translated Bohlen. He added that Stalin had outlawed the building of single-family housing and constructed large, drab, boxy complexes that had to be at least six stories high.

Jack was surprised at the large number of horse-drawn carriages. Although it was a city of more than four million, Moscow had no subway. Still, he was impressed by Red Square and Saint Basil's Cathedral, its colorful towers jutting skyward. Next to it, the plain and dreary Kremlin, the seat of the government, stood in stark contrast.

As he and Bohlen crossed Red Square, Jack glimpsed a Russian woman and a man behind a kiosk whispering to each other. He saw the man gaze past him as if he didn't see them. A few minutes later, Jack saw them again. They were being followed.

In his subsequent travels, Jack visited Leningrad, Kiev, and Crimea. When his energy faltered, Jack used the scalpel to insert a pellet, and by the next day he was revived and eager to push on. He left the Soviet Union convinced that life in a Communist country was usually harsh, inflexible, and backward. Still, he knew that those in power were determined to take their place on the world stage, and it would be foolish to discount or ignore the possible threat they posed.

Chapter 13

From the bow of the steamer, Jack viewed the hills of Istanbul, intrigued to be entering the city that straddled Europe and Asia. During the voyage, he learned from *Inside Europe* that Turkey was in the process of westernizing under the "blonde, blue-eyed combination of patriot and psychopath" dictator Kemal Atatürk, who had changed his name seven times, abolished the fez, turned mosques into granaries, and ordered every Turk to assume a last name in the Western tradition. After Atatürk's death the previous year, he was succeeded by his right-hand man. Should be an interesting visit, thought Jack.

After boarding the ship in Crimea, Jack had crossed the Black Sea. Before that, he'd toured Hungary, Lithuania, Latvia, Estonia, and Romania. He had stayed just long enough in each country to familiarize himself with the capital cities and meet with a dignitary or two who might offer expertise on the European situation.

His lodging in Istanbul's Old City was a short distance from the Grand Bazaar, so Jack headed there first. Traders had haggled with buyers under the bazaar's arched ceilings since 1455. Jack walked past local women wearing long, colorful skirts, their heads modestly covered with scarves. But many were also wearing western skirts with a Parisian flavor. Turkey seemed to be in transition.

As he neared the market, he took a moment to breathe in scents of cardamom, bitter orange blossom, and tobacco gurgling in hookahs. Reflecting on the trip and various moments of enjoyment, he realized he had learned more than he ever would have had he relied solely on books. He'd concluded that Europe was a powder keg waiting to be lit. It appeared to just be a question of when. He had to get what he needed now before it blew up. There was no time to waste.

As he arrived at the market, Jack's thoughts were interrupted by the mustiness emanating from rolled woolen rugs, goats, and uncleansed humans. Covering more than fifty-eight streets, the bazaar teemed with rows of stalls showcasing furniture, jewelry, carpets, leather goods, and everything in between. Vendors selling freshly picked fruits and vegetables encircled the cobblestone streets of the market.

A vendor made eye contact and presented his goat. "You like? Very good price."

A few minutes later, a merchant unfurled a carpet in Jack's path. "Special for you. Make home nice."

Jack wondered what his mother would say if he brought the rug back to their residence in London. Probably throw it in the trash. The sights, sounds, and smells made him ravenous, so he stopped at a stand. He pointed at the open brazier of roasting meat.

"American?" said the vendor. "First time here?"

"Yes."

"Eat this," the vendor said, handing Jack his kebab, "but you must also try raki, our national drink." He took out two cups and poured them both a drink. He quickly downed his cup. "Now you."

To refuse would be disrespectful, and Jack was curious, so after a bite of his kebab, he took a gulp. The strong anise-tasting liquid was different from anything he'd ever drunk. He hoped it wouldn't cause a stomach flare up. He thanked the man and munched on the kebab while crossing the Galata Bridge. As he arrived at the Palazzo Corpi, Jack marveled at the residence that housed the consulate general of the United States in Turkey. Marble floors and Italian Rosewood gave it an opulent quality. He'd made an appointment to see John MacMurray, the U.S. ambassador to Turkey, eager to learn his views on China and the Far East. MacMurray was a former assistant secretary of state and minister to China.

"My father sends his regards," Jack said, shaking hands with the dapper MacMurray. He was stylishly dressed, his outfit topped off by a summer white fedora.

"And please send him mine. In these times, we must stick together and try to prevent war."

Over Turkish ravioli at a cafe, they talked about a variety of issues, including those in the Far East. "I'm concerned that U.S. policy toward Japan in China could lead to trouble," said MacMurray. "America should accept Japanese domination in China. If it doesn't, there will be trouble."

Jack hadn't thought much about this theater of the world, but now MacMurray was suggesting further world conflict was possible. From his vantage point on the East Coast of the U.S., and lately Europe, the small remote island nation of Japan seemed an unlikely threat to the United States. Jack knew about Japan's dominance over Russia during their war earlier in the century. Now Japan had conquered a large part of the enormous nation of China. How had they done it? Jack wondered. Small nations could also be powerful. He promised to follow the developments more carefully.

When Jack asked for a recommendation for engaging the local community, MacMurray suggested smoking a hookah and gave him an address not far from the consulate. "It is a very relaxing experience and brings people together. People have been enjoying the custom here for several centuries. I assure you it will be a good opportunity for you to learn something about the Turks and how some of them view the world situation."

I've never smoked, thought Jack, but it will be worth it if it helps me gain an understanding of the local culture. He walked down a narrow street and entered the darkly constructed café. Inside, he saw mostly bearded men drinking sludge-bottomed Turkish coffee huddled around the hookah water pipe. Istanbul, like this café, had become a melting pot in recent years. It was a city of many ethnicities and religions. Jack recognized French, Arabic, and Greek accents and words.

Jack sat down, and after a few minutes, the hose was put on the floor in front of him. He picked it up and inhaled the shisha, pleased that the hookah smoothed the inhalation. He inhaled again deeply, exhaled, and joked, "We should bring this custom to the United States. I'll talk to Roosevelt."

"Yes, and tell your Roosevelt he may find himself in the middle of something over here," a gaunt, subdued Turk said. "I don't know what. But it won't be good."

Jack nodded. "Yes, I think you are right. The situation is becoming dangerous. But I have great faith that Turkey will prosper. You are a relatively new country and have a great future. And I have always admired your achievements in art, science, and medicine. But there is no doubt the Great War changed everything. Were you involved in that struggle?"

"We were part of the Ottoman empire before the war," the man said. "We got mixed up in the war and ended up on the wrong side, the losing side. The empire is no more." He waved his hand. "We deserved our fate. We did terrible things during the war. Things the world does not know much about."

Jack sensed the man had something important to say—something he badly wanted to get off his chest. "Yes, war can bring out the worst in man," Jack said. "I don't think any country, and that includes my own, didn't participate in dishonorable acts during the conflict."

"Yes, I suppose that is true." The man lowered his voice and became solemn. "But how far can a country at war go? Is it permissible to wipe out an entire population to justify itself?"

"I don't think so. Do you have any knowledge or experience with what you're talking about?"

"Do you know of the Armenians? They were part of the empire. Our leaders believed they wanted to leave it, and did not want that to happen."

"What did they do?"

"I can only say the Armenians were treated very harshly. Very badly."

Jack noticed the other Turks nodding.

The man looked away and then back at Jack. "I was there. I helped. I was very young—only twenty. But I cannot forgive myself," he continued.

Jack had no idea what the man was talking about, but he discerned it had to do with some sort of atrocity.

"The Armenians were sent on death marches to the desert," the man went on. "A million or more died. I was there. I will always be there."

The room went silent. Jack took one more puff before excusing himself. As he walked back to the hotel, Jack thought if what this man was saying was true, the Turkish Empire had tried to erase an entire people. Within a single month, he had learned about Stalin's mass cruelty and that the Armenians had been subjected to mass slaughter. He wondered what awaited him in the roiling Mideast.

Palestine was his next stop.

Chapter 14

Hundreds of women congregated in front of the pink limestone King David Hotel as Jack arrived in Palestine in late May 1937. At the front, Jack could see a blue Star of David flag. The demonstrators were blocked from coming closer to the hotel by British police in khaki shorts and sun helmets. After retrieving his trunk from the taxi, Jack asked a woman wearing a white, wide-brimmed hat what was going on.

"We are protesting the British White Paper," she said. "It is complete nonsense."

The White Paper stated that Palestine would be neither a Jewish state nor an Arab one but an independent state to be established within ten years. Jewish immigration to Palestine would be restricted to seventy-five thousand, and there would be stringent limitations on acquiring property.

"The British are denying us our rights," she continued. "It would relegate us to minority status in what would be a future Arab-majority state. We cannot allow this. This is our homeland."

"Seems that the other side believes that too. I hope a resolution is possible," Jack replied.

"Yes, but that is a long way off, I'm afraid. It is a very dangerous time here. You must be careful."

A Palestinian woman wearing a wrap-around cloth, her head covered in a veil, and a demonstrator engaged in a heated debate off to the side. Nearby, Arab men viewed the demonstration with thinly veiled anger. Some of them shouted and shook their fists at the demonstrators.

Jack had arrived in Palestine at a critical juncture, and tensions were high. He was aware of the conflict, having read reports of the three-year-old Arab revolt against the British, who had controlled the territory since

BECOMING JFK

1920. The Palestinian Arabs demanded independence and railed against the idea of a Jewish national home. The revolt had faded by March. But now the Arabs were incensed by the White Paper because it allowed an intolerable five more years of Jewish immigration.

Jack maneuvered through the demonstrators and was allowed to enter the hotel. Two-thirds of the building was leased to the British Mandate administration.

After unpacking, Jack went to the rooftop, which overlooked the old city and Mount Zion. As he surveyed the magnificent scenery below, he was cognizant of the terrible strife between Arabs, Jews, and the British. He would have to be careful not to get caught in the crossfire.

On his way out of the hotel to take an early evening stroll, Jack examined himself in the lobby mirror. He was pleased that he had filled out. Dr. Taylor's medicine seemed to have done the trick. He looked forward to exploring the immediate area. Jack straightened his tie and continued toward the exit. The hotel's high ceilings, marble floors, and painted accents successfully created an ambience reminiscent of the opulence of the King David era. British government and military personnel were clustered in conversation near the hotel entrance and lobby.

Boom!

A terrific roar rocked the building. Jack was thrown against a marble column. He ran to take refuge in a corridor. Screams erupted from guests as they raced to huddle under tables. The hotel became eerily silent for a long minute as everyone waited for more explosions. Police sirens wailed, and British soldiers drew their weapons. Jack wondered if the hotel might be under full-scale attack and what he would do if it was. Luckily, he hadn't made it out the door when the bomb hit. The bomb turned out to be the only violence at the hotel.

The next morning, Jack saw the results of the previous night's assault.

A large crater disfigured the hotel grounds. He'd thought he would be safe at the hotel. The next day, he saw a Jewish bus equipped with a wire screen to protect passengers from rocks and grenades thrown by Arabs. During the rest of his stay, Jack witnessed actual violence between Arabs and Jews. He also met with consuls and officials, then spent several hours synthesizing the information before cabling his observations to his father.

> *I see no hope for the working out of the British policy as laid down by the White Paper. The important thing and the necessary thing is not only a solution that is just and fair but a solution that will work.*

He felt that the only possible resolution was to break the country up into two autonomous districts that would safeguard British interests. He continued:

> *I have never seen two groups more unwilling to try and work out a solution that has some hope of success than these two groups.*

Jack visited the Western Wall and the Temple Mount. The Holy Land brought out his latent religious interest. Jack wondered if peace would ever be possible in this land where three religions met. He wrote:

> *I saw the rock where our Lord ascended into heaven in a cloud, and in the same area, I saw the place where Mohammed was carried up to heaven on a white horse.*

On June 8, his final evening in Jerusalem, thirteen bombs rocked Jewish neighborhoods, which he reported to his father were set off by Jews. Jack thought it ironic. He wrote:

BECOMING JFK

The Jewish terrorists bomb their own telephone lines and electric connections and the next day frantically phone the British to come and fix them.

Jack made his way to Egypt, where the focus returned to the evolving events in Europe. He arrived at the American legation in downtown Cairo. Two scimitar-bearing, fez-wearing guards, holdovers from the Ottoman Empire were at the gate. Jack presented his diplomatic passport and was allowed to proceed. The minister's luxury Packard Super Eight car was parked outside. Jack mounted the steps and entered the building.

The sixty-four-year-old minister, Bert Fish, used a cane. After general greetings, Jack said, "I'm sure you're glad to be away from the turmoil in Europe."

"I don't know about that," said Fish. "War hasn't started down here, but things are definitely heating up."

"What's happening?"

"With Italy and Germany signing their pact of steel, Mussolini is going to make his move. He'll want the Suez for himself and his partner Herr Hitler. Control the Suez and you control access from the Mediterranean through Africa all the way to the Arabian Sea. You can see what an advantageous position that could be for Italy and Germany."

"How will they do it?"

"They'll move from Italian Libya along the coast to Egypt and then to the Suez. I don't think the Brits will stand for it. They'll put up a fight. And because the Italians aren't great fighters, the Germans will have to come down and join the battle. Who knows what will happen from there."

"So the war won't be confined to Europe?"

"I'm afraid not. I suggest letting your father know. Might change his mind about appeasing the Germans, although I think the only thing that could is if the Germans invade Cape Cod!"

Later that week, Jack hired a guide who took him out on a camel to see the Great Pyramid at Giza. Getting there was difficult—and the bumpy camel ride tortured his back. Still, when he gazed at the majestic pyramid, he considered it worth doing. He thought about the workers who had spent their entire lives hauling great blocks of stone to honor their masters and was reminded of slavery in the United States.

Jack left for Bucharest and thereafter made stops in Beirut, Damascus, and Athens before returning to Great Britain.

Chapter 15

In the U.S. Ambassador's office in London, Jack watched as his father flung down the document. "Hitler sent British Foreign Secretary Lord Halifax his demands, Jack. He insists that Poland return Danzig to Germany. Halifax wants help in preparing a response." Throwing up his hands in frustration, the ambassador added: "Jack, is there anything you can contribute from your experience in Germany?"

Jack took a moment to properly phrase what he wanted to say, feeling privileged that his father would consider his opinion. "From what I learned, the German majority there agrees with him. Hitler's not going to stop until he gets Danzig."

Since his return, Jack had seen a distinct change in conditions in London. Ordinary Britons were digging air-raid shelters in the gardens behind their houses. "Got to be prepared," a man warned, shovel in hand. "Jerry is coming. Won't be long. Up there." He pointed to the sky. "Dropping bombs on us. You Yanks are safe—for now."

On June 27, Jack joined his father at 10 Downing Street, the prime minister's residence, for a reception thrown by Chamberlain. From the outside, the terrace house was modest looking, but there was more than met the eye behind its black front door. One hundred rooms in several larger houses were connected by a warren of hallways and staircases.

Once inside, Jack became instantly aware of the somber mood. There wasn't a smile to be seen. People chatted in muted tones. The prime minister, attired in a dark suit and striped ascot tie, made the rounds. He greeted his guests, trying to put up a good front, but the tall, gaunt Chamberlain looked worn down.

It had to be an awful burden, thought Jack, to carry the weight of a nation's hopes and fears. Jack mused on whether Chamberlain was going to ride out the conflict or give way to a new leader. He might not have a choice, Jack guessed. Britain needed somebody more forceful and energetic. Chamberlain had the past written all over him.

Jack had gone back to work in the embassy, his duties now enhanced. He worked in an office with other staff, became familiar with his father's diplomatic correspondence, and was requested to help draft his reports and telegrams. And he became acquainted with prominent British politicians coming to and going from the embassy. The tension between England and Germany escalated as June came to a close. His father grimly carried on.

A few days after the prime minister's reception, Jack entered his father's large second floor office overlooking the central gardens of Grosvenor Square. "What's the latest?" Jack asked, handing his father a preliminary version of a report he had written.

"The situation isn't dire yet," his father said, "but it's getting there. The agreement between the French and British to help Poland if the Germans attack is a disaster," he said, slamming down his glass. "It will surely lead to war."

"Why?"

"Hitler is taking that as an insult. He'll attack and destroy the French and British. They don't stand a chance. Hitler has a war machine that's unstoppable. In their hearts, all Englishmen know this to be true."

His father's rhetoric sounded dangerous to Jack. Give a bully something, and he only wants more. But he didn't have very good answers himself. "Do you think giving up Poland would satisfy Hitler?"

"I don't know. The problem is a small group of brilliant people has created a public feeling, which makes it impossible for the government to take a sensible course."

Jack didn't know what a sensible course was, but if war was imminent, he needed to go back to the heart of the continent before it erupted. This time he'd have companionship.

In early July, Jack and his Harvard roommate Torby left London, taking the ferry across the channel. Torby had come over to compete in track in London—and to woo Kick. He'd had no luck with either, finishing well back in the pack in his race and unable to make time with Kick.

"Jack, do you think your sister could ever fall in love with a guy like me?" said Torby, as the ferry departed.

Jack looked at Torby, moving his head to stare at him from different points of view. "A guy like you, Torb, but maybe not you. I don't know what it is, but she's got a thing for these English guys. Can't get enough of them. Perhaps if you take on a British accent, drink more tea, and acquire a stiff upper lip, she might consider you."

As he stared out at the sea, Jack's mood turned serious. His father had called them before they left and warned, "Don't have a smart mouth or antagonize those people. The Germans are ready for war, and you aren't German. Don't start anything."

"I suppose we should be careful in Germany," Jack said to Torby. "Still, I've been there before, and he hasn't. Anyway, we'll have Byron with us, so I feel a little more protected. But I don't think they have much of a problem with Americans—yet."

Burly, lantern-jawed Byron White, a Rhodes scholar he'd met at the embassy, was a former all-American halfback who'd finished second in the balloting for the nation's best college player that year. He went on to play professionally in the NFL and acquired the nickname "Whizzer" because he had a knack for whizzing by defenders.

Jack and Torby made stops in Paris before meeting White in Munich. It was apparent that Germans was more ardent and fierce than a couple of years before. That included the women, unsmiling and aggressive as they went about their shopping. The Germans were preparing to march; they were just waiting for the Fuhrer's orders. Jack and Torby waited for White at the Hofbräuhaus, where he and Lem had been assaulted two years earlier. They were surrounded by inebriated, loud-mouthed brownshirts.

When White arrived, he invited them on a tour of the city. "A friend of mine in London lent me his car," said White. "I'll show you all the Nazi highlights."

"Sounds like my kind of tour," Jack said sarcastically, "although I've probably seen some of it before. But it will be good for Torb."

It was an abnormally hot day, and the sun beat down on them as they exited, but Jack was glad to be out of the obnoxious atmosphere of the tavern. They got in the car, and Jack took the front seat and Torby the back.

After driving for a few minutes, White said, "This is the Field Marshall's Hall." He pointed to a large, open-sided building fronted by two large statues of Bavarian military heroes. "In 1923, Hitler tried to overthrow the local government with his Beer Hall Putsch. He failed, was arrested, and spent a few months in jail."

"Not enough," said Jack. "Should have added twenty years."

As they passed the Old Town Hall, White said the site was where propaganda chief Joseph Goebbels gave a speech that initiated *Kristallnacht*, "the night of broken glass," that targeted Jewish businesses, buildings, and synagogues the year before.

"Broken glass," muttered Torby, putting his head between Byron and Jack. "Big deal. They deserved it," said Torby, who was virulently antisemitic.

Jack turned around to face Torby and threw him a dirty look. "Hey, Torb, feel free to keep your stupid opinions to yourself."

"You're starting to sound like the Nazis," chimed in White. "Maybe we should turn you over to them."

Torby shrank back in his seat. "Hey, give me a break."

"If you like propaganda, Torby," said White, "and from what is coming out of your mouth, I think you do, then you'll enjoy this next stop." Nearing a multi-level stone monument, he said, "The Nazis put this here to commemorate one of their heroes. This guy Horst Wessel, a brownshirt, wrote a Nazi fight song that became a national anthem. But he got killed in a dispute with Communists, so Goebbels made him a martyr. Here's what he built."

When White slowed down in front of the monument, they all felt the car shake. Something had hit them. And then another.

"What the hell was that?!" shouted Torby.

A mob had formed almost instantly. Shouting and waving, the furious crowd pelted their car with stones and bricks. Angry Germans pressed their noses to the windows like hungry pigs, bellowing as they pounded the car's glass with their fists.

"Why are they going all crazy after us?!" yelped Torby. "We haven't done anything."

Jack was angry and confused. He wondered if the irate Germans thought they were going to do something to the monument. In his previous visits to Germany, he'd been roughed up, spat on, and treated rudely. Now they were being targeted for simply slowing down around a stupid monument.

"These people are nuts," Jack said. "What the hell's the matter with them?"

"Maybe we should take them on," said Torby.

"No chance," said Jack, who was anything but a brawler. And he recalled his father's warning about the danger of inciting the Germans.

The situation was worsening by the moment, as the crowd grew in number. Behind the mob, Jack saw a dozen armed brownshirts approaching the car. Now they were in real trouble.

"Byron, Nazi soldiers are coming! Get us the hell out of here! These crazy people are dangerous!"

White blasted his horn, found an opening, and zoomed away.

"Do you think they'll send somebody after us?" said Torby after they'd driven several miles.

"I think we're in the clear," said Jack, looking back. "Byron, that was better than anything you did on the football field. But why were they giving us such a hard time?"

"It's the English license plates, dammit," White said. "They hate the English. That's all they need to get them agitated. And we aren't even English."

"How can we avoid having a war," Jack asked, "if this is the way these people feel?"

Chapter 16

After visiting Italy in August, Jack and Torby hired a car and headed for the Kennedys' rented villa on the Riviera, just outside of Cannes. "This car is a wreck," Jack said, struggling as the vehicle shook and bucked to the right.

"Then why are you driving so fast?" said Torby, gripping the door handle.

"The sooner we get there, the sooner we can ditch this car and see all those beautiful women lining the boardwalk." Jack smiled at Torby and sped up. "We're not even halfway there."

"Look out, Jack!" yelled Torby.

The car was veering off the shoulder. Jack sharply turned the steering wheel to avoid a stone outcropping on the right. They swerved; the tires squealed. Jack felt weightless as the car turned upside down in the air. Time stopped as Jack braced for their eventual return to earth. Finally, the car landed on its back and skidded for endless seconds before stopping with a screech. Jack had been thrown against the floor gear shift, which dug painfully into his back. He and Torby looked up at the car's roof.

Jack turned to Torby and said, "Well, pal, we didn't make it, did we?"

They wiggled out the window. Their luggage, which had been strapped on the tailgate, had come free. Underwear, shoes, books, and scraps of food were strewn all over the road. When Jack took a step back, the pain in his back was so bad he could barely move. He made an attempt to pick up a shoe but couldn't bend over.

"I'm going to have to rely on you to get our stuff," Jack said sheepishly. "Seems my back is out of whack. I owe you."

"You sure do," Torby said angrily as he picked up their belongings.

Jack was always in a hurry. Once he got going, he found it almost impossible to slow down. Sometimes it got him into trouble.

After the car was taken away, they rented another, and Torby drove most of the way to Cannes.

After the accident, the south of France proved to be a godsend. Jack spent most of the day at the beach, and the sun's warmth seemed to ease the pain in his back. After a few days, he could move without wincing.

On one of those hot days in early August, he, Torby, and Claiborne Pell, an acquaintance of Jack's at Princeton and heir to the Lorillard tobacco fortune, relaxed outside the Kennedys' cabana at the Hotel Du Cap resort.

"Excuse me guys. I see an old friend." In the distance, Jack had zeroed in on Marlene Dietrich. A chance to renew acquaintances. Dietrich was filming unsuspecting beachgoers with her movie camera.

"Hello," said Jack, walking up to her. "Remember me? Jack Kennedy." The German beauty was resplendent in white billowy trousers, white shoes, and a tight, short-sleeved blouse that accentuated her breasts.

"I remember," Dietrich said in her throaty voice. "I believe we had a dance."

"Would you like me to film you? If so, don't be too hard on me. I'm no Sternberg. But I did enjoy you in *The Devil is a Woman*. You were quite devilish."

"That would be nice." Dietrich lowered the camera and gave it to Jack. "As long as you make me look *fantastisch*." Dietrich arranged herself on the sand, leaning back against a lounge chair. Jack filmed while

Dietrich posed, putting her right hand in her pocket, and throwing back her head.

"Anytime you need somebody to film you, let me know," said Jack, returning the camera.

"It depends," she said slyly, "after I see how this comes out."

The next day, Jack donned cabana attire—a white terrycloth robe trimmed in black—threw a towel over his shoulder, and strolled the boardwalk. There was Dietrich again, this time in a stunning white swing skirt bathing suit.

"May I return the favor?" asked Dietrich in a dusky tone, as she raised her camera. "Go back there. Then walk toward me."

Jack strode forward flashing a brilliant smile while Dietrich filmed. "Now I can say I've been in a Marlene Dietrich film. It's your turn," said Jack, reaching for the camera. "Let's have you stand on the platform." He was directing a famous movie star.

Dietrich didn't need any encouragement. She hopped up on the ledge. Fluffing her hair, she put one foot behind the other, faced her hips away from the camera, and turned her shoulders toward Jack.

"That's great," said Jack as he filmed. "Now show me you are happy to be an American citizen." (Dietrich had recently obtained United States citizenship.)

Dietrich laughed and flashed a winning smile. She stepped down and retrieved her camera. "*Danke*," she said, giving Jack a kiss on his cheek.

"By the way," Jack said, aroused by her affection, "do you have a cabana around here?"

"Yes, I do," said Dietrich. "Why do you ask?"

"Perhaps you'd like some company. I'm told I make excellent company."

Dietrich hesitated. "Well, let's see if you do." They retired to her cabana.

On his way back, Jack ran into Pell and bragged. "The Blue Angel has fallen."

Jack visited Dietrich several more times, but while he and his friends lounged on the beach and enjoyed the boardwalk, events in Europe were spinning out of control. Hitler was now spouting false tales of Polish atrocities against Germans in Poland as a pretext for an invasion. Germany doubled down on its control of Czechoslovakia and allowed only Germans to cross its borders.

Jack had been thinking about his next step. With war on the horizon, he felt the urgency to do some final research.

"What's next?" said Torby as they strolled the town of Cannes. "Any plans, Jack?"

"Need to do one more trip. Gather a bit more information and nail things down for my thesis before school. It's back to Germany and then Prague. Also report anything interesting to Dad. Going solo on this one, Torb."

Ambassador Kennedy expressed reservations about Jack heading into the maw of the looming conflict, but said he'd wire George Kennan at the American legation in Prague to get Jack a diplomatic passport, assuming one was still possible.

A few days later, Jack sat in on a call with Kennan.

Kennan's voice was tense as he spoke: "No trains are running, no planes are flying, no frontier stations exist, and yet we have received a telegram from you who have chosen this intense and confusing time to send your young son on a fact-finding tour around Europe. And it's up to us to find a means of getting him across the border and through the German lines. Just so he can include in his itinerary a visit to Prague. Outrageous!"

His father and Kennan went at it a few minutes before Kennan relented. Soon, Jack had his documents.

Outside the Kennedys' rented chateau on August 12, Jack waved goodbye to his family. It would be a long trip—nearly six hundred miles. His route would take him east via northern Italy through Innsbruck to Vienna and finally to Czechoslovakia. Jack knew his documents didn't guarantee his safe passage through Germany and on to Czechoslovakia. An imperious German patrol could stop him and send him back, or shoot him and dump him in the forest. They could say he had tried to run a checkpoint, and no one would know the truth.

He decided to drive more cautiously than usual, so he slowed down and monitored his turns. Going in the opposite direction was an endless line of dirty cars crammed with passengers and suitcases strapped on top. Thousands of Poles were seeking escape from the imminent German invasion of their country.

Jack climbed north through the Brenner Pass to Switzerland. He stopped to rest and eat in the picturesque Swiss village of Stein am Rhein before crossing the Rhine into Germany. His diplomatic papers allowed smooth sailing at the checkpoint, and he continued on to Austria. After an uneventful night in Vienna, Jack departed for Czechoslovakia.

The fun and games were over, thought Jack, as he neared the Czech border. His pulse quickened. Ahead was the checkpoint, and he could see a dozen or more German soldiers dressed in field gray. When he stopped, a soldier brandishing a Mauser rifle approached his window. Another flanked the passenger side.

Jack extended his documents.

The soldier grabbed the documents and scowled. He rapped his gun on the door. "Closed. Go back." He pointed the way Jack had come.

"American," Jack said. "I go to Prague. Promised a German escort."

The guard shook his head again, which caught the attention of an officer.

The man looked familiar. "Heinz?" said Jack, recognizing him as one of the Germans he and Lem had picked up back in 1937. In full military uniform, Heinz wore the peaked cap of an officer. "It's me, Jack Kennedy. Your tour guide from a couple of years ago. Heinz, how are you?"

"*Guten Tag,* Jack. We meet again."

Jack and Heinz chatted amiably about their lives since they'd last met. Heinz was now married and had a child. When he asked Jack why he was traveling to Czechoslovakia during this tense time, Jack said it was for his university studies and changed the subject. Jack handed Heinz a typed letter that authorized him as a special envoy.

Heinz read the letter. "Yes, I've been expecting you. I got word from your Mr. Kennan. I take you to Prague. Follow me."

Jack trailed Heinz's swastika-emblazoned car. The idea of having a Nazi escort was revolting—but necessary. Several hours later, they arrived in Prague. Jack continued to follow Heinz as he sped through the narrow streets until they arrived at the city's historic Malá Strana district where the American legation was located.

After a brief time in Prague, Jack headed for Berlin, where the plan was to meet brother Joe. They didn't know it at the time, but on August 19, the day Jack arrived in Berlin, the first German divisions began marching toward the Polish frontier. He and Joe were staying at the Hotel Excelsior, a short distance from the Reich Chancellery. They ate a traditional breakfast of rolls that came with plates of cheese and meat and talked about their respective traveling experiences.

"I almost didn't make it out of Spain," said Joe. "I was traveling with Franco's Nationalists when the Loyalists captured us."

"What happened?"

"They were getting ready to shoot when I pulled out my passport. Saved my life."

"Quick thinking, Joe. But why were you with the Nationalists? Hitler's been quite happy to support them by bombing the cities."

Joe shrugged. "I didn't say I was for them. They offered me a ride."

After recounting his own experience evading an angry German mob when he was with Torby and Byron, Jack asked what Joe was doing that day.

"I'm going to visit Unity Mitford. Want to come?"

Jack had other plans, but even if he didn't, he had no interest in spending any time with Unity or her sister Diane. They were part of the declining British aristocracy who fawned over Hitler. The two sisters had lived in Germany for five years. Hitler had attended Diane's wedding at Joseph Goebbels' house.

"Isn't she the one Hitler said was the perfect Aryan type? Are you sure that's something you want to do?" Jack asked.

Joe didn't seem aware of the possible political implications of associating with a Hitler acolyte. "Why not? It will be fun."

"No, that's all right. You enjoy yourself."

Jack went back to the hotel and picked up a copy of the *Berliner Zeitung*. The headline read: Poland: Look Out!

As August drew to a close and knowing his days in Europe were coming to an end, Jack made arrangements to talk with Alex Kirk, the American chargé d'affaires in Berlin.

More vigilant now, Jack exited the hotel and looked around at people in the immediate vicinity. At the next corner, he lingered a moment to see if any of the faces at the last corner had now turned up at this one. Didn't appear to be.

BECOMING JFK

The embassy was on Pariser Platz, across the street and to the right of the stallions atop the Brandenburg Gate.

Jack guessed the mustachioed Kirk was about fifty, but something about him gave the impression of a much older man—perhaps the pressure of his job.

Kirk lit a cigarette before extinguishing the one he was smoking. "Welcome to Berlin, although there's nothing welcoming about it at the moment. It's crazy around here. Every day they send a bunch of Nazis parading through the plaza just to keep their citizens in a state of frenzy. It's working." He waved his cigarette to illustrate his point, creating circles of smoke.

After some discussion about Jack's thesis, Kirk motioned for him to go outside. On the patio, standing within inches of Jack, he said, "They are listening to me. Bugged my office. Today, Hitler and Stalin announced something they are calling the Nazi-Soviet Non-aggression Pact. Hidden in the protocol is an agreement between the two countries to partition Poland and much of Eastern Europe."

Jack tried to grasp what that meant. Either way, it wasn't good. Especially for Poland.

"When we go back to the consulate, I'll give you an envelope. Give it to your father immediately."

Inside, Kirk pressed the envelope into his hand and wished him good luck. *What could be of such importance?* Kirk could have telexed or phoned his father. Perhaps he figured that giving it to Jack was safer.

A few days later, Jack returned to London and delivered the letter to his father at the embassy. The ambassador opened the envelope and took out a piece of paper. Scanning the contents, he shook his head and then put the paper on the desk.

"What does it say, Dad? Since I'm the one who carried it, I think I deserve to know."

"Kirk says there will be war within a week." The ambassador threw up his hands in defeat. "God help us."

Since all hell was about to break loose, Jack decided he'd have as much fun as possible before returning to school. "I have the feeling an era is ending," Jack said to a friend. "Let's hit the 400 Club." Several times late that month of August, Jack donned his tux and made his way to the basement nightspot of the high society club in the West End. Its dimly lit dance floor and romantic music played by the large band made it the perfect escape. But he couldn't escape for long.

On September 1, German troops invaded Poland, and Nazi planes bombed Polish cities. The war had begun.

The next day, Jack and Joe joined other members of the family enroute to the family residence from the embassy. Intending to cut across Hyde Park, they were interrupted in their journey by the first prolonged air-raid alert in London.

"There!" said Joe Sr., pointing to a shelter. The Kennedys bolted for the entrance. They huddled in the brick cellar of a dressmaker with dozens of other frightened Britons and Americans.

"Get me ships! Get me out of here right away!" shouted a white-faced American in a suit. Jack guessed he was a businessman who now realized his business was no longer viable in England. The all-clear finally sounded. No bombs had been dropped.

A day later, Jack, Joe, and Kick emerged from the car in front of the House of Commons. The brothers wore double-breasted suits, a light one for Jack in contrast to Joe's dark pinstripe. Jack realized it was a monumentally grave day, but he was eager to see history being made.

They flanked their sister, who was adorned in a wide-brimmed black hat, a black dress trimmed in white, and white gloves.

As they strode toward the House of Commons to hear the declarations of war, Kick asked, "What do you think this means for our country?"

"Not much," said Joe. "It's none of our business."

"That's true," Jack said. "For now."

The young Kennedys found seats with their parents in the Strangers' Gallery, where at noon Chamberlain urged Parliament to declare war on Germany.

Just before the proceedings began, the ear-splitting sound of an air-raid siren blasted. Everybody was hustled to a shelter in the House of Commons. When the all-clear sounded, they returned to their seats.

Jack listened in rapt attention as Churchill spoke. He recalled Churchill's words in *The World Crisis* about the Great War. Warning of a perilous future, he had written, "Will our children bleed and gasp again in devastated lands?"

Apparently so.

Before dawn the next morning, Jack was blinded by lights. His father was looming over him in his bathrobe, minus his glasses, his hair disheveled.

"Wake up, Jack! You're going to Glasgow as my representative." He explained that the *SS Athenia*, an English ship carrying 1,400 passengers en route to Canada, had been torpedoed and sunk by German submarines More than a hundred people had been killed or drowned. That included twenty-eight of the three hundred Americans aboard. The majority of survivors had been sent to Scotland, and the ambassador was tasked with safely repatriating the remaining Americans. "Tell them the United States will pay for their passage home."

Jack pulled on a shirt and trousers, wondering why his father had chosen him to go. Perhaps because he was the least important, and the ambassador's staff, including Joe, was occupied and he was the only one available. He steeled himself to face the frightened Americans. He would do whatever he could to distinguish himself in such difficult circumstances.

Jack flew to Glasgow and spent much of the day at the hospital. He did his best to comfort the wounded survivors. He sat at the bedside of a woman whose head was bandaged. Her eyes were glazed, and her hands shook. Jack wasn't sure if she saw him. "I'm from the American Embassy in London. I want you to know we will get you back home to America safely. Is there anything else I can do for you?"

"You don't know what it was like," she said, still in shock. "I don't know how I made it. Did I make it?"

"You did. And soon you will be going home. I will see to that."

Emerging slightly from her stupor, she stared at him. "But you're just a boy. What can you do?"

"I'll do everything I can," said Jack, touching her on the hand.

After consoling others, Jack went to the lounge of the Beresford Hotel to meet with the other survivors. Looking out over the troubled, agitated faces, Jack felt fear, anger, and mistrust. Many of the survivors were in blankets draped over old, ill-fitting clothes. Some were bandaged and sported ugly bruises. Others stared at the ground, still in shock.

Jack wondered what it must have been like to be asleep when the torpedoes struck, unable to express immediate physical and mental distress before realizing that the ship was sinking. No doubt there was chaos, and the passengers were hysterical. Those who acted swiftly and donned lifejackets—nothing more than floating blocks of cork held together by

BECOMING JFK

canvas—and got to the lifeboats had the best chance of surviving. How well the ship's officers were trained to handle the emergency was paramount. Cool heads needed to prevail if lives were to be saved.

Jack introduced himself, aware that what he was about to say would be met with contempt. He steeled himself for the response. "I want you to know a chartered freighter is on its way from New York to pick you up. I talked to my father this morning. He asked me to tell you that the government has plenty of money for all of you."

"We want a convoy!" several shouted, shaking their fists.

"I understand your concern. But President Roosevelt has said there is no need for a convoy because American ships would not be attacked," Jack said, raising his voice over the clamor. "We are still neutral, and the neutrality law still holds. It is much better to be on an American ship now than on a British ship even if it is accompanied by the whole fleet."

But many would have none of it and shouted, "You can't trust the German Navy! Tell that to Hitler!"

A gray-haired man stood up. "We demand American ships to protect us going back! I read where ninety destroyers have just been commissioned by the government. Surely, they can spare a few for a couple of days. All that money and they cannot do this for us?!"

"Yes, I understand your concern."

The hostile crowd continued to protest. Keeping his composure, Jack restored order while allowing individuals a chance to voice their frustration.

"I'd like to hear from those who want to express their opinions about the situation. You sir," he said, pointing to a man in the crowd. "What do you want to say?"

"Two years ago, the whole Pacific fleet was sent out for Amelia Earhart. And we get nothing?"

Jack nodded and pointed to a young woman about his age. "We refuse to go until we have a convoy," she said. "You have seen what they will do to us," she said.

Jack allowed all who wanted to talk to express their view, then reiterated, "You will be safe in a ship flying the American flag under international law. A neutral ship is safe."

After promising to inform his father of their demands, he departed and caught the night express train back to London. Among his recommendations was that a convoy be sent for the survivors.

His father disagreed. "That is impossible and unnecessary," he said.

"Hey, little brother," said Kick at breakfast a few days later, holding up a copy of the *London Evening News*. "From now on, I'm your older sister."

"What?" said Jack.

"First, let me congratulate you on a job well done. The paper says, 'Mr. Kennedy displayed the wisdom and sympathy of a man twice his age.' It says the 'Ambassador of Mercy'—that's you—'is nineteen-year-old Jack Kennedy.' You lost three years, little brother, during your trip to Scotland. And since I was born in February and you in May, I'm your older sister. I'll expect a lot more respect from you from now on. And if you need any advice about the ladies, you can always come to me."

Jack laughed. Kick was something else.

Before returning to the states, Jack assisted with arrangements for the survivors. They returned home aboard the *Orizaba*—without a convoy.

In a stroke of luck, Jack got a last-minute seat aboard the September 21 flight on one of the new luxurious Pan American Clippers. It was called a flying boat because it could land and take off on water. In the dining room, he was attended by formally dressed waiters. Jack ate his grilled filet mignon and contemplated the last seven months abroad. Since leaving New York in the dead of winter, he had traversed the continent and beyond through the heat of the summer. He'd acquired a wealth of knowledge about the political situation and experienced a wide variety of cultures.

Now with fall approaching, he was leaving behind a country ill-prepared for war to complete his thesis and final year at Harvard. If the air raids he had experienced were a portent of things to come, then the English might soon have to defend themselves from German bombs. Jack thought about the horrors that might engulf this part of the world. He had been shocked to learn that Stalin had killed millions of his own people and that Hitler seemed hell bent on wreaking havoc on the world. Could something be done to prevent a catastrophic war? Jack wondered. Maybe it was too late—at least it was for the Poles and Czechs.

Chapter 17

"Where have you been?" Torby asked, as Jack swept into F-14, their first-floor suite. Located inside the brick residence hall called Winthrop House, their modest rooms at Harvard overlooked a courtyard and the Charles River. Jack exhaled as he dropped his trunk in the center of the room. He'd arrived after school started because of the business with the *SS Athenia*.

"Trying to prevent war. Looks like I didn't have much luck," Jack said.

"Can't stop Hitler. Doesn't seem like anybody can."

"Yeah, probably right. The Brits don't seem ready. And I need to figure out why."

Already behind, Jack knew it would be a frantic rush to finish his thesis by the March deadline. He had enrolled in four courses that he hoped would help narrow his thesis focus: Elements of International Law, Modern Imperialism, Principles of Politics, and Comparative Politics. He bored into the major political ideologies. Jack read ferociously and listened closely to lectures on Fascism, Socialism, Capitalism, Totalitarianism, Imperialism, and Militarism.

"How's the research going?" asked Professor Bruce Hopper, his thesis advisor, when Jack arrived at his office. Hopper was a former World War I aviator and newspaper reporter.

"There's something about the Brits—their attitude about Hitler and their unwillingness to re-arm," Jack began.

Hopper took a puff on his pipe and got up to put a log on the fire. "Might be onto something there. Tell me more."

"The way I see it, Chamberlain was just mirroring the wishes of

BECOMING JFK

his people," Jack continued. "They didn't want another war, didn't want to prepare for one, or at least do the dirty work of re-arming in the last decade to deter a new war. Look where that got them. Into another war."

"Seems that way. Now you've got to prove it." He encouraged Jack to use all his resources to gather material.

"Send immediately pamphlets, etc., Conservative, Labor, Liberal Pacifist," wrote Jack to his father's top aides in London. Soon, boxes of books and other materials filled his room, along with detailed statistics on Britain's defense budgets.

"My father might be digging himself a hole," Jack said to Torby one night after returning from a late night at the Spee Club. He often went there to spread out, do research, and compose his longhand drafts. "It just doesn't go over well to talk publicly about being defeated and to say democracy might be on its way out." Jack had been astonished to read in *The Boston Globe* that his father had said, "Democracy is finished in England. It may be here."

"Yeah, that was something."

"I'm tempted to talk to him, but I'll stay out of his way. Certainly he can get better advice."

Throughout the winter and into 1940, Jack worked harder on his thesis than on any project he ever had before. His grades so far had been mediocre—mostly Cs with a scattering of Bs. But the deadline of mid-March was approaching fast. Miss it, and he'd be doomed. He needed help. After finishing the research phase, he planned to dictate his planned text and have typists shoot out fresh drafts. But there was a complication: He had already left for a wedding in Chicago and wouldn't be available to interview typist candidates.

"Get a pencil," Jack told Torby over the phone from Chicago and read him this classified ad:

WANTED. Stenographer, young, to furnish typewriter, assist on thesis, capable of taking shorthand. $20. Apply Wednesday, F-14 Winthrop House Harvard College.

"Help me out here, Torb. If there's anybody who knows a good candidate, it's you. I put 'young' in the ad. And if you like them, but they can't type worth a damn, feel free to see if there are any good candidates to date the captain of the football team."

The ad in the *Boston Herald* attracted sixty applicants.

Marie, a pretty eighteen-year-old, was hired and labored on the project for three weeks. Jack added other typists, slipping them in late at night at Winthrop or at the Spee. A knock at the Spee's door usually meant a delivery of new drafts.

"The first factor to be discussed," Jack dictated to Marie from handwritten notes, "is the almost complacent attitude with which the German re-armament was regarded by Britain in the first few years of the thirties. Got that, Marie?"

Stenographers and typists had completely taken over the sitting room, much to Torby's dismay. Four young women typed ferociously, two on opposite sides of a table and another stationed at Jack's desk. The clatter of the keys forced Jack to shout as he dictated. "England was fortunate in having the period after Munich; we are fortunate in having a broad ocean. But if the dictators win the present war, we are going to have to be prepared to make the same type of sacrifices that England made during the last year."

Jack stayed cool-headed, although his typists occasionally became flustered under the pressure. "We'll be all right here," he frequently said.

Using all his resources, Jack cajoled Joe's old roommate to check for weaknesses in spelling and syntax. Joe was now at Harvard Law School, and Jack wondered if he'd follow in his brother's footsteps after graduation, but he didn't want to do it just because his brother had.

On March 15, Jack grabbed his finished typewritten document and dashed to his advisor's office, trying to avoid taking a pratfall on the slushy path. He had only a few minutes to make the deadline. He submitted the manuscript, entitled "Appeasement at Munich: The Inevitable Result of the Slowness of Conversion of the British Democracy from a Disarmament to a Re-armament Policy." It totaled 147 pages, including six pages of an annotated bibliography. In the thesis, he concluded that Britain's belief that world security would be provided by the League of Nations, its unease about the financial weight of re-armament, the gnawing fear about another war, and the unwillingness of its statesmen to stand up against pacifism were the main reasons why England hadn't re-armed starting in the early to mid-thirties.

As he exited the building, Jack exhaled in relief, emitting cold vapors in the late winter. *What a relief to drop the damn thing off.* He allowed himself a grin of satisfaction.

There were only a few months of school remaining before graduation, but Jack began to think about his next step. The logical choice was law school, and Yale was his first choice. Jack was still considering Harvard Law, but a new environment seemed in order. While he waited for his thesis grade, Jack contemplated other options.

He chaired the student Red Cross committee for the war relief fund, but after a few weeks, the results had been disappointing. "Gentlemen, twelve hundred dollars means less than fifty cents from each student in the college," Jack said, addressing the committee. He raised the timbre of his voice. "There need be no fear that contributing to the Harvard Red Cross fund approaches even psychological involvement in the European war. That this money will be used to aid the suffering civilians of the invaded Allied countries is simply because they are providing the battleground this time. We wish to help their innocent civilians. We need to do better. Let us focus on the houses and the Freshman Union."

His plea was successful. The committee fanned out and raised $1,700, more than $500 over quota.

"*Cum laude*-plus, Torb," Jack said discontentedly, reclining on his bed. It was the lowest passing grade. "I would have gotten magna cum laude, but they knocked me down a little for being too long and some unconvincing judgments. Had some spelling and grammar problems too. Could have cleaned that up if I'd had more time."

"Cum laude plus is ok. You passed."

"Yeah, I guess so. Well, done with that."

Overall, Jack graduated *cum laude* with a Bachelor of Arts in international government. While he thought about law school, his plans were put on hold by a recommendation from Arthur Krock, a *New York Times* Pulitzer-Prize-winning columnist—and also his father's ghostwriter. The elder Kennedy had paid Krock $5,000 to edit and rewrite a short book in his name called *I'm for Roosevelt* that was used during the 1936 presidential election.

"I think you should publish it," said Arthur Krock, holding Jack's thesis, while the elder Kennedy looked on. Krock was staying at a mansion a few doors down from the Kennedy property in Palm Beach. He'd asked to see the thesis after Joe Sr. mentioned the topic. "It's very timely, given the European situation."

Jack restrained his enthusiasm, but his insides churned. "A book?" Jack had toyed with the thought of a writing career, occasionally mentioning it during casual conversations. Publishing a book at his age would be a great step in that direction. He pictured his name prominently displayed on the cover. It gave him chills.

"Improve the writing yourself," his father said. "After you are satisfied with it, ask Arthur to go over it again."

Krock directed his agent to seek publishers, renaming it *Why England Slept*, a nod to Winston Churchill's *While England Slept*.

Jack took up Krock's invitation to ensconce himself in his work at Krock's Georgetown library in Washington, DC, and bring things up to date—if that was possible. Events were moving swiftly. By this time, Germany had invaded Denmark and Norway.

"We're having trouble finding a publisher, Jack," said Krock, puffing on his pipe. "The manuscript needs opinions that would appeal more to an American audience. I'd suggest taking a more strident and fulsome tone. Make the point that Britain hadn't been prepared, and have people wondering if the U.S. would be ready? Do you see where I'm going?"

Jack nodded and went to work. He frequently asked Krock questions or sought clarification to develop this new focus. They had a pattern. In longhand, Jack revised old chapters and wrote new ones, then handed them off to Krock, who edited as he typed. Bright and vastly more experienced as a writer and journalist, Krock attacked Jack's preliminary effort, urging him to write in a more commanding, authoritative tone.

The revised content was much improved. "We must always keep our armaments equal to our commitments. Munich should teach us that; we must realize that any bluff will be called. We cannot tell anyone to keep out of our hemisphere unless our armaments and the people behind these armaments are prepared to back up the command, even to the point of going to war."

Occasionally, Jack wondered if he had borrowed too much of Krock's views, suggestions, and words. But he recognized the fleeting opportunity. He needed to get the manuscript published *now*. It might be worthless in a few months.

There was an offer from Harper and Brothers, but it was withdrawn as events in Europe made the work untimely.

Jack called Lem. "It looks like things are going nowhere," he lamented.

"For the moment, maybe," said Lem, ever encouraging and devoted. "Something will turn up."

And it did. Krock was soon on the phone with Jaxk. "You got it. Just received word from the agent that we've got a buyer."

"That's great," Jack said, letting out a sigh of relief and punching his fist in the air.

The manuscript had found a home with the small publishing house of Wilfred Funk, a publisher of encyclopedias. Moving quickly, the book was finished in June and in stores in late July.

The timing was perfect. France had just been swallowed up by Germany, and the American public was jittery, worried that the United States was unprepared if war should come. *Why England Slept* took off.

In his wet bathing suit in the sun room at Hyannis Port, Jack stared at the gaudy hardback cover emblazoned with the red, white, and blue British Union Jack flag. The words "John F. Kennedy" appeared below the title and above the image of a sleeping lion. It felt damn good to be an author. He hadn't expected it so soon. Certainly not at twenty-three … and maybe never. But an opportunity had presented itself and, strenuously urged on by his father, he had gone after it.

Jack gazed at the pile of books to sign and congratulatory letters at his feet. President Roosevelt had sent a warm post, praising the book for providing a great argument for acting and from a position of strength. He'd also received laudatory correspondence from prime ministers, business executives, and local politicians. His father called from London to offer praise, even if it deviated sharply from his isolationist views.

In between touch football games, Jack did interviews over the phone. He posed sheepishly for a publicity photo with his left hand on an open page of the book while he grinned at a typewriter. Although he'd received a number of invitations to speak, for the moment Jack was content to stay home and enjoy the summer pleasures of the Cape.

Jack took his newfound fame in stride, pleased with the book's reception, but it wasn't his way to project an effusive confidence, or boast to others—unless it involved his sexual conquests. Success was enough. But he wondered what this success meant for his future. He wasn't sure whether he should consider a career in letters or continue on the path to public service.

Joe had returned to Hyannis from Chicago. He was being groomed for politics and had been a delegate to the Democratic Convention in Chicago, which was held just before Jack's book had come out. But he'd done a curious thing, voting for James Farley on the first ballot instead of Roosevelt. Farley had no chance to win. He'd never even held elective office. That would surely displease the Democratic establishment, and it wouldn't help Joe if and when he decided to run for office.

Jack queried him about his experience in Chicago while they sat in the living room. "Didn't realize you were such a Farley fan."

"Yeah, well, I never liked how Roosevelt treated JP," Joe said, clenching his teeth. "Putting out a bunch of bunk about him. Remember that 'high administration official' who said in the *Chicago Tribune* that Dad would put all his kids in an orphanage one by one to get himself into the White House? Made me sick to my stomach. I'm sure Roosevelt was behind that. So, it was the least I could do. Quite happy to vote against Roosevelt."

Jack remembered his father complaining about the ill-treatment he had received from Roosevelt. "If you say so," Jack said. "But publicly stating your opposition might not do you any good. Roosevelt people aren't going to like it. And they probably have long memories."

"That's too bad for them. Did what I had to do. Roosevelt has left JP twisting in the wind once too often. Besides, Farley's Irish Catholic."

Pointing to a copy of Jack's book on a table, Joe said, "Congratulations on the book." He paused and added. "Heard Krock gave you a lot of help."

Jack had expected the dig but said nothing.

"How are sales?" Joe asked.

"Pretty good. No complaints." In fact, it was doing more than okay. It had appeared on *The New York Times* and *Washington Times-Herald* bestseller lists. The reviews had been good too.

Jack mused at how his literary success was outpacing his brother's. Joe's attempt to publish a book based on his reports from Spain had never materialized. For the moment, Joe was playing second fiddle. Not that he would shove it in his brother's face, but Jack intended to seek his own path with little concern for what his brother might do… with one exception: running for office. His father said Joe had first dibs, though Jack didn't understand why. *Just because he is the oldest?* That wasn't much of a reason. He thought about trying to usurp Joe's position as the Kennedy standard-bearer. After all, he no longer avoided competition with his brother as he had at Choate.

Perhaps he'd run for another office so they wouldn't be directly competing. He didn't think his father would have a problem with that. Maybe in another state. The family had a home in Bronxville, New York, in addition to their Hyannis Port residence. Then let the chips fall where they may. Or he could bide his time and wait until Joe ran for Congress and then president—or didn't. A lot could happen before then.

To be honest, Jack couldn't see his brother as president. As much as his father wanted to help his oldest son achieve that goal, Jack didn't think Joe had the intelligence or acumen to make important decisions. In fact, he considered himself smarter than Joe. His brother was a straight-ahead thinker, lacking much in the way of imagination or vision. Joe was good at regurgitating facts. He was also a hothead. Jack recalled the time Joe had thrown Teddy into the ocean, angry after they'd lost a race. Jack didn't think those traits were a good combination to lead the nation.

In the meantime, there was law school. Jack wasn't excited about the prospect, but he would go.

Chapter 18

Jack was in discomfort, and it wasn't going away. He grimaced, adjusted his clothing, and left the bathroom. Later, he noticed an unusual discharge and began to suspect the consequences of not taking precautions. Reflecting on the spring, he recalled several fleeting encounters—perhaps too many. Now, he needed medical attention.

Adding to his troubles, his back was acting up, a lingering pain aggravated by a recent tennis game. His stomach issues had also returned. It seemed everything was catching up with him at once.

By late August, Jack sought treatment at the Mayo Clinic for his various ailments, including issues with his genitals, spine, spleen, and stomach.

"We've successfully treated the gonorrhea," the doctor assured him after a course of antibiotics.

"That's good to hear," Jack replied.

"However, the burning sensation during urination is due to urethritis, a residual condition linked to the infection. Unfortunately, it's likely to be chronic. I strongly recommend using protection in the future to avoid further complications."

"Thanks for the advice, Doctor," Jack said, masking his disappointment. While the diagnosis wasn't ideal, he reasoned that it wasn't the worst of his health concerns. He could manage it. Besides, he had no regrets about his choices.

Jack's thoughts drifted to the possibility of unintended consequences—what if someone had become pregnant? It wasn't a concern he dwelled on. In his mind, the responsibility would fall to the woman. There were ways to address such situations, and if she chose to have the child, paternity was never certain.

Jack had queried a doctor and learned there was no reliable paternity test. A blood test had become available in the 1920s, but it was anything but accurate. Jack wondered if his father had impregnated another woman besides his mother. If so, he might have siblings he didn't know about.

When the doctor recommended he rest and delay the rigor of full-time law school until next year, Jack agreed. To be honest, a break suited him. The best alternative for the present was to get some sunshine and go west.

Jack checked into the Hotel President in Palo Alto, which was south of San Francisco and had been named to honor Herbert Hoover, the former Stanford student who became president. California had beckoned again, partly based on a friend of Joe's who said Stanford was a very agreeable place with plenty of coeds—an advantage over all-male Harvard.

He found a furnished rental for $60 a month at the back of 624 Mayfield.

"You'll have to get your own bed, though," said Gertrude Gardiner, his landlord.

"Don't need one." With his back acting up, Jack found it comfortable to sleep on a plywood plank.

The campus was dominated by a quadrangle of sandstone buildings, all of which had red-tiled roofs. After walking a campus dotted with palm and eucalyptus trees, he sat in the red seat of his new green Buick convertible coupe. He'd purchased the car using his book royalties. It felt good to earn his own money. Jack studied the school schedule, thinking he might try something different in his new locale. He circled a few classes to audit at the Stanford Business School.

He attended a business class but daydreamed while the professor droned on about monetary theories. After a few minutes, he slipped out and found a seminar on contemporary world politics, which analyzed the ongoing presidential race.

"In my view," said Jack during the seminar, "Roosevelt will win a third term, although that hasn't happened before. These are unprecedented times. I think the American electorate will stick with him."

After class, Jack drove to L'Omelette, a French-themed restaurant, and sat at the bar. A tri-color canopy extended over the seating. He ordered his favorite meal of steak frites.

"Excuse me, aren't you the guy who wrote the book about England sleeping?" said a middle-aged man, well into his third drink.

"Well, something like that."

"Well, I hope your book wakes them up," the man said with a laugh. They chatted for a few minutes before Jack excused himself.

Jack had become recognizable. After the *Stanford Daily* ran a story about him which mentioned his book and that he was the son of the one-time ambassador, he'd become a minor celebrity on campus. Requests for interviews or a picture became commonplace.

As he walked through the campus, Jack was often flanked by students wanting to meet the local celebrity. "You're Jack Kennedy, aren't you?" said a tall, handsome student, maneuvering between admirers. After reading the interview, the post-graduate student in English literature had tracked him down. He'd attended dances with Kick back East. "I'm Henry James and I'm from New York and Yale and I, er, is there any chance we could get together sometime?" he suddenly asked. Flustered, he'd forgotten to mention he knew Kick.

"Oh," said Jack. "I'm very busy. I've got to go—I'm afraid it's really not possible. But thanks for coming along anyway. Nice to see you. Good luck!"

A few days later, Jack parked in front of the post office and again ran into Henry. Jack remembered his face. When Henry finally mentioned he'd known Kick, they joked around for a few minutes before Jack all but ordered, "Come have lunch with me."

They walked to a nearby cafeteria. After getting their food and sitting down, Jack probed, per his custom, "Where are you from? Where did you graduate? What did you study at Yale? How did you do? What are you doing here?" In five minutes, Jack had his life story.

Jack took a liking to Henry, and they became friends, often attending Stanford football games together.

At L'Omelette one day after a game, the talk turned to women. Henry said, "My psychiatric counselor at Yale told me that the ideal marriage of two people occurs when the man says, 'I want to devote myself to this one woman, who is going to be the mother of my children, and the keeper of the feminine flame in this relationship, while the man will in turn be conveying the masculine side of things.' I haven't quite made up my mind about that sort of thing yet."

"Hmmm," said Jack doubtfully. "Perhaps I have."

Henry took out a letter. "Let me read this to you. It's a letter from my girlfriend back east."

"Okay, just so it's not too long," said Jack, his eyes sweeping over the room to see if any women there interested him.

Henry read, "'I can't tell you how devastated I am. I walked past your house on Seventy-Fourth Street, and I wept so copiously I almost stumbled and fell.' Isn't that beautiful?" Henry wiped away a tear.

Jack wasn't moved. "Oh, it may be romantic to you, but that's not the kind of thing I'm looking for." Jack instantly regretted his rebuke. "I'm sorry, Henry. I guess we're just different."

Dismayed by Jack's curt, unsentimental response, Henry said, "Then what are you looking for?"

Shrugging, Jack said, "Once I get a woman, I'm not, for the most part, interested in carrying on."

Henry crossed his arms in disbelief. "So, once you've bedded them, you don't care about them much?"

"That's right, Henry." Jack saved his hands. "To me, it's the conquest. That's the challenge. The chase. Not the kill! I like the contest between male and female. That's what excites me."

"Interesting point of view, Jack. Do you think that will ever change? You know, fall in love, find a wife and have kids?"

"I don't know about the falling in love part. As for the rest, I'll wait and see." Jack thought about his first conquest at Stanford a few nights previous. He'd taken Susan Imhoff back to his cottage, and they'd had sex on his plywood bed board with her on top, which was preferable when his back hurt.

Jack had begun to enjoy Stanford and the beauty of Northern California. The school had a country club feeling about it and was dominated by Republicans. He made a habit of driving over to nearby Lake Lagunita, which offered swimming and boating.

One day after taking a swim, his attention became riveted on a young woman who slinked around, animal-like, in her bathing suit. He'd never seen anybody walk that way. Perhaps she was self-conscious about exposing her voluptuous figure. "What's your name?" Jack asked, cutting her off before she could return to her friends.

"Harriet Price," she said, "but my friends call me Flip."

"Flip? I hope I become one of those who are allowed to call you that," he flirted. "How did you get the name Flip?"

"Apparently, because of my lively personality."

"Well, there's no doubt about that!"

Jack took her to Dinah's Shack, to sporting events, and to Carmel. But he hadn't taken her to bed. Then in his car one night, when Jack tried to move things along, Flip was insistent, removing his hands from sliding up her dress, ending their kissing just as it appeared she'd lost control.

He decided to take a different tack and tried the like-father, like-son approach.

"My father treats my mother well, Flip," said Jack as they strolled past Memorial Church. "He used to go on long business trips—especially when he had the movie business in Hollywood—but he always brought back something special for my mother, a big Persian rug or nice jewelry. And everything was all right. And it's being Hollywood, I guess things happen."

"Oh, did they?" She looked away.

"Yes, but he was still faithful to the family. I guess they worked out an arrangement. I mean as long as everybody is happy, right?"

Later that night, Jack made a last-ditch effort to bed Harriet, and he took her to his cottage "for some tea."

After a few kisses, she pushed him away. "I can see where this is going."

"Well, let it go there."

"If you think you are going to take me to bed, then you don't know me."

"Oh?"

Flip got to her feet. "Listen to me. Here I am at Stanford, and I'm just a poor little girl from Little Rock." She put her hands on her hips. "I belong to this good sorority, and the girls in this sorority all have more of a pedigree than I do, and they're all brighter, and they're all everything."

"So?"

"Now, I have very good looks, and I am sought after by men."

"And one of them is me."

"But I have decided, if I want to get a good husband, I have to go to that husband as a virgin. I don't want to lie. That's just the way I am. Don't you understand? It's just not worthwhile losing my virginity to a guy who's going back East in a short time whom I may never see again."

"We might be good together, Flip."

"Like I told your buddy Henry, I'll keep you guessing, I'll toy with you, but you will never get anywhere with me. I *won't* go the whole way."

Jack threw up his hands, defeated, but respectful of her clearly stated boundaries.

"Now take me home," she said.

Once his relationship with Flip went as far as it could, Jack felt the urge to go back to Hollywood. Now that he had a bestseller, he was curious if he might attract a few Hollywood actresses—a step above the starlets he'd pursued on his previous trip. He went to Los Angeles with a list of contacts his father had given him.

While Jack was hanging around a Hollywood set, a handsome, deep-voiced man introduced himself. "Robert Stack," he said, offering his hand.

After talking about their respective careers, Jack found he had much in common with the young actor. Stack was an avid sportsman, owned two world records in skeet shooting, and had taken drama classes at Bridgewater State in Massachusetts. He was only twenty, but he had a strong presence.

"Do you like war movies?" Stack asked Jack. "I'm in one, and it's my first major role. Come out and see it with me."

They went to a screening of *The Mortal Storm*, starring James Stewart and Margaret Sullivan. The movie was about a German family

BECOMING JFK

and how Fascism impacted them.

As they walked out, Jack kidded, "You were pretty good. Did a great job of playing a Nazi. I was in Germany recently. You nailed it. But you were a lot more likable than the ones I saw over there. Interesting ending."

"Wasn't it?"

In the last scene, Stack's character couldn't decide if he should return to his Nazi comrades or reject Fascism.

"A great many countries are going to have to determine which side to take in the very near future," Jack said. "Including the United States."

They stopped at a restaurant and sat at the bar. Stack ordered a martini and Jack a ginger ale. They both chose the lamb chop dinner. The talk turned to the Hollywood starlets for which they both had a strong desire. Stack said he had a hideaway in the Hollywood Hills where he took them.

"A hideaway?"

"A friend and I told our mothers we needed a place for meditation and study. They agreed. Want to see it? You might want to use it sometime."

Whitley Place was a small curving street in the Hollywood Hills. Stack's place was amidst a jumble of apartments heaped atop one another like building blocks. "Watch your head," said Stack, outside the door to the room.

The room was so small that standing upright was practically impossible. There was only space for a bed. On the ceiling were plastered flags of almost every country in the world.

"I call it the Flag Room," Stack said with a wicked grin. "This is where I engage the ladies in a game of memory."

"What?"

"I give the gal a test. She has to memorize the country and their flag in a given time. If she fails, she has to pay the penalty."

Jack was both amused and mildly shocked at the subterfuge. "I can guess what that is."

"Well, she is already in a horizontal position, so paying the penalty is usually no problem. Feel free to try it out."

Jack took him up on the offer several times—not caring if the women matched the flag with the country. If the flag was matched correctly, Jack honored her with a bout of lovemaking; if she failed, she got the same treatment.

Jack opened a copy of the *Stanford Daily* dated October 30, 1940. His picture was on the front page. He'd received his draft number. "The holder of 2748 for the Palo Alto area is Jack Kennedy, son of Joseph P. Kennedy." The article went on to mention both his attendance at Stanford and his book.

If there was going to be a war, Jack wanted to be in on it. He was not interested in being on the sidelines. He wanted an active role. No desk job for him. If he had his choice, given his love of the sea and sailing skills, he'd rather be on a ship than in the army or air force.

But with all his physical problems, he doubted the military would take him. "This draft has caused me a bit of concern," he wrote Lem, thinking about how it might affect his future. "They will never take me into the army—and yet if I don't, it will look quite bad for me."

The fun and games of his West Coast trip took a different direction when his father, under considerable domestic criticism for his controversial stance on appeasing Germany and not aiding Britain, arrived in San Francisco on November 14.

"Jack, it's good to see you," Joe Sr. said when Jack met him at the airport.

It had been more than a year since he had seen his father. German

BECOMING JFK

bombing of England had begun September 7. His father appeared hollowed out from the ordeal, although each evening he departed Central London for his sixty-room rented mansion in Windsor and escaped the German bombing blitz. The British press, who initially embraced him, now called him "Jittery Joe."

Reporters surrounded the ambassador at the San Francisco airport and began shouting questions at him. When he and Jack escaped the press, Joe Sr. pursed his lips and said to his son, "My policy is only to keep the United States out of war. I will work toward that end as long as I live."

Jack nodded, unconvinced.

"Stay the hell out of Europe," he continued. "It's a no-win situation. There's nothing we can do. Lindbergh's seen the German Air Force. He's made it clear that England is no match for it."

They got into Jack's car and drove north to media mogul William Randolph Hearst's ranch at Wyntoon in Siskiyou County, near the top of California.

"Jack, you might as well know it," said his father, after they'd been driving for a couple of hours. "I'm not going to return to England."

"What?" Jack said, although not completely surprised. His father's viewpoints weren't popular, especially with Roosevelt.

"Yes," he sighed. "Roosevelt very happily accepted my resignation. As soon as he finds a successor, I'm done."

"Probably for the best, Dad."

"I think so. But I need you to do something for me. With your book and travels, you've become fairly fluent in the situation over there. I want you to put together a draft for an important newspaper or magazine article that would run under my name."

"About what?" Jack appreciated his father's confidence in him, although he was surprised he hadn't tapped Joe or one of his staffers for the job.

"I realize that my position—staying out of that mess—has not been well received. I want to begin rehabilitating my standing here."

"Oh." The last thing Jack wanted to do was develop an article regarding a viewpoint he didn't share. Even if it was his father's.

"Once a successor has been found and I'm no longer ambassador, I want to publish a major article detailing my opinions. Putting something in print will be beneficial. Plenty of facts to back me up. Like you did with your book."

After Jack returned to Stanford, he hoped his father would forget about, or at least delay, his request. He put it out of his mind and made several more trips to Hollywood, again taking advantage of his father's connections.

On the Metro-Goldwyn-Mayer lot, Jack surveyed the comings and goings of stage technicians, press assistants, and gophers involved in the filming of *Edison, the Man*. During a break in the action, a stocky man with a shock of red hair, dressed in late-nineteenth century period clothing, approached him. Jack recognized Academy Award-winning actor Spencer Tracy.

They exchanged pleasantries, and after Tracy asked about Jack's father, he said, "Jack, I've heard a lot about your book. I'd be honored if you'd autograph a copy for me."

"You're in luck," Jack said, opening his briefcase. "I've got an extra."

"Come over tomorrow for a set party," Tracy said. "Gable's coming by and there'll be plenty of pretty women. You might be autographing a few more books."

Jack brought Henry along with him. When they arrived, the party's hostess rushed over, gushing, "Oh, Jack, dah-ling! Lovely to see you.

How handsome you are. Your book is *so* exciting—a best-selling author—oh my goodness." Leaving Henry behind, she grabbed Jack's arm. "I want to introduce you to some people."

As they made the rounds and engaged in small talk, Jack gauged his chances of being alone with any of the famous actresses present. Or were they still above his rank?

The air was thick with smoke, but through it he saw the hard-drinking Tracy holding a cocktail glass, teetering on his feet.

"Let's sit here," Jack said to Henry, seeing on a nearby couch several beautiful young women. One of them looked familiar. She was dark-haired, voluptuous, and alluring. Where had he seen that face? *Life* magazine, publicizing a feature about starlets. The one sitting next to him had been on the cover. Lana Turner. A few years younger than him, she was known as the "sweater girl" because of the form-fitting sweater she wore in *They Won't Forget*. His prodigious memory had come in handy.

"Jack Kennedy," he said to Miss Turner. Remembering the *Life* cover photo of a shaggy unattractive dog that Turner had on a leash as she descended the stairs, Jack said, "Had I been taking that picture, I would have gotten rid of the dog so the attention would be focused on you."

"Thank you," Turner said appreciatively. "I couldn't agree with you more. I only wish they'd have listened to me."

Jack felt he was making time and was about to ask if Turner wanted to get some fresh air. See what happened while they stargazed. But his move was interrupted when one of the women asked them what the difference was between East Coast and West Coast girls. Henry chirped, "About three thousand miles."

It wasn't much of a joke in Jack's opinion, so he was surprised to hear Turner and the others laugh uproariously. Jack raised his eyebrows at this unexpected turn of events. Normally, he was the one who drew the guffaws, giggles, and exclamations of "You are so funny!" Jack had never been desperate for attention; others were naturally attracted to his lively personality. But tonight, Henry was on a roll. It was like watching a .200 hitter get four hits in a game.

Anxious to draw the attention back to him, Jack blurted, "That's his only joke, so—"

"I also sing and dance," Henry said, "but I need a couple of volunteers. Ladies?"

Eagerly, the women got to their feet, ready to perform. After all, that's why they were in Hollywood. With Henry in the middle, his arms around the gals' waists, he sang Bing Crosby's big hit "You Must've Been a Beautiful Baby." The women chimed in, kicking right and left, and the guests stopped to watch the performance, clapping along to the beat.

Jack sat alone with his arms crossed watching the spectacle. Henry's usurpation of the women's attention was bewildering. He hadn't seen this coming.

The women sat down, breathless and reveling in their performance and the attention. To Jack's surprise, Henry continued to be witty and charming for the rest of the evening.

When they got back to the hotel, Jack parked the car, then turned to his friend. "Henry! You were quite the star tonight," he said laughingly. "Although I don't know if I liked playing second fiddle, no doubt you were the life of the party. I didn't know you had it in you."

"Neither did I. Maybe I learned from hanging around you."

But when they returned to Stanford, Jack couldn't resist introducing Henry to friends with a backhanded compliment. "You know this guy here, he doesn't look like anything, but boy, he really was a smasheroo hit down in LA!"

BECOMING JFK

Jack had only a couple of days left at Stanford before he would attend the Institute of World Affairs in Riverside, California, after which he'd fly home. He hoped to relax, but a cable from his father made that impossible. "When will outline on that appeasement article be ready?" it read. He couldn't get out of it now.

Jack composed his ideas in his head and began dictating to a secretary. In the cover letter to his father, he said the outline showed an approach to the problem that differed from his long-standing isolationist stance. Above all, he wanted his father to sound positive—not defensive or unpleasant. Jack advocated emphasizing opposition to dictatorships. "You hate them. You have achieved the abundant life under a democratic capitalistic system, and you wish to preserve it. But you believe that you can preserve it by keeping out of Europe's wars." *Now the crucial point.* Jack added that it would be beneficial to shed the skin labeling him an appeaser. It could never do him any good. Nobody likes somebody who bows down to another.

As he dictated, Jack felt himself something akin to a statesman or key advisor. It was almost an out-of-body experience. He hadn't deferred by writing son-to-father, but as man-to-man on nearly equal terms. He had become a strategic consultant and speechwriter.

With the draft completed, Jack said his goodbyes to Flip and a few others. He packed up and boarded a United Airlines flight from San Francisco to Los Angeles. But shortly after takeoff, Jack realized he had more to say. He had not addressed a critical issue, so he took out pen and paper. "Dear Dad," he began the note. Writing feverishly, he added a supplementary nine pages, pressing for his father to reverse his position and advocate for the United States to come to Britain's defense. That

America had to help its allies. The great debate over the Lend-Lease Act was raging, and his father was against the program that would provide food, oil, and munitions for the Allies. If Britain went down, the United States would be "alone in a strained and hostile world." He added:

> *You are an appeaser + against aid—this you have to nip. I do not mean that you should advocate war, but you might explain with some vigor your ideas on how vital it is for us to supply England.*

Jack finished just before landing. He drew a deep breath of relief and satisfaction, then folded the pages and stuffed them in an envelope. He mailed the package to his father on his way out of the Los Angeles airport.

On January 18, after discussions with Roosevelt and others, Jack's father did a three-sixty. Speaking on NBC Radio, he reluctantly agreed to support Lend-Lease. His announcement surprised everyone—including Jack. As he listened closely to what his father said were his reasons, Jack heard a few of his own phrases come from his father's mouth.

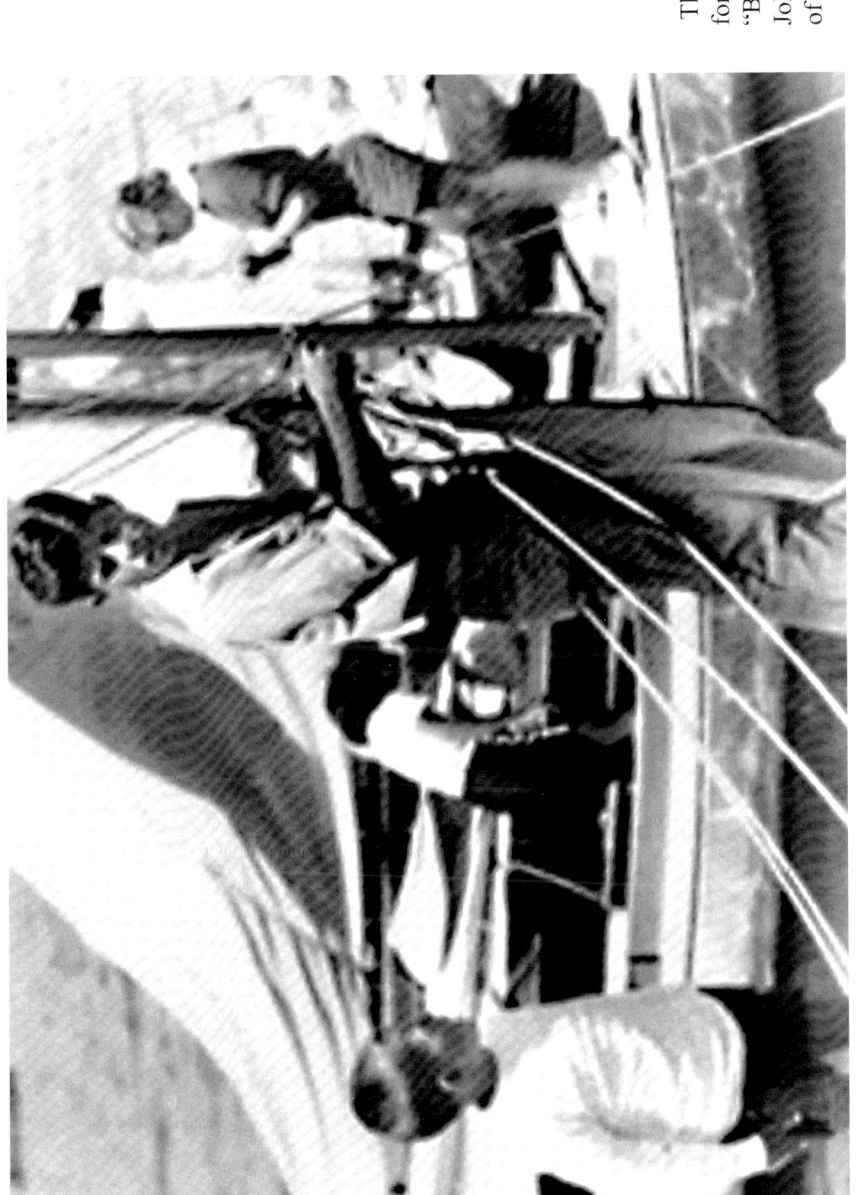

The *Boston Globe* caption for this 1934 photo read: "Bob advises his brother John how to bend the jib of the Victura."

Jack poses with fellow Muckers (from left) Ralph Horton, Lem Billings and Charles Schriber while at the Choate School in Wallingford, CT.

With sister Rosemary behind him, Jack holds a snake at a zoo in Jupiter, Florida, April, 1936.

Hoping to bulk up to play Harvard football, Jack toiled as a ranch hand at the Jay Six Ranch in Arizona.

In Hyannis, for a family portrait. Seated from left are: Patricia, Robert, Rose, Jack, Joseph with son Edward on his lap; standing from left are: Joseph, Kathleen, Rosemary, Eunice (rear, in polka dots), and Jean.

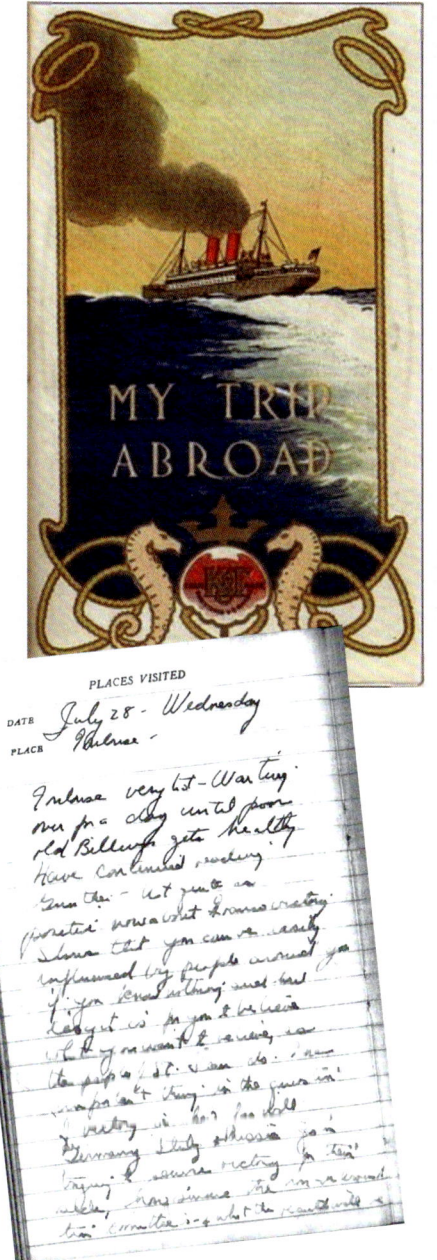

Kathleen gave her brother a travel diary for his trip to Europe in 1937.

During their tour of Europe, Jack and Lem visited the Chateau de Chambord, famous for its distinctive French Renaissance architecture.

Lem wrote in his diary, "the leaning towers of Pisa & Kennedy."

In Venice, Jack feeds the pigeons.

On the way up Mt. Vesuvius, they picked up two Germans soldiers on holiday.

Finding respite from the Nazi fervor in Nuremberg, Jack practices his juggling.

Jack acquired a dachshund, "Offie," in Germany. Allergies forced him to give the dog away.

Nearing the end of their trip, Jack is photographed in The Hague, Netherlands.

1937 HARVARD Junior Varsity

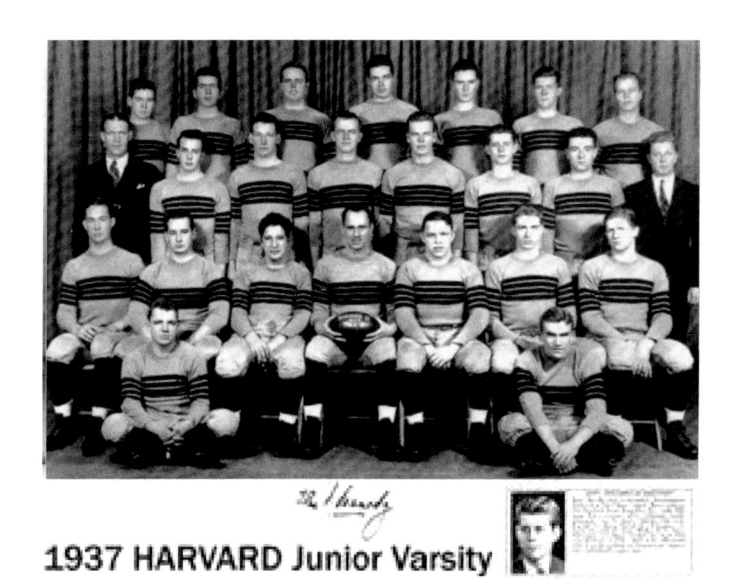

John F. Kennedy poses with the 1937 Harvard Junior Varsity football team. Persistent health issues, including debilitating back pain, forced him to abandon his football aspirations shortly thereafter.

John F. Kennedy, pictured in swim trunks at Harvard, competed on the varsity swim team, where he focused on endurance and teamwork despite ongoing health challenges.

U.S. Ambassador Joseph P. Kennedy returns to England with his sons Joe Jr. and Jack.

Jack arrives with his sister Kathleen and brother Joe at the House of Parliament on September 3, 1939 to hear Prime Minister Neville Chamberlain's announcement that a state of war existed between England and Germany.

When the British passenger liner *Athenia* was sunk by a German submarine at the beginning of World War II, Jack's father sent him to Scotland to soothe the fears of surviving American passengers and arrange transportation home.

Thanks to his father's connections, Jack was a frequent visitor on the set in Hollywood, 1940.

During his stay in California, Jack autographs a copy of his book, *Why England Slept*, for actor Spencer Tracy.

While auditing classes at Stanford in 1940, Jack signs up for the first draft in the nation's history.

Sister Kathleen (left) and Lem (far right) with Jack in Palm Beach, Christmas, 1940.

The Kennedy house in Hyannis Port, Massachusetts.

Jack in Hyannis Port during the summer of 1941.

Bobby (in back) and others join Jack at the wheel in Hyannis Port.

Jack relaxes in Hyannis Port.

At the end of 1941, Jack became involved romantically with Inga Arvad, who wrote for the Washington Times-Herald, and had interviewed Hitler in the 1930s.

Shortly after meeting Jack, Inga wrote a column about him that was mounted on a plaque and presented to him as a gift from the newspaper.

A somber Jack separated from his true love. Suspecting Inga was a spy, the government separated the couple and transferred him from Washington D.C. to Charleston, South Carolina.

Lieutenant Kennedy and Ensign Joe Kennedy in 1942 before they shipped overseas.

Jack at the wheel of the PT 109.

The PT 109 crew. Jack is on the far right.

An oil painting commissioned by the Navy in 1961 recreates the moment when the Japanese destroyer Amagiri struck PT 109.

Jack used a cane while recuperating from the PT 109 catastrophe.

With Secretary of the Navy James Forrestal (far left) in Berlin, Jack tours the Reich Chancellery in 1945 while a Russian soldier looks on.

In his Beacon Hill Boston apartment, Jack takes a moment to relax while running for Congress in 1946. A picture of his parents sits on the mantel.

During the campaign, Jack was said to have "stolen the city's heart" when he walked a billy goat around Boston.

On June 18, 1946, Jack won the Democratic Party nomination for Congress in the 11th District in Massachusetts. Flanked by his mother and father, he celebrated at his campaign headquarters.

As his Doberman Pinscher "Mo" looks on, Jack chats with Bobby in Hyannis Port after his primary win.

During a series with the Detroit Tigers at Fenway Park in Boston, the Democratic nominee examines Hank Greenberg's bat while Red Sox teammates Ted Williams and Eddie Pellagrini look on.

PART THREE
LOVER BOY

Chapter 19
February 1941

Jack was reading the Miami newspaper when his father entered the living room. He had arrived back in Palm Beach in March. "Just the man I wanted to see," his father said and sat down. "Great job on that article."

Jack's commentary for the *New York Journal-American* had addressed the question of whether Ireland should give naval and air bases to England. In it, he posed the question, "Is Ireland, by her refusal to do so, sleeping the same sleep that brought England to the brink of disaster?"

"You're becoming quite the scribe." his father said. "Adds to your fame as a best-selling author, which I, uh, helped you become."

"Thanks for suggesting I work with Krock."

"No, I meant sales. In your best interests, I bought a few thousand. Well, a bit more. There's a big difference between being an author and being a best-selling author."

Jack sagged, dismayed that his success had been artificially contrived. Joe Sr. had ginned up sales by purchasing boatloads of the book so his son would be on the *New York Times* best-seller list. Of course, he hadn't asked Jack beforehand and, as usual, acted on his own. But what Jack would have answered if his father had asked him to approve the idea, he couldn't be sure. It didn't matter now. He wasn't completely mad at his father; he was well aware he would do most anything to help his sons achieve success. Still, it took some of the joy out of his accomplishment.

"It was selling well, but I wanted to put it over the top. You can thank me later. Now, let's talk about your future. That work you did for me on the appeasement article was outstanding. You probably recognize some of your words in that radio speech I made a couple of months ago."

BECOMING JFK

Joe Sr. clasped his hands together. "So, now it's time for a new project. Which I think you need since you won't be going to law school until September, or later. It will be an extension of what you've already done, but more in depth."

What could this be? thought Jack, who was feeling a tightness in his gut. "Yes?"

"I believe there is great interest in my years as ambassador. I want to produce a chronicle of everything that transpired during this time and, of course, my important role in those events. That is something you can do and do well. You were there for some of it."

"Yes, but—"

"Jack, as of this month, I'm no longer an ambassador. But I'm still fresh in everyone's mind, especially after my well-received speech supporting Lend-Lease, for which you are due credit. Anyway, we have to keep the momentum going."

"Whatever I can do to help," said Jack uneasily. He was already thinking of how to avoid the project.

"Thatta boy."

His father got up to leave the room. "Oh, take a little time off before we start. Your mother and Eunice are leaving shortly for South America. I think you should join them."

Jack exhaled after his father had exited. The last thing he wanted was to be his father's scribe. It would take a year or more to complete the project, and it wasn't something he wanted to do anyway.

Before he made his way to South America, Jack hurriedly sent off a letter to writer John Hersey, who was the husband of a former flame, Frances Ann Cannon. He hoped a woman Jack had met at their wedding would be interested in the project. After persuading his father that she was more skilled at writing the chronicle, a meeting was set up between the two. It went well. He was out of it.

By that time, it was too late to get the required visas to accompany his mother and sister, so Jack flew alone, later, to Rio de Janeiro from Miami. He toured the city with them, visited Sugar Loaf Rock and Copacabana Beach, and then left on his own for Argentina. He'd met the daughter of the Argentine ambassador during the Pope's investiture two years previous, and she had invited him to stay at their property. After enjoying the pleasures of the ranch and the ambassador's daughter, Jack flew to Montevideo, Uruguay, and then to Santiago, Chile. From there, he boarded the SS *Santa Lucia* from Valparaiso bound for New York. He'd been out of touch regarding world events during his stay, but the liner received regular communications on the war in Europe.

During his idyll in South America, Japan had become more threatening, prompting President Roosevelt to declare a full state of emergency as Japan aggressively pursued expansion in the Far East, driving further into China and securing possession of Southeast Asia. He also learned that Germany had invaded Russia.

"Cable for you," said a ship orderly, handing Jack an envelope while he ate breakfast.

He nearly dumped his coffee on his lap when he read: *Joe has volunteered for military service.* He couldn't believe it. Joe, who had argued vehemently against U.S. involvement in Europe's mess, who admired Hitler, and who co-founded the Harvard Committee Against Military Intervention, had quit his final year of law school. He'd been accepted into the navy's aviation cadet program in May and was sworn in as a seaman second class. Jack was flummoxed. Either Joe had changed his view of America's involvement in European affairs or something else had prompted his enlistment.

A few days after Jack returned home, Joe stopped by. Based at a station in Squantum, near Boston, he was home for the weekend. Joe wore his uniform of cadet khaki shirt and pants. Jack thought he looked more like a boy scout than a soldier.

"Didn't figure on you joining up," said Jack, as they stood outside on the veranda in Hyannis Port. "Thought since you wanted the U.S. to stay out of the conflict that you'd do your best to keep out of it yourself." Jack rubbed his chin.

"Listen, Jack, I haven't changed my political views, but if I hadn't enlisted and been drafted instead, they'd have put me somewhere I didn't want to be. I'd be a lowly private. By joining voluntarily, I was able to choose where I wanted to go. I have a chance to distinguish myself once I get through training." He huffed up. "I intend to be a navy pilot."

Nodding, Jack said only, "That's good." He was surprised his brother was choosing the fly-boy route over being on the water, but what he said about the advantage of enlisting made sense.

"Whether or not the U.S. becomes involved in the war," Joe continued, "it's important our family is represented in the military. And that responsibility falls on me. Of course, it can only help my political prospects."

Joe glanced at the choppy waters of Nantucket Sound, then back to Jack. "It's going to be tough on you, though," Joe said solemnly.

"What's going to be tough?"

"I told JP you're perfectly capable of taking care of everything when he's gone. You are, aren't you?"

"I am," Jack stammered, not fully understanding what Joe meant.

"With your health and everything, they won't take you. That's not your fault. Not serving in the military will be tough. But you'll be the one to handle things when JP travels or Mother goes on one of her trips. The kids will be looking to you. Can you do it?"

So, Joe assumed they'd never take him because of his poor health, and he might well be right. Jack didn't know himself, though he had his doubts.

"I could," Jack added. He didn't say he would.

"Good," said Joe, and walked into the house.

Jack didn't like the idea of Joe dictating his new role. *I'll decide that*, thought Jack.

A few days after Joe returned to his base, Jack set sail with Eunice and Bobby for Martha's Vineyard. Jack guided the *Victura* within sight of Edgartown Harbor. From the starboard, Bobby pointed and yelled, "Jack, look at this!"

"Eunice, take over," Jack said, and handed over the tiller to join Bobby up front. Adjacent to the usual fishing boats, sloops, and yachts was a sleek, gray, compact military vessel. It was unlike any boat Jack had ever seen. "That's really something." Jack said. "I've got to get on it."

Preparing for potential war, the navy had put the boat on an exhibition tour and opened it up to the public. Jack docked the *Victura* and beelined for the boat like a magnet was pulling him. There was something about the trim lines and scrappy look that captured his attention. The vessel bristled with torpedoes and mounted machine guns. Most of all, even though it was stationary, Jack sensed it had speed and maneuverability.

His heart racing and his curiosity piqued, Jack explored the vessel, poking into the sleeping quarters, stepping into the machine gun turret and, best of all, sitting in the cockpit. He imagined himself climbing behind the wheel, then opening the throttles and bouncing off the waves.

Eunice and Bobby had come aboard, but Jack was oblivious to their presence.

"What kind of boat is this?" he asked an officer.

"It's a motor torpedo boat," the officer said. "But everyone calls them PT boats, which stands for Patrol Torpedo. It's fast and can turn on a dime. It's almost all mahogany planks. We've got a crew of twelve. She's got torpedoes, mounted machine guns, and depth charges. Like it?"

"You bet I do," said Jack.

Barely able to contain his enthusiasm, Jack peppered the officer with questions and learned that young officers just starting out had a good chance of commanding one. He thought something like this might be right up his alley.

The rest of his Martha's Vineyard vacation with Eunice and Bobby went by in a pleasant blur, but the image of the PT boat was never far from his mind.

Chapter 20

By the time he returned to Hyannis, Jack had made up his mind to not only enlist, but to request sea duty. He couldn't let his brother have all the military glory. And physically he was feeling pretty good. Yes, his back ached a little more, but he could live with that. The big question still was whether they would take him.

In early July, both the army and navy officer candidate schools rejected him because of his back, and Jack had all but resigned himself to attending Yale Law School. But he had a final card to play before that happened. He didn't want to use it, but he had no other choice. Jack asked his father for help.

"I know just the guy," said Joe Sr., as they drank coffee in the sun room. "My former naval attaché in London, Alan Kirk, is now director of Naval Intelligence in Washington. He was impressed with your efforts during the *Athenia* crisis. Let me see what I can do."

Wanting Jack to join him in Naval Intelligence, Kirk had a medical friend examine Jack and write up a clean bill of health for him. After impressing his interviewers, Jack was commissioned as an ensign without attending officer school. He was assigned to the Office of Naval Intelligence in Washington, DC. Jack was a little disappointed not to be out on the high seas, but it was a step in the right direction.

Jack reported for active duty in late October. On his first day, he proudly put on his new black uniform that sported one gold bar and made his way to the Office of Naval Intelligence.

Things were looking up. Jack found lodging at the Dorchester House on Sixteenth Street. He was excited about this new military endeavor, and he would be living in Washington at the same time Kick would be in DC working at the *Washington Times-Herald*. As she had in London, Kick had a toe-hold into the social scene, even though she'd only arrived shortly before Jack had.

While naval intelligence sounded thrilling, the work was pure drudgery. Six days a week, he toiled in a sparse room filled with rows of metal desks. His job was to collate, edit, and condense intelligence reports from foreign outposts into departmental bulletins.

Right from the start, Jack began forming connections thanks to Kick. She introduced him to the *Times-Herald's* colorful publisher, Eleanor "Cissy" Patterson, at a party.

"Jack," Patterson said, "I'm quite impressed with your book. And that you had it published so soon after graduating college. Perhaps you'd be interested in meeting some of the more interesting people in Washington. I'd like to invite you to a dinner I'm hosting."

The guest list at Patterson's mansion in Dupont Circle included the undersecretary of the navy, financier Bernard Baruch, isolationist Montana Senator Burton Wheeler, and Pulitzer Prize-winning journalist Bernard Swope. Several commented positively on his book. The discussion was lively, and although he was many years younger than most of the guests, Jack held his own.

"In my view," he said, "America is a participant in the war in many ways other than sending troops to the fight in Europe. I believe it is best to go after the Germans now," he said during one discussion. "If we wait and our allies fall to the wayside, we will have to take them on alone. I don't want to write a book called *Why America Slept*."

Kick hosted her own party at the F Street Club, an historic nineteenth-century mansion. She sidled up to Jack and made an introduction. "Jack, I'd like you to meet Inga Arvad. Inga's a reporter for the *Times-Herald*. I'll let you two get acquainted," she said and slipped away.

Jack could only stare. Inga was honey-blonde, blue-eyed, and statuesque, with full lips and a perfect complexion accentuated by high cheekbones. Even a minor flaw—a slight gap between her two front teeth—Jack found appealing. He was further intrigued when she told him she'd been a student at the Columbia Graduate School of Journalism.

"How was it for you there?" he asked.

"Difficult in some ways," she said, sipping on champagne. "Trying to find my way. I was older, and if I may say so, a little more sophisticated than many of the other students."

"I believe that."

Inga laughed. "I probably overdressed. Sometimes I wore a long black dress to class. And I smoked cigarettes from a cigarette holder. I wanted to impress people."

"How did you happen to come to Washington and get a job at the *Times-Herald*?" asked Jack, impressed by her rapid professional progress.

"A chance meeting. The Pulitzer board is headquartered at Columbia, where I was a student in the graduate journalism program. The day after that year's prizes were announced, I spotted this man waiting for a taxi on Broadway. I walked up to him and said, 'Are you Mr. Krock?'"

Jack told her his father worked with Krock and that he had made valuable contributions to his book.

"Really?" said Inga, delighted at the coincidence. "Anyway, I introduced myself and said I would like to work on a newspaper in Washington. He told me to look him up if I happened to be in Washington."

"Here you are. So, I guess you did."

"No promises were made. He didn't know me or my qualifications, but he was kind and helpful, and I moved here based on that conversation. He had me out to his wonderful home in Virginia and began introducing me to important people. One of those was Mrs. Patterson. I told her I could get an interview with Axel Wenner-Gren. He's one of the richest people in the world and owns the *Southern Cross*, the largest yacht in the world."

"Yes, I've heard about him."

"I didn't know then if I really could get the interview, but I got an exclusive with him, and it ran on the front page. And here I am."

The next day, Inga rang Jack up to say that she had been ordered by Patterson to get an interview with him for her column.

Jack met her at the venerable Mayflower, the beaux arts hotel a short distance from the White House. When the interview was over, Jack said, "Why don't we take a walk? I'm tired of giving answers, and I've got some questions for you."

As they walked along Connecticut Avenue, Jack learned Inga was fluent in four languages and a former Miss Denmark. But her good mood disappeared when she mentioned her husband, Paul Fejos, a Hungarian filmmaker many years her senior. She hadn't seen him in a year and a half. No love lost there.

That was good because Jack was captivated by Inga. Although he'd enjoyed the pleasures of a variety of women, he'd never become intimate with a married woman. He hadn't wanted to get caught up in the complications. There were enough single women around to occupy his time. But Inga was different—irresistible somehow.

"Where's your husband?" Jack asked casually.

"He's in Peru, hoping to find the lost cities of the Incas."

"Good luck to him. Lost cities can be hard to find." Jack longed to touch this mysterious, alluring woman. When they reached Farragut Square, he said, "Let's sit." They had been seated only a moment when Jack put his hand on Inga's leg. "I wouldn't mind if he stays lost."

Inga looked at his hand. "Jack, you are my subject. Do you think it's appropriate to be doing such things?"

"I do. Extremely appropriate."

"You do?"

"Yes." He kissed her full on the lips.

"Yes, perhaps it is appropriate," she said.

Several days later, they found themselves in Inga's bed on the fifth floor of her art deco residence on Sixteenth Street.

When the interview came out, Jack called her from Hyannis Port, where he was celebrating Christmas with the Kennedy family. The interview lauded him, mentioning his "much praised book" and that "elder men like to hear his views, which are sound and astonishingly objective for so young a man."

"My favorite part," said Jack, "is when you say, 'The twenty-four years of Jack's existence on our planet have proved that here is really a boy with a future.' So you think I'm a boy with a future?"

"You could be," she parried playfully. "It's up to you."

"Except I wish you hadn't called me a boy."

It was good to hear Inga's voice. He missed her, especially the touch of her skin. Talking with her buoyed him because there was a cloud hanging over the Kennedy family. Rosemary was missing. She'd been enrolled at a convent school in Washington, DC. Having only arrived in October, Jack hadn't seen her. He, Kick, Rosemary, and their father were supposed to attend a college football game in Baltimore on November 8, but Rosemary hadn't made it. Dad had said only that she wasn't feeling well. Now, nobody was saying why she wasn't here with the rest of the family.

The clan gathered at the table for their holiday dinner. There would be no small talk tonight—no 'what did you do today?'—but then there never had been. The patriarch had always demanded that discussion at meal time revolve around what was happening in the world. He expected everyone, but primarily his sons, to bring a topic of interest to the table. And he was happy to hear viewpoints different from his own as long as they were supported well by facts and reason..

But tonight was different.

After the blessing of the food, Joe Sr. said, "Rosemary won't be joining us. We've decided she will be better off for the time being at a different school where she can get the instruction she needs."

Jack was sitting next to Kick, who began to quietly cry.

"But when is she coming back?" Eunice asked, almost jumping out of her seat.

"I'm not sure. I know we all miss her, but it's for the best." The patriarch paused and then said sternly, "And it's best that we don't talk about her. It will only have a negative effect on our family. So that's it. I won't have anything more to say on the subject. Is that clear? Now let's eat."

Jack's mother looked down at her plate. Eunice crossed her arms and looked straight ahead. Jack met Kick's somber eyes, and Joe stiffened for a moment, then shrugged.

"Let's take a walk," Jack said to Kick after the early meal was over. They grabbed their heavy coats and silently trudged close to the water. The wind was fierce and cold. When they stopped, Jack asked, "What do you know?" He'd seen his sister's anguish at the dinner table.

"Oh, Jack," she said. "They operated on her. Daddy had it done."

"What do you mean? What kind of operation?"

"On her brain."

"What? Why would he do that?" Jack recalled the last time he had seen Rosemary. It had been in London in 1939, just before he'd returned to Harvard. He remembered dancing with his sweet sister and making sure she had partners. He hadn't noticed any difference in her behavior.

"She'd been escaping from school at night. Walking the streets until the early morning. Who knows what she was doing? According to Mother, the staff at the school said she'd become very difficult to deal with. She'd often go into a rage."

"Mother told you that?" He hadn't noticed any violent outbursts or other behavioral issues when they were together in London.

"Yes. When she found out Daddy was planning to do some sort of operation, she asked me to look into it."

Jack thought it surprising that his mother had asked Kick instead of her older sons for assistance. But she was closer to her daughters. "What did you find out?"

Kick said she talked with a reporter at her paper who had been researching mental illness and treatment for a series of stories. He told her that the results from the operations weren't good. Patients after surgery didn't worry much, but they lost all normal capabilities.

"When I heard that," Kick said, "I told Mother it's nothing we want done for Rosie. Daddy did it anyway. Oh, Jack, I'm sure it didn't go well. And I could have stopped it." She embraced him, burrowing her head in his shoulder.

"I doubt that. We both know that when Father has his mind made up, it's difficult to change his mind. Don't blame yourself, Kick."

Jack returned to Washington and found Inga's compassion and nurturing essential after the news about Rosemary. He and Inga were rarely apart. Much of their time was spent in bed, but this relationship was more gratifying and deeper than any he'd ever experienced. He'd never met a woman as beautiful and as worldly as Inga. Having trained with the Danish Royal Ballet, Inga had poise and moved with grace. He was

BECOMING JFK

entranced by her lovely, warm laugh and quick mind. She was four years older than him, and she was an accomplished and resourceful woman.

There was undeniable passion between them, but it was more than just physical—a meeting of minds as well as bodies. Inga was a confident and attentive partner, her desires matching Jack's own. Yet, after one intimate encounter, she gently challenged him.

"Jack, you've got a lot to learn about how to satisfy a woman," she said with a teasing smile.

Surprised, Jack propped himself up on one elbow. "What do you mean?" he asked. His experiences had been brief and routine, marked by quick embraces that ended with his own gratification.

"I'm going to teach you," Inga replied. "For starters, slow down." She guided him with patience, encouraging him to take his time, to pay closer attention to her needs and desires. She showed him how to move in harmony with her, leading him to discover the deeper pleasure of truly connecting.

Under her guidance, Jack began to appreciate a new dynamic in their intimacy—one that was not just about release but about mutual fulfillment. Inga's confidence and ability to communicate transformed their encounters, teaching him to listen, to respond, and to truly engage.

Still, there were moments, particularly after days apart, when Inga gave him the space to seek his own release first, knowing it would help him relax and refocus on her the next time.

For Jack, Inga represented a first—not just in the physical sense but emotionally as well. Their connection was unlike anything he had experienced before. When work or travel separated them, Jack wrote heartfelt letters to her, expressing a sincerity he rarely revealed to others. In one, he confessed, "To you I need not pretend. You know me too well."

As time went along, Jack learned more about Inga's life—and it had been quite a life. Arriving in the United States in February 1940, Inga announced her age as twenty-three, figuring it would help her job prospects. Women of twenty-seven (her actual age) were supposed to be married and have children.

One day after lunch in Inga's apartment, she shared that she had lived in Southeast Asia and Malaysia. She also let it slip that she'd married an Egyptian she'd met at seventeen while traveling in Egypt. And she'd even stayed with headhunters on the island of Nias, off the coast of Sumatra.

"Headhunters?" Jack said. He put down his fork and stopped eating.

"Yes, I even dined with one."

"And kept your head?"

"Yes, but while we were dining in his hut, I saw a strange object." Inga made a circle with her thumb and forefinger. "It was a smoke-darkened, shrunken, but still recognizable head of a red-haired German missionary. And I'd met him only a few months earlier!"

Jack drew back, shocked at the image.

"I asked the chief why the missionary had met this ghastly fate, and he said, 'Bad manners.'"

"Maybe," Jack quipped, "he was a Nazi."

Inga also told him about a previous relationship she had with a fellow Dane, Nils Blok, who was also enrolled at Columbia. "We had some fun times. But he was nothing special. And I came out ahead."

"Ahead?"

"Yes, we were out for a drive one day. I was at the wheel, though I didn't have a driver's license or insurance. I got into a bit of a crash and chipped my tooth. Nils was nice enough to say he had been driving. Anyway, I got a nice settlement from the insurance company, so it worked out. Would you have done the same for me, darling?"

BECOMING JFK

Jack thought back to when he'd been caught speeding with Lem when they were students at Choate. Hearing the police car siren, Jack had pulled over and convinced Lem to switch seats with him. Another speeding ticket and Jack would have lost his license. Lem received the citation, although Jack paid for it.

"Sure," he said. "Why not?" Suddenly, Jack felt pangs of hunger and the urge to be outside. "Let's take a walk along Pennsylvania Avenue. Get something to eat." After they'd been walking for a few minutes, Jack asked if she had ever interviewed anybody famous.

"Yes, although I don't know if I am proud of it now. But I was then. At Columbia, I thought it might increase my stature if I mentioned I had interviewed famous German people."

"Oh?" Jack perked up. "Like who? Marlene Dietrich?"

"No. Adolph Hitler."

Jack halted. "You interviewed Hitler?"

"Yes, and a bunch of his sidekicks like Göring and Goebbels. I met Himmler too."

While Inga talked, Jack sensed trouble—for him as well as Inga. If what Inga was saying was true, and he had no reason to believe it wasn't, J. Edgar Hoover and the FBI probably knew all about it, and likely were already listening in on her conversations and following her. Any person who had fraternized with Hitler and top Nazis was going to be a person of interest to the FBI. Now that he was involved with Inga, he too was probably under suspicion. Guilt by association.

Jack casually looked around, curious to see if they were being followed. He didn't spot anybody. "Tell me more."

Inga said she had been invited to a luncheon at the Danish ambassador's house in Berlin in 1935 while working as a reporter. She learned Hitler's second in command, Hermann Göring, intended to marry Emmy

Sonnemann. Surprised to find Sonnemann's number listed in the phone book, Inga called her, and Sonnemann invited Inga to interview her, which led to an invitation to their wedding. At the wedding, Inga chatted with Goebbels. Looking to promote Hitler, Goebbels arranged an interview with Hitler.

"I told him I didn't want a political interview and that I didn't know anything about international relations. I wanted the little things about the Fuhrer. He was one of the most famous people in the world. Why wouldn't I desire an interview with him?"

"What happened at that meeting?" Jack grabbed Inga's elbow and stood facing her.

"It was very strange. Dr. Goebbels called me and said a car was on the way. I was taken to the *Reichskanzlei* and rushed into a room. Hitler was seated way in the back."

Jack tried to imagine the scene of Hitler and Inga in the same room. Did he shake her hand, or embrace her?

"What happened next?"

"I raised my arm and said, 'Heil Hitler.'"

"You what?! Why the hell did you do that?" Jack said, disgusted. "You're not a German citizen."

"I know," Inga said, looking at the ground. "I thought I was supposed to. I wasn't pledging loyalty to him or anything. Forgive me, Jack. I was only twenty-two. Anyway, Hitler was baffled and didn't respond. I'm ashamed to say I repeated it when I left. Hitler was very obviously embarrassed, but I had no idea why. He led me to an overstuffed chair and complimented me on my German. Then suddenly he said, 'What happened to Dr. Goebbels?' I didn't know the usual protocol and looked rather blank. Later, I was told that Hitler never received anyone alone, and the person by whom one has been introduced always stays there with the guest."

"So, you embarrassed Hitler. Not many people can say that. What else?"

"I frisked him."

"You frisked Hitler?!"

"At one point, I asked him, 'Are you wearing a bulletproof vest?'"

"Why did you ask him that?"

"I was curious how vulnerable he might feel. From his answer, perhaps one could say he felt invincible. He said, 'Frisk me.'"

Jack's mouth gaped at the idea of his lover groping Hitler.

"So, I did. He wasn't wearing one. I didn't do a thorough examination, Jack. I just touched him briefly on his chest. Nothing special."

"And did he touch you, Inga? I don't like the idea of this guy threatening the world having his way with you."

"He doesn't have a wife or girlfriend. From what I gathered, it's not an interest of his. He seems to believe having a woman would interfere with his mission."

"What? To conquer Europe? What else did he say?"

"He told me I was the perfect example of Nordic beauty. When a world leader tells you something like that, I'll admit it does have an effect on you. I tried to get away when it seemed like the interview had lasted long enough, but Hitler kept me going. A little later, Dr. Goebbels joined us. It was about two hours later before I left, and when I did, Hitler said, 'I have enjoyed myself so much that I beg you to visit me every time you return to Berlin.'"

"I've got a bad feeling you took him up on his offer."

"I did. I had a private lunch with him. He had Danish food for me. We started out with tea, which Hitler sent back three times, demanding it be made right."

"Did he ever go after you romantically? Try to kiss you?"

"No."

"I don't get it. He invites you to his place, arranges a second date, and doesn't do anything."

"Jack, I was there to interview him, not have sex with him."

"And if he said he wanted you to see his bedroom, would you have agreed?"

Inga hesitated. "I don't know. He is very charismatic. I might not have been able to help myself. Let me ask you the question: If you were president, as you say you'd like to be, do you think a young girl in the presence of President Jack Kennedy would be able to resist?"

"I hope not," said Jack.

"As I was leaving, Hitler gave me a framed autographed picture of himself. It said, 'To Inga Arvad, in friendly memory of Adolph Hitler.'"

Jack shook his head. He stopped and faced Inga. "Based on what you've told me, about your association with Hitler and the rest, I have no doubt the U.S. government is on your tail."

"But that was many years ago," Inga protested. "And I didn't do anything wrong. I was just trying to move up in the world."

"I know. But the FBI doesn't know that … and they don't care. So they're going to make sure you aren't in deep with the Nazis."

Inga dismissed the idea that the FBI would be interested in her. "I was just trying to advance professionally, Jack. Doing so can be hard for a woman. I don't think you realize that. I have to use every advantage." Inga smiled wistfully. "And one of them is that I'm not that hard to look at. I was just covering the human interest beat when talking with these Nazis. Mostly what they thought of marriage, what they ate for breakfast. That kind of thing."

"I probably should say goodbye now and never see you again. But I don't think I can. So, you have to promise me something."

"What?"

"That you never talk with me or anybody else about your time in Germany with the Nazis. Not at your place or on the phone. I have no doubt that you are under suspicion, and that means me too."

"Okay. I understand. I know I didn't do anything wrong, but they don't know it. I don't want to get you involved, Jack."

"Looks like I already am," he said, laughing sardonically. "But I do want to read what you wrote about him."

They went back to Inga's, and she retrieved the articles and put them in an envelope before they went back outside. Her interview had run in Copenhagen's largest daily, the *Berlinkski Tidenade*.

"I'll read them to you. They're in Danish," Inga said.

"What does the headline say? I can make out Hitler."

"An Hour with Adolph Hitler." Inga took a deep breath. "Hitler asked me about Germany: How did I like it? Little by little, we warmed up and sat back comfortably in our chairs. He became exceedingly human, very kind, very charming, as if he had nothing more important in this world than to convince me that in National Socialism lay the salvation of the world."

"Hitler charming, eh? He's doing a hell of a job trying to charm the British to death," Jack said sternly. "Go ahead, keep reading,".

"I'm ashamed to read it now." She paused, took a deep breath, and continued. "One likes him immediately. He seems lonely. The eyes, which are tender-hearted, look directly at you. They radiate power."

"The poor guy is lonely and has a tender heart," Jack said bitterly. "Tell that to the British, the Poles, the Czechs, and the Dutch. I don't think they'd agree."

"Honestly, Jack, I wrote what I saw. He fooled me. I admit it. I couldn't see beyond the face. But did anybody see it coming back then? Did you?"

"During my visits, I was appalled at the arrogance of the German people, but I didn't have a notion Hitler was going to be the scourge of the world. That's it then? You interviewed him a couple of times. Nothing more?" he said hopefully.

"I wish I could say that. You might as well know. Hitler invited me to the 1936 Olympics."

"And did you go?"

"I sat in his box. He came in for a few minutes at one point, and I conducted a short interview."

On her last trip, Inga said, a top Nazi asked if she would go to Paris and work for the Germans. Another German officer, who had been a minister to Denmark after the Great War and took a liking to her, intercepted her on her way out. Aware of what was going on, he told her that there would be a price to pay if she refused. Himmler would be informed, and the Gestapo would pay her a visit. "Leave immediately," he warned. "I packed that night and took the first flight back to Copenhagen."

"I'm glad you did. But shortly after your last chat with Herr Hitler last year, he invaded the country of your birth."

"Yes, that's true."

It was easy to be hard on Inga, knowing what he now knew, but Jack couldn't be certain if he would have seen the evil had he been in the same room as Hitler those several times.

Chapter 21

As he stepped outside Inga's apartment building the next morning, Jack tried to act casual. He scanned the street. Nobody to his right or left, but across the street a man wearing a fedora sat in a car. When he saw Jack glance his way, he raised the newspaper to conceal his face.

Could be a guy wasting time until he had to clock in, Jack thought. Or the FBI. From here on out, he'd just assume he was being followed whenever he visited Inga and that her house and telephone conversations were being monitored and maybe even taped.

Jack walked in the opposite direction the car was facing. Was he being duped? he wondered. Perhaps Inga really was a spy. She might be working for the Nazis. He believed her, but he had no proof she was telling the truth. But if she wasn't, what could she gain from cavorting with a lowly ensign—even if he was a member of a well-known American family? It didn't make sense. Still, there was good reason for him to stop seeing Inga. It certainly wasn't going to help his future. In fact, no good could come of being involved with a woman who had willingly associated with Hitler and other Nazis.

But he'd never met a woman like Inga. Unlike his mother, Inga expressed genuine concern for his health. True, his mother had cataloged all his illnesses on cards since his time as a toddler, but he'd never felt loved by her; Inga offered a kind of motherly concern.

"It is because you are dearer to me than anybody else that I want to be with you when you are sick," she had written when they were apart. "Maybe it is my maternal instinct."

She had a grip on him, a hold on his heart, like no other woman before. No, he couldn't give her up. Besides, Inga hadn't done anything

BECOMING JFK

wrong. She had only been trying to do her job and, as she put it, "make her way in the world."

Jack was alarmed when Inga informed him that a co-worker at the *Times-Herald* told her the FBI was tapping her phone and bugging her apartment.

"I hear the phone click every time," Inga told Jack as they strolled the Washington Promenade, "I'm sure it's the FBI. And every man who looks at me twice or follows me for a block, I'm convinced must be an FBI agent."

Apprehensive and needing a break from the situation, Jack asked Lem in early December to come up to DC for the weekend. There was nobody better to take his mind off his troubles. Because of his poor eyesight, Lem hadn't been drafted. He was working in sales and advertising in nearby Baltimore.

"Let's go find a game," Jack said. He drove to a park near the Washington Monument, where a half dozen guys were playing touch football It was one of Jack's favorite things to do—find a game and invite himself to play.

"Looks like you could use a couple of extra players," Jack said. "Mind if we join in?"

Shifty and nimble, Jack excelled, while Lem, a lineman when he was at Choate, was overmatched. Jack played ferociously, forgetting the last few fretful days with Inga and her tales of Hitler and the Nazis. Once, Jack caught a short pass and had only Lem to beat for a touchdown. Jack faked right and went left. Lem slipped, falling in a heap while Jack trotted in for a touchdown.

"Lemmer, you can't tag anybody when you're sitting on your ass," he said with a laugh.

They played another hour before Jack drove them back to his

apartment. The radio blared the Andrews Sisters hit "Boogie Woogie Bugle Boy."

"If they had let me play at Choate, we'd have gone undefeated our last year," Jack joked.

"But we did go undefeated," Lem reminded him. "Without you."

"Well, we would have been even more undefeated with me in there."

"More undefeated?" Lem shook his head. "You're a nut, Ken."

The music cut off.

A serious voice came on: "We interrupt this program with an important announcement."

Jack and Lem looked at each other.

"We have received word that the Japanese have attacked Pearl Harbor in Hawaii," the voice on the radio continued.

"Now everything is going to go to hell," Jack said. "Get ready for war."

Driving on Pennsylvania Avenue, they witnessed people streaming to the White House as if drawn by a magnet. Washington was the center of their universe, and people wanted to feel as close as possible to the greatest source of power in the country. It made them feel safer and gave them comfort for what they sensed would be ominous days ahead.

The next day, Roosevelt addressed the nation and Congress declared war on Japan. A few days later, Hitler announced that Germany would join Japan in fighting the United States.

Immediately, the Office of Naval Intelligence moved to a 24-hour a day schedule, and Jack was slotted into the 10:00 p.m. to 7:00 a.m. shift. As he worked on documents late at night and early in the morning, Jack's mind drifted to Inga and how their relationship might change now that the United States was at war.

BECOMING JFK

Later that month, Inga greeted Jack with a forlorn face when he visited for an afternoon dalliance. What's up, Inga-Binga?" he said, using his new nickname for her.

"Darling," she said through moist eyes, "I won't be able to see you for a while."

"Why not?" said Jack, concealing his alarm.

"Paul, er my husband, is coming. He won't be here long." She told him that her husband, whom she hadn't seen for two years, was returning to the United States. They had been apart for most of their marriage, but now the filmmaker, at 45 roughly the same age as Jack's father, had departed the jungles of Peru and arrived in New York.

Jack's thoughts darkened as he imagined Fejos asserting his marital rights. He looked away, then back at Inga, unable to contain his frustration. "Are you going to be with him?" he asked quietly.

Inga sighed, avoiding his gaze as she ran a hand through her hair. "I was afraid you'd ask me that. The truth is, I don't know. Maybe he won't want to, considering how distant we've become. Or maybe he will try to repair things, thinking intimacy will bring us back together. It would be hard to refuse, Jack—we are still married. But if it happens, I want you to know it won't mean anything to me."

"It will to me," Jack said, his voice tight.

"Please try to understand. This isn't easy for me," Inga replied softly.

Jack stood and took her by the waist, his determination overriding his doubt. "Let me make things less complicated," he said, guiding her toward the bedroom. "If this is what might happen, I want to be the one you turn to first."

Inga gave a small smile, her eyes filled with both affection and resignation. "You're first in my heart, Jack. Let's make this time ours."

Their moments together that afternoon were charged with an intensity Jack hadn't felt before. Later, as they shared a quiet lunch, he found himself drawn to her again. Unable to resist, he swept her into his arms and carried her back to the bedroom.

"What are you doing now, Jack?" she asked with a teasing laugh.

"Maybe I want to make sure you're so tired that Fejos won't even try to win you back," he said with a mischievous grin.

Inga chuckled, her playful spirit matching his. "Well, I suppose it's worth a try," she said, leaning into him. "Ensign Kennedy, I leave myself in your capable hands."

"As you wish," Jack murmured, pulling her closer with a tender determination.

But later that night, Jack had a heated phone conversation with his father, who seemed well aware of what was going on. He demanded Jack end the affair immediately. Once again, his father was getting involved in his love life. Jack refused. "If and when I do, I'll decide." Just to get his father's goat, he added, "I might even marry her."

"Damn it, Jack!" his father shouted. He was so loud that Jack moved the receiver away from his ear. "She's already married!"

But the noose was tightening on Inga. The next night, before Jack's shift began, Kick phoned and said it was urgent that they meet. It had to do with Inga.

"I'll come over," Kick said.

"No, that's okay," Jack said, wary that their conversation might be bugged. "I'll meet you over by the Lincoln Memorial."

The rushing figure of his sister emerged from the gloom. This wasn't going to be one of their friendly visits, which were usually full of gossip and laughing.

"Jack, they're onto Inga," Kick said breathlessly.

Jack nodded, already aware of the surveillance, but wanting to see if Kick had more information. "What do you know?"

Kick said a co-worker at the *Times-Herald*, Page Huidekoper, who'd formerly worked for their father in London, had been told that Inga might be spying for a foreign power. "The word around the office is that a guy in Purchasing told Page that some old Berlin newspapers had a picture of Inga taken with Hitler at the Olympic games. My boss marched Inga and Page down to the FBI to make a report."

Jack processed the information. Inga had been forthright in telling him of her visits with Hitler. But she hadn't mentioned being photographed with him. Jack imagined Inga and Hitler smiling and laughing in his private box. A smiling picture of the two together would be damning for the both of them.

"Now I'm sorry I introduced you. But I swear I didn't know any of this about Inga. Jack, please be careful."

"I know, Kick. It's not your fault."

"And there's something else."

What other bad news could there be?

"There are rumors about Inga's husband. He may have German connections. I'm sure he, too, is being watched."

Working in Naval Intelligence gave Jack access to people in the know. Jack made some quiet queries about Fejos and Wenner-Gren. The news was disturbing. The Wenner-Gren yacht, the *Southern Cross*, was the largest private luxury yacht in the world. It was equipped with up-to-date radio equipment, machine guns, and rifles.

"We believe it is currently being used to refuel German U-boats," his contact said.

"We should keep a watch on him," Jack said.

"Yes," the man said, "and also Fejos."

"Of course."

He looked hard into Jack's face. "And Fejos's wife."

Jack decided to play dumb. "Why Fejos's wife? What's she got to do with anything?"

"She's been seeing some guy around town who is not her husband. And she has a background that is a bit suspicious, if you know what I mean." He paused. "And I think you do."

Jack gave a blank look.

"I'd suggest very strongly that that guy find another gal. It can't end up good for him."

"Thanks for the info," Jack said, and returned to his desk. But his mind wasn't on his work. He'd been given a warning—albeit an unofficial warning. But Jack didn't like being told what to do, especially for what he considered a lousy reason. And this didn't sound like a legitimate reason to him.

So Jack continued seeing Inga despite the warning. Even when he was away from Washington, Jack wrote often. He telegrammed from New York:

> *I won't be there until 11:30 by train. I would advise your going to bed, but if you come, buy a thermos and make me some soup. Who would take care of me if you didn't?*
>
> Love,
> Jack

Inga was the best damn thing that ever happened to him.

"Did you have relations with him?" blurted out Jack. They had agreed to meet at a park in the late afternoon after her husband's visit.

BECOMING JFK

Inga recoiled. "I have to compliment myself on my performance. It was one of my best roles ever. Did I ever tell you that I acted for a bit? Paul put me in one of his films. It was called *Millions in Flight*."

"I don't care about that," said Jack tersely. "What happened last night?"

"He knows about us. He asked if I love you, and I said I do. We talked about divorce but didn't make any decision."

Jack's heart warmed over this news. He held Inga in his arms and kissed her.

"So you have nothing to worry about," she said, wrapping her arms around his neck. "I made him sleep on the couch. He left in the morning. If you don't already know, Jack, I was interviewed by your FBI."

"Not much of a surprise," said Jack, pretending he hadn't heard. "How did it go?"

"I told this agent that I detest Hitler and their form of government. And if necessary, I would bring suit against Page Huidekoper to clear my name."

"That's good. Shows you're willing to go on the offensive."

Inga turned inward. "Your FBI tried to pressure me. They showed me a still picture from that movie I was in."

"So?"

"The International News Service sent out the picture in 1936." Inga looked down, nearly in tears. "I hate what those people did. Underneath the picture, the caption said: 'Meet Miss Inga Arvad, Danish beauty, who so captivated Chancellor Adolph Hitler that he made her Chief of Publicity in Denmark.' He never did any such thing!"

Jack shook his head. From the inaccurate caption, readers would falsely assume Inga had agreed to serve the Reich when she had done no such thing.

"It didn't go well from there, Jack. I demanded a letter from the FBI stating that I was not a spy, but they refused."

"Why?"

"The agent said he was terribly sorry, but he couldn't give me such a written assurance because if he did, I might become a spy the next day even if I wasn't today."

"I see their point. Anything else?"

"I left there in a terrible mood. I went home feeling as if I had all of the FBI trailing me. I kept looking over my shoulder. Jack, I've heard of innocent people spending years in jail!"

Jack motioned to a bench, and they sat down. "I don't know if anything was gained by going to the FBI, but it was the right thing to do. Not that you had much choice."

"I suppose you'll want to leave me now, Jack. I wouldn't blame you if you did. I'm only causing you trouble."

Jack put his arm around Inga's shoulders. "You can't get rid of me that easily, Inga-Binga." They kissed and chatted for a few more minutes before Jack had to report for duty.

On his way home from work the next morning, Jack bought the *Washington Times-Herald*. He sat at the counter and ordered coffee. Along with millions of other Americans on January 12, he skimmed Walter Winchell's column looking for something of interest amidst the usual blend of gossip and commentary. But under the headline "On Broadway," between an item about a spat between two Broadway actresses and a report about jazz greats Louis Armstrong and Gene Krupa making the rounds, were two scintillating sentences. "One of Ex-Ambassador Kennedy's eligible sons is the target of a Washington gal columnist's affections. So much so she has consulted her barrister about divorcing her exploring groom. Pa Kennedy no like."

BECOMING JFK

Jack choked on his coffee. Her name hadn't been mentioned, but Inga was the only columnist with an explorer husband.

Pa Kennedy no like. Jack ruminated over that phrase. Somebody had tipped off Winchell. It wasn't good publicity, Jack thought, but it could have been worse. Winchell could have mentioned Inga's former connections to Hitler and the Nazis. Jack wondered who had contacted Winchell. It could have been Fejos. Or the FBI. Or his father. They all had motives for breaking them up. Maybe it was all three.

The next day, Jack received a phone call from the Office of Naval Intelligence. He was ordered to report to the navy base in Charleston, South Carolina. *That was more than five hundred miles from DC and from Inga.* And unless he had special permission, he'd be restricted to travel within seventy miles of the Charleston Navy Yard.

Jack slammed down the phone. *They moved me out of town just to break us up.*

Chapter 22

Jack's work was no more interesting in Charleston than it had been in Washington. He deciphered naval signals and taught air raid precautions to munitions workers—but now he didn't have Inga. He'd found quarters by the water with a friend of his family on Murray Boulevard. It was only a few blocks walk to Battery Point, the tip of the Charleston Peninsula, where he worked in a three-level Victorian.

In his room, he reread Inga's letter.

> *Go up the steps of fame. But—pause now and then to make sure that you are accompanied by happiness.*

Jack looked up for a second, touched by her eloquent counsel, before continuing:

> *Maybe your greatest mistake, handsome, is that you admire brains more than heart, but then that is necessary to arrive.*

Inga had discovered something about him he didn't know. It was true he was a man of intellect—not feelings. Detached from his emotions, he regretted not being able to display more sentiment. That was the way he was. His demeanor had its drawbacks, but also advantages for a public future where having a cool head was paramount. Jack recalled his comportment under pressure during the *Athenia* furor. He had dealt with the situation, hadn't lost his composure, and reassured the survivors that help was forthcoming.

Jack phoned that night from the vestibule downstairs, whispering into the receiver. He couldn't stand being away from her womanly charms, intellect, and even the way she spoke English. (She pronounced a *v* as a *w*. *Would you like more wegtables?*)

But more importantly, Jack was able to confide in her as he'd never been able to in any other woman. To her, he'd more than hinted at his interest in running for higher office, but he hadn't told any other friend—not even Lem.

"Why don't you come down here for a visit?" Jack said.

"I may," Inga teased.

"Don't say you may."

"Isn't that sweet? I'll come, maybe."

"I hate for you to come all this way just to see me."

"Darling, I would go around the world three times just to see you. Do you very much want me to come this weekend?"

"I would like for you to."

"I'll think it over and let you know. So long, my love."

Tired of dealing with interminable reports, Jack couldn't wait for January 24 to end. He clocked out at 5:30 and went back to his room to clean up and wait for Inga's call. He had just gotten out of the shower when the phone rang.

"Jack, there's a lady with a funny voice on the phone for you!" called his landlord.

Jack wrapped a towel around his private parts and prepared to bolt down the stairs.

"Now stop right there. Go back and put some clothes on!" his landlord said, pointing to his room. "That is not the way we do things around here, ya hear?"

Sheepishly, Jack returned to his room, put on pants and a shirt, and came back down.

Giving him a disdainful stare, she said, "That's better," and handed him the phone.

"Jack, I'm here. Will you come see me?" Inga said, giving her room number at the Fort Sumter Hotel, only a few blocks away.

He dashed to the hotel and sprinted up the stairs to her room. Inga had dolled herself up, but she wore only a light bathrobe with apparently nothing underneath.

"Hello, Ensign Kennedy," she said.

Jack found solace in Inga's presence, her warmth easing the restlessness that so often stirred within him. Their connection felt effortless, a brief reprieve from the constant churn of his thoughts. After their tender intimacy, they shared a shower, their laughter mingling with the steam, before heading to the hotel restaurant for dinner.

The next morning, as sunlight filtered through the curtains, Inga turned to him with a smile and suggested they visit the picturesque Middleton Gardens.

Jack balked at the cost. "Pay that much to walk in the park? The hell with that. Let's find another park or stroll through town."

Inga fumed. "I come all the way down here and you are not going to take me to see the gardens? It's like you'd rather chew one of your fingers off than pay the $2 for me. I might go back to Washington right now."

"Two tickets, please," Jack said to the ticket agent. *Damn*. Sometimes he was just like his father, trying to save a few bucks for no reason.

"Enjoy yourself, ya hear," drawled the ticket agent who handed Jack the tickets. "It's something you and your lady friend will appreciate."

Holding hands, they wandered through the vast, geometrically shaped garden and lagoon.

"It's beautiful, isn't it, Jack?"

"It's quite nice."

A few minutes later, Inga became morose and began to cry.

"What's the matter?" Jack asked. "I'll try not to be so stingy. You can blame it on my father."

"No, it's not that." Inga wasn't able to speak for a moment and then began sobbing uncontrollably. "The FBI snuck into my apartment while I was at work. They looked through everything. Read those stories I wrote about Hitler and Germany."

"They didn't find anything they didn't already know."

Inga took out her handkerchief and dabbed her eyes. "It feels so awful to have someone break in. I know I'm being watched. But now they go in whenever they want to."

No doubt they were being watched and listened to here in South Carolina.

On the way out of the gardens, the ticket agent asked if they had enjoyed their visit.

"Wonderful," said Inga.

"How was it built?" Jack asked. "Took a lot of work."

The ticket agent beamed. "Well, the nigras deserve the credit. They're the ones that did it. Did a nice job, didn't they?"

The Middleton Plantation had been created using slave labor. "Did they have any choice?" retorted Jack. "C'mon, let's go."

Jack and Inga spent most of the next day in bed, interrupted only by a brief window-shopping trip to Schindler's Antique Shop on King Street. They returned to the room and more lovemaking. Jack couldn't get enough of Inga.

After Sunday morning's session, Inga gave Jack a gentle shove. "Jack, we've made love a number of times."

"Yes, I've noticed."

"I thought I might become pregnant." Inga said she had twice visited labs to determine her status.

"Why would you think that?"

"It could happen. You don't use anything. You take every pleasure of youth but not the responsibility."

Jack stared at her blankly. It was true. He had thought briefly about what he might do if Inga became pregnant. He wouldn't marry her, but would she have the baby? She was twenty-eight, and still married. That would be quite a complication for him. He'd hope that she'd end a potential pregnancy, but he knew if he suggested it, she'd be angry.

Jack took her to the train station. From her window seat, she waved goodbye as the train pulled out. Jack felt a fluttering in his stomach and an immediate emotional loss.

After Inga left for Washington, Jack returned to his rented room. The landlord eyed him suspiciously and said: "You take care of this bill now, ya hear?"

Jack called Inga that night. "For what it's worth, I've heard that my own landlord is a government investigator."

"I wouldn't worry that much," said Inga. "In one way or the other, you'll be shipping out sometime soon. When do you leave?"

"I don't know. Nothing yet."

"By the way, I'll be going to New York," Inga said.

"What for?"

"I'm going to have dinner with Nils."

"Oh."

"But you have nothing to worry about. I'll be staying at the Barbizon Hotel for Women."

When she returned to Washington, Jack called her and teased, "I heard you had a big orgy in New York."

"You wish." Inga laughed but hesitated when Jack said he wanted her to come back to Charleston soon.

Feeling tense after their conversation, Jack walked to the White Point Garden at Battery Point. Here, the Ashley and Cooper Rivers converged to form Charleston Harbor. In the distance, Jack could see Fort Sumter, where the Civil War began. A sign said colored people were prohibited from using the park.

He continued walking up King Street, heading north toward downtown. A restaurant posted a "colored only" sign outside the dilapidated lavatory. He passed an African-American man, and a few moments later heard a loud grunt. He looked back to see several young white men standing over the man, now sprawled on the ground.

"Watch where you're going, nigger," one of them said. "You nearly ran into us."

Jack had seen enough of the Jim Crow South in his short time there. The South, from what he'd remembered in New Orleans and here, wasn't his kind of place. They were friendlier down here with their "How y'all doing?" greetings, but they treated Black people like dirt.

He walked the downtown's cobblestone streets and lunched at a diner. Seated at the counter, he stared absent-mindedly at the menu. Would Inga come? he wondered. Perhaps she was toying with him. She said she'd travel around the world three times to see him but hesitated about coming to visit him in Charleston.

Disturbed about the day's events, Jack returned to his apartment and penned a letter to Lem, letting loose his frustrations.

> *Have I discussed Southerners with you? It's not so much that they say 'ya hear' after every goddamned remark*

but all the rest of the shit that convinces me we should have let them go their own way."

He added he was pursuing ways to get out of his desk job—one was an assignment to Pearl Harbor and another to a battleship.

Two weeks after their first rendezvous, Inga flew to Charleston for a three-night stay. This time "Barbara Smith" had a room at the Francis Marion Hotel downtown. While they breakfasted downstairs the next morning, Inga said she was considering having her marriage annulled.

Jack's mood again dipped with Inga's departure. A few days later, Jack received her letter.

In a noisy place, I met a boy who was supposedly brilliant, and who laughed the whole time. There is determination in his green Irish eyes. When you talk to him or see him, you always have the impression that his big white teeth are ready to bite off a huge chunk of life. I love him more than anything. In reality, we are so well matched. Only because I have done some foolish things must I say to myself no. At least I realize that it is true what they say. We pay for everything in life.

Not only was he heartbroken by what sounded like the end, but his back was also acting up. Wanting to get out of Charleston, he asked for leave and went to Palm Beach.

Jack and his father chatted amiably in the living room about life in Charleston. His father looked away and then back at Jack. "I want to talk with you about this thing you are doing with this woman. What do you think you're going to get out of it?"

"I know I like being with her more than any other woman I've ever met."

"Yes, but listen to reason. You've got to think about your future. She's four years older than you and is on her second marriage. And she's not Catholic."

"That's true. So what?"

"You'd never marry somebody like that, and I don't think you are even thinking about marriage at this point." He waited for an indication of his son's intentions.

"No, I suppose not. But I also don't want to be without her."

"I had nothing to do with it, but I'd hoped having you sent to Charleston would put a damper on that. Apparently, it hasn't."

"No, it hasn't."

"I want you to stop seeing her."

"I'm not surprised."

For a few more minutes, they went back and forth. Jack stubbornly refused to give in.

When Jack wouldn't agree to end the affair, his father pulled out his ace in the hole. "This gal of yours, do you think you are the only one?"

Jack's voice tightened. "You're telling me I'm not, or just throwing it out there?"

"They have her apartment bugged. After she came back from Charleston the last time, she was immediately in touch with a former boyfriend. His name is Nils Blok."

"So?"

"She stayed with him overnight at his place in New York."

Jack processed this information. She had lied to him. The same day they'd made love, she'd made arrangements to rendezvous with another lover. It was disturbing. Hadn't he given her enough loving on their weekend? Did he believe his father, knowing he'd do anything—even lie—to break them up?

"Interesting."

"End it, Jack. It's the only thing to do."

"To you. But maybe I don't think so. But if it is, I'll decide when." He didn't want his father making the decision for him.

For the next few days after his father left, Jack agonized over what to do. Why shouldn't he stay with Inga? She hadn't done anything wrong. She'd had the opportunity to interview a head of state and taken advantage of it to advance her career. Back then, the United States didn't see Hitler as the threat to world peace he had become. Nobody did. But that didn't seem to matter to anybody, including his father. And, for the time being, he wasn't going anywhere. He was committed to serving overseas, to getting in the action. But that could be another year yet. And who knew if that would ever happen? In the meantime, he could see Inga, at least occasionally.

Jack considered how continuing the relationship could affect his future. But Joe was the one destined for political success, not him. Jack had no idea what he would do after the war. Writer? Professor?

But he also began to realize the affair was about more than him. It could result in a permanent black mark, not only on him but on the Kennedy family. There was more at stake here. Perhaps that was the primary reason his father demanded he stop seeing Inga. He couldn't allow something like this to hurt the Kennedys. It could damage Joe's political chances. Jack imagined more newspaper gossip: "Kennedy Son's Gal a Hitler Favorite." Or "Ambassador's Son Dating Hitler's Chief of Publicity." That would be devastating.

One way or the other, this relationship was probably going to end. Perhaps it already had, if what his father said was true. He might be transferred or shipped out. Jack wasn't ready to end it now, but he couldn't expect Inga to keep traipsing down to Charleston to see him… assuming *she wanted to see him.* And he couldn't visit her since he was restricted to the local area. Still, he wanted more time with her. She had a hold on him like no other woman had.

Jack arranged for leave and flew to Washington on February 28.

"What's the news, lover boy?" Inga asked, as soon as he entered her apartment. She looked ravishing in an A-line dress that accentuated her great figure.

They took a walk. Jack said now was a good time to put an end to their relationship. He repeated what they both suspected—that her apartment was bugged, and all their conversations and lovemaking had been recorded both here and in Charleston hotel rooms.

"I hope they enjoyed it," Inga said.

"You weren't acting for them."

"No, dear. There was no need."

Tempted to mention her visit with Blok, Jack refrained. It couldn't lead anywhere good.

When they returned to her apartment, she put her arms around his neck. "I'll never forget you, Jack," she said, kissing him sweetly.

"Well, I'm not gone yet." He led her to the bedroom. "One more for the road."

Jack left in the morning. Though his back definitely ached, he was more wounded by the gaping hole in his heart.

A few days later, Jack received a letter from Inga.

> *Some birds sing cheerfully, some mourn, others are envious and nasty. Mine always sang. It did especially for a few months this winter. In fact, it sang so loudly that I refused to listen to the other little creature called*

> *reason. It took me, the FBI, the U.S. Navy, nasty gossip, envy, hatred, and big Joe, before the bird stopped.*

Jack looked away, moved by Inga's heartfelt, poetic prose. He read on.

> *If you feel anything beautiful in your life—I am not talking about me—then don't hesitate to say so, don't hesitate to make the little bird sing. It costs so little: a word, a smile, a slight touch of a hand. The beautiful things in life cost nothing. We shall realize all that in the near future, because life is going to be tough and double hard for the people who have ideals, who have hopes, who have someone they really love; who understand humanity.*

Jack put the letter down. Inga was some woman. She just wasn't his anymore.

With his relationship with Inga over and upset over the American military defeats in the Philippines during the first quarter of 1942, Jack was restless. He wasn't in the action. All he'd done in Charleston was complete a compulsory correspondence course in naval regulations and maintaining a ship's history.

He was afraid of getting physically soft, so he'd sent for the Charles Atlas strength and health program, hoping the regimen might help his back and overall fitness. He didn't want anything to prevent him from getting sea duty. Alone in his apartment, he sweated and pushed himself through an assortment of finger lock chest pulls, bicep curls, squat thrusts, and other resistance exercises championed by Atlas.

He wrote Lem:

> *The exercises are very enjoyable and most helpful. I only succeeded in throwing my back out on exercise 1, lesson 4.*

Jack gritted his teeth as he gingerly sat down to attend to paperwork in his office. Over the last few days, his spine had become inflamed, and that pain plus the return of severe stomach cramps had him walking around like a cripple.

He took leave and went both to the Mayo Clinic in Minnesota and the Lahey Clinic in Boston. Both agreed that the only possible way he could serve at sea was to have an operation on his spine. They recommended fusion of the right sacroiliac joint.

Jack tried a different course of action, checking himself into the naval hospital in Chelsea, outside of Boston. He told the doctor, "I feel that I am not getting ahead going from hospital to hospital. Everybody has their opinions, as I'm sure you will, but I want to get sea duty. I am here for a check-up. Nothing more."

The doctor's report, Jack was pleased to see, concluded his back pain was due to "tight muscles in his legs and abnormal posture consequent thereto."

Jack's stay at the hospital was enlivened by one of Inga's touching letters. She was in Reno, where she was in the process of getting a divorce. She pleaded with him to "duck when the Japanese or German bullets aim at that handsome chest or bright head. You are just too good—and I mean good—to be carried home."

Jack returned to Charleston in late June, optimistic about his chances for sea duty. When the navy sought officers seeking sea duty, Jack applied, along with thousands of others. He didn't make the first round only because there was nobody to take his place in Charleston. Jack could only wait. But he knew his time would come.

In the meantime, he was assigned to give a speech to fire up the new recruits. From the podium, attired in his dress blues, Jack surveyed the hundred or so men. Speaking from notes, he used his history chops and fervor to carry his message: *For What We Fight.*

"A number of years ago in a room in Philadelphia, a group of men signed their names to a Declaration. For that, they could have been hanged. That was treason and the penalty for treason was death. And yet, these men signed. Today, 166 years after the signing of the Declaration of Independence, we, in America, are faced with a similar decision. The men who signed the Declaration of Independence met their issue squarely, and with their lives, they affirmed their beliefs. You men, today, by stepping forward have pledged a similar faith.

"The sacrifice is not too great. As young men, it is, after all, for our own future that we fight. And so, with firm confidence and belief in that future, let us go forward to victory."

Surprised to see the recruits applaud vigorously, then get to their feet shouting, "To victory!" Jack nodded his appreciation. In that moment, Jack realized he had a talent for energizing people with his words and his voice.

He added, "There's no doubt in my mind, and sooner or later in our enemies' minds, based on what I've seen here today, that triumph will soon be ours. Thank you."

In a few weeks, Jack got the news he'd long been craving. He'd been accepted into the midshipman training school on the campus of Northwestern University. He arrived in late July.

Chapter 23

During the physical examinations at training at Northwestern, Jack successfully covered up his bad back. No doubt the bucking broncos of the sea would be murder on it, but he was determined to get in the fight. Impressing his interviewers with his knowledge and self-confidence, he was selected to go to the PT boat training center in Rhode Island in late September after completing instruction at Northwestern. He joined about eight hundred other trainees who would cycle through the eight-week program. Ten PT boats were waiting for them to train on.

As he had at Stanford, Jack required a wood plank for a bed, so he enlisted Fred Rosen, who had become a friend when they worked together in Charleston, to help. He and Rosen drove all over Newport, Rhode Island searching for a plank of plywood to put under Jack's mattress. They finally found a lumber yard that would cut one, brought it back to the barracks, and put it on his bed. Rosen agreed to keep quiet about Jack's bad back. He didn't want the commanding officer to know.

"Hopefully, I won't be sleeping on this long," said Jack, trying out his new mattress. "I want to ship out as soon as possible, though I suppose not everybody does. Oh, have you heard?" he kidded Rosen, who was Jewish. "All the Jews are going into the Quartermaster Corps to be away from the front lines."

He'd bantered with Rosen before, lobbing semi-offensive Jewish stereotypes at him. In that respect, he aped his father, who used Jewish stereotypes to taunt Arthur Krock, among others.

But Rosen had had enough. "They must be good at trigonometry, Jack," Rosen retorted.

"Why?" Jack said, ignorant of the sleight he'd made on Jews and his friend.

"Because the navy's navigators are drawn from the Quartermaster Corps. They'll be in harm's way. So maybe it would be a good idea if you shut up."

Jack hadn't meant to offend his buddy; he'd just been emulating his father. He wished for nothing so much as for the conversation to end, but Rosen wasn't finished.

"I know you Irish take a liking to shoveling horse muck. What is it about the shit shoveling that gets you all excited, Jack?"

"Hey—"

"And always wanting to tie one on, hit the bottle, get drunk. Oh, that's right, you're not much of a drinker, are you, Jack? Sure you're Irish?"

"Last time I looked," Jack said grimly.

After finally realizing how his assumptions and parroting of his father had sounded, Jack apologized. "All right, Fred, I'm sorry. Went up a one-way street the wrong way." Jack offered his hand. "Thanks for, uh, teaching me a lesson."

Shaking Jack's hand, Rosen said, "My pleasure, Jack. But don't make me teach you another. Now let's go into town and have some fun."

Jack completed the training process, surprised that he never fired a torpedo and only training at night. The boats were considered too vulnerable to enemy aircraft to operate during the day. Rather, they got only the basics: information on how to bring the boat in along the pier, how to care for the engine, how to fire the torpedoes, and how to operate the on-board radios. They'd have to learn the rest by actually doing all those things later.

The more Jack learned about PTs, the less impressed he became. His instructors informed him the PT torpedoes traveled at 28 knots, which was well below the speed of Japanese battleships. The torpedoes, he also learned, were not accurate at long ranges of a few thousand yards, and often failed to detonate. Jack mused in a letter to Lem:

> *Add into that equation our frighteningly inaccurate deck guns and you've really got something to laugh or cry about. Right now, I'm thinking Mr. White should write a sequel to his bestseller about the PTs,* They Were Expendable, *and title it* They Are Useless.

Yet, Jack figured he was ready to take command of a PT and ship out. He'd been promoted to lieutenant. But it wasn't to be. In November, he was told he wouldn't be going overseas, that he'd be staying in Melville, Rhode Island as a PT trainer.

Jack walked into the Quonset hut and announced, "I got shafted. They got me staying here as a professor while you guys go off to action." He slammed his hat on his bunk.

The next day, he met with his commanding officer but failed to convince him to send him overseas. Jack stomped his way back to the hut, contemplating his options. There was no way he'd spend the war training others. That would not constitute a successful war record. Jack decided he'd take the risky step of going over his CO's head.

"Here comes Shafty!" came the catcalls when Jack walked in. "Did you get shafted again today, Jack?" somebody said. "No? Maybe tomorrow."

Jack offered a tight smile. "All right. Guess I've earned it." *Shafty*.

The only way to lose the nickname was to get shipped out. This time, Jack decided to go around the military chain of command as well as bypass his father. He rang up his grandfather on his mother's side, John

BECOMING JFK

"Honey Fitz" Fitzgerald, the former mayor of Boston and still a power broker.

"Grandpa, I need to go where the action is. I might go out of my mind if I'm stuck here. You don't want that on your conscience, do you?"

Honey Fitz laughed. "No, I guess I don't. Your mother would never forgive me."

Jack had done his homework. "Senator David Walsh from Massachusetts heads the Senate Naval Affairs Committee. You got any pull with him?"

"Sure, I know him. And he owes me a favor. Or at least I'll tell him he does."

"Good. Can you set up a meeting with him? I want to talk with him about having my change of assignment order approved. So I can go to the South Pacific."

"If you're sure that's what you want, Jack."

"I'm sure."

When he met with Walsh, Jack won him over with his knowledge of war strategy and international relations. Walsh got the ball rolling to get Jack out of his duties as a training instructor. In the meantime, Jack was awarded command of PT-101, a 78-foot training boat. His first mission was to take it along with three other boats to Jacksonville, Florida. Relieved to get away from the Melville facility, Jack stood at the wheel, leading the flotilla headed south.

The squadron was off the coast of Virginia when Jack felt his hull scraping. He'd run aground! Embarrassed by his inattention to the tides, Jack awkwardly announced the development to his crew. "We'll be out of here in a few minutes."

Jack threw a towline out to one of the other boats so the 101 could be towed to deeper waters. But the towline drifted and became wrapped in his own boat's propellers.

"I'll go in to see what I can do," Jack said, grabbing a knife from his sheath. He took a breath and jumped into the frigid winter waters. It was the coldest water he'd ever been in, and he knew he couldn't take more than a few minutes before becoming incapacitated. Working feverishly, Jack began to feel numb. He didn't have much time. With a final stroke of his knife, he cut the towline. He scrambled aboard and went below deck, shivering and coughing, and wrapped himself in blankets in an attempt to stem the chills.

Finally, the incoming tide allowed his boat to continue on its way. But the next day, he was in worse shape, with continued chills, a temperature, and the sweats.

"Don't ship off to war without me," Jack said wanly to his crew as he was taken off the boat and driven to the local hospital. Jack spent three days in bed at the base hospital while the convoy went on without him. He was diagnosed with acute gastroenteritis.

Jack worried that this latest illness or his tidal miscalculation might wreck his chances to go overseas. Finally recovered, he checked himself out of the hospital, boarded a train, and rejoined the convoy in Jacksonville, then visited his family farther south in Palm Beach.

Joe was there too, and he smugly talked about his experience piloting large, cumbersome airplanes that could land on water. They sat outside smoking cigars in the warm Florida weather and complaining about their current military situations.

"I've got new orders and I'm not happy about them," said Joe, flicking his ash. "I requested Europe or the South Pacific, but they're sending me to Puerto Rico to be on the lookout for German submarines. None has been seen yet. Wouldn't be surprised if JP had a hand in this."

"Neither would I," said Jack, puffing on his cigar. "They've got me teaching. I'm a goddamn professor."

Jack had other disappointing news. He'd been ordered to Panama—a safe backwater if ever there was one. "Could be JP's work too. I don't know why he believes he needs to protect the enemy from you and me. What have they ever done for him?" Jack laughed.

The brothers nodded in unison, used to years of excessive supervision and spying from their father.

Their discussion was interrupted by Joe Sr. "Let's get some pictures of you two in uniform. Mother wants them. The photographer will be here soon."

They put on their dress blue uniforms for the studio session.

"Put Joe in front," said his mother. Joe was now an ensign—Jack's old rank—and sported the golden wings of a Navy flier. Outranking Joe, Jack had two gold lieutenant's stripes decorating his sleeve. He mused that he was above his brother in rank. He'd never force him to do it, but in theory, he could make his brother address him as "sir." Just the thought delighted him. *Take that, Joe.*

When he returned to base, Jack immediately set about reversing the order to Puerto Rico and asked for a change of assignment. On February 20, it was approved. "You can't call me Shafty anymore," he announced to his hut mates. "I'm on my way to the Pacific."

PART FOUR
SKIPPER

Chapter 24
March 1943

On March 6 in San Francisco, Jack boarded the USS *Rochambeau* bound for the South Pacific. For eighteen days, the troop carrier chugged toward the Solomon Islands.

"I don't think that guy's going to make it," said Jack on the deck to a naval officer, nodding at a jittery pilot who was smoking nervously. "If I was to guess, I'd say he might get a government gravestone."

"Why do you say that?"

"You've got to have a feeling you're going to make it," said Jack. "Otherwise, there's a good chance you won't. I had a friend who'd turned shaky and then died on Guadalcanal... I'm not like that. I'll make it."

Recent efforts in the war were promising. Victory at the Battle of Midway and Guadalcanal in January turned the Pacific war in the Allies' favor. But the Japanese still controlled many islands nearby.

Events had also been fortuitous in Europe, where the Russians had taken Stalingrad back from the Germans. In North Africa, where Lem was stationed with the Red Cross, a combined Anglo-American contingent had forced the Germans out of Morocco, Tunisia, Algeria, and Libya. Then, a major victory was achieved when General Erwin Rommel's Afrika Korps was defeated at El Alamein.

Coming into the island of Espiritu Santo, Jack and another serviceman were struck by the lush tropical beauty. Before them were verdant rainforests that ended in sublime white beaches and turquoise waters.

"What a sight!" said Jack. But his reverie was interrupted when he saw the hulk of a ship. "Look over there," he said, pointing to the remains of a bombed-out transport vessel. How many men had gone down with

BECOMING JFK

the ship, Jack wondered. "We'll be taking one of those soon," he said. "I'd prefer it if ours doesn't meet the same fate."

A few days later, Jack boarded the transport vessel LST 449, headed for Guadalcanal and accompanied by the destroyer *Aaron Ward*. Nice to have protection, thought Jack. Otherwise, this tub is a sitting duck.

Jack had been surprised at the sheer number of islands that were simply coral outgrowths, reef upon reef on which the waves unleashed an endless spray. Beautiful lagoons cut a swath through the islands.

He was also glad he still had a few of Dr. Taylor's pellets, his Victrola, and a few records, but mostly what he brought with him were books. Nearing their destination three days later, Jack was looking forward to setting foot on land. In his underwear, he hunkered down in the small cabin aboard the transport ship. He was reading *Pilgrim's Way*, a fascinating memoir set during the first four turbulent decades of the twentieth century in Britain.

Suddenly, the ship lurched. Jack was nearly bounced off his bunk. He threw on his pants and sped up the stairs. The ship's alert pierced the air. The transport listed and the stern lifted out of the water—the result of a 500-pound bomb exploding a few feet off the starboard bow. As he emerged into the daylight, Jack was surrounded by a flurry of men rushing to battle stations. He looked up to see a formation of enemy planes targeting the transport, which was loaded with fuel and ammunition.

The screaming of the planes made it impossible to hear and to think.

Womp! Womp! Womp!

A bomb exploded near the port bow, sending out a great geyser and spraying Jack with saltwater. The captain was catapulted across the bridge, breaking his neck. Two more explosions close to the starboard bow obliterated lifeboats, burst bulkheads, and destroyed electronics.

Jack ran to the stern and began passing shells to an anti-aircraft gun station knee-deep in water. Overhead, Japanese planes whizzed by. Explosions and plumes of water covered the transport in a fog. He couldn't see the water. When the haze cleared, Jack was alarmed to see the *Ward* tilting precariously after having taken several direct hits.

Allied planes arrived to counter the Japanese assault. The battle seemed to rage for eons, but only minutes passed. Every few seconds, enemy planes zoomed in, strafing and bombarding the freight vessel from different directions. Finally, there was a lull as the Japanese regrouped for another strike. Two minesweepers tried to tow the *Ward* to safety. Six hundred yards from shore, Jack saw it go down.

Nearby, like a falling star, a white cloud made a splash. A Japanese pilot's parachute had hit the water. The pilot flailed helplessly as he tried to extricate himself from the fabric. The transport maneuvered toward him. Would he surrender, Jack wondered, or be killed? The LST was now within twenty yards of the pilot, close enough for Jack to see he was young with close-cropped black hair. Mesmerized, Jack watched as the pilot threw aside his life belt, pulled out a pistol, and took two shots at the ship's bridge, trying to kill the captain.

Crew members returned fire, and the ocean boiled around the pilot like a school of fish. Everybody missed. "Fuck this shit," said a seasoned veteran. He grabbed his rifle, aimed, and blew the top of the pilot's head off. The Japanese aviator threw his arms up, plunged forward, and sank beneath the sea.

Jack returned to passing shells, but he slowed down, stunned that the pilot, singlehandedly, had tried to defeat an entire ship.

Finally, the planes disappeared and the all-clear sounded. The battle over, Jack exchanged expressions of gratitude with his battle station mates. They'd survived. He learned later that it had been the largest Japanese air attack since Pearl Harbor, consisting of sixty-seven Japanese dive bombers protected by 110 Zero fighter planes.

That night, before falling into a fitful sleep, Jack reflected on the battle. He couldn't forget the image of the Japanese pilot sitting in the water, helpless but unwilling to surrender. Jack had never seen anyone die before. The soldier might have lived had he not fired at the bridge. Jack learned that Japanese officers were duty bound to go down fighting—an attitude that suggested this would be a long war.

He recalled the frantic activity as crewmen sprang into action, many taking fearful glances at the skies. The terror on the men's faces. A boy sailor, who looked so young he must have faked his way into the military, shaking uncontrollably.

Jack felt a sudden revulsion. During the attack, he had felt trapped, stuck on an unwieldy transport ship and dependent on other ships and planes for protection. Better, he thought, to be in command of one's own ship and able to control one's own destiny.

Chapter 25

"You'll love it here," said Barney Ross, whom Jack had come to know from Melville. It was late April at Tulagi in the Solomon Islands—PT boat headquarters for the Southwest Pacific. Jack had just arrived.

"I'm sure I will," Jack said to Barney, scanning his new home. "But where are the girls?"

The naval facility consisted of a floating dry dock, a machinery shed, and a PT supply ship. The island had once been the capital of the British Solomon Islands Protectorate. Neglected roads, water towers, and Western-style homes dotted the landscape.

Jack found shelter with Johnny Iles and Leonard Thom in a hut. They had cleaned it out and used planks for flooring and orange crates for storing their clothes. Although it was the dry season, there were days and nights of consistent showers. The rapid-fire of rain against the hut's exterior produced a constant drip from the roof to the ground. And a sea of mud flowed just outside the door.

"What the hell is this?" Jack said to Thom a few days after settling in. Jack scraped at an ugly green substance on a book. The fuzzy mold permeated his clothes, bed, writing paper—even the Victrola.

"Get used to it," Thom said with a chuckle, "because the mold will always be with you."

The men weren't alone on the small island. It was also inhabited by Melanesians, who loved to trade.

"All they seem to want is a pipe, and they will trade you canes, pineapples, anything—even their wives," an officer told Jack. "You'll notice a small percentage of the Melanesians have blonde hair and blue eyes.

Some of them are cannibals. Heard they do it for a variety of reasons—retaliation, to insult an enemy people, or to absorb a dead person's qualities. So don't get on their bad side."

"Thanks for the tip."

Jack kept up his correspondence, and to Inga he wrote sardonically about life on the island:

> *It's the end of my greatly illusioned dream about spending the war sitting on some cool beach with a warm Pacific maiden stroking me gently but firmly, while her sister was out hunting my daily supply of bananas. But I can hear you saying, "You asked for it, honey, and you're getting it!*

Jack got to work assisting other PT boat captains while waiting for his own assignment. Often shirtless in the humid climate, he wore a cadet cap and kept a Bowie knife secured to his web belt. He had just finished refueling a PT when Lieutenant Bryant Larson approached.

"Here's your boat, Kennedy," Larson said, pointing to a dilapidated, radar-less eighty-foot vessel. PT-109 was one of two remaining PTs in the squadron—the rest had been lost in action. At the beginning of the year, it had been in the thick of the action north of Guadalcanal. "It used to be mine," Larson said. "Let's take a ride."

Jack scrambled aboard and into the cockpit. He was greeted by several rats that scurried out of his way. His foot crunched on roaches. When moored, the boat was covered by jungle bushes to conceal her from enemy planes, but the vegetation functioned as the perfect bridge for rats and cockroaches to come aboard. His heart swelled. It wasn't the most beautiful boat in the American fleet, but it was his. It seemed like forever since he'd begun his campaign to captain a PT. He finally was going to do it.

"Let's get her going!" Jack shouted to the motormac below deck. The three 1250 horsepower Packard engines coughed and sputtered before settling into an uneven cadence.

"It needs work," Larson said, as Jack took the 109 through basic maneuvers. It ran rough.

When they returned to the dock, Larson said, "The mechanics will give it an engine overhaul, and you and your crew—start getting one together—will take care of the cleaning and painting. *Me?* I'm going home."

Jack was glad to have one holdover from the previous crew, his housemate Leonard Thom, whom he named his executive officer. Larson had only good things to say about Thom.

"He's got your back, and he's a good guy to have around if things get a little out of control." Larson tipped an imaginary cup down his throat.

A favorite drink of the men was fruit juice mixed with 190-proof torpedo fluid. Since Jack wasn't much of a drinker, he didn't hang out much at the Tulagi officers' club, known as the Royal Palm Club. Every night around 7:30, the tent would swell. It wasn't long before men would crash out, blow their dinners, and stagger off to bed.

Jack hired on twenty-year-old Gunner's Mate Bucky Harris, but others were doubtful about joining the crew of the young, skinny skipper. "Geez, I don't know if I want to go out with this guy," said one. "He looks fifteen."

Torpedoeman Andrew Jackson Kirksey, Radioman John Maguire, and Seaman Edman Mauer put that aside and signed on. Mauer had been on the *Niagara*, a tender supplying PTs with fuel and provisions, when it was sunk only a few days earlier.

"Ed, I'm going to do my best to make sure another ship doesn't go

BECOMING JFK

down while you're aboard," Jack said. Mauer had lost everything. "We'll have to do something about that." He got Mauer a change of clothes at the Navy store, though they didn't have any shoes his size. Making the rounds of the Marines, Jack persuaded a few of them to give up shoes, dungarees, shirts, socks, and underwear.

Jack set about establishing a seaworthy team, quietly asserting himself and pitching in. Once the 109's engines had been overhauled, Jack stripped to his shorts and joined his crew in scraping the bottom, cleaning the bilge, sandpapering, and refreshing the paint with camouflage green.

Everybody was cross-trained for a variety of duties, but some crewmen were still learning. As they prepared to test fire, Jack was alarmed to see Harris trembling at the machine guns. He'd never fired them without an instructor nearby.

"Now you're on your own," ordered Jack. "Start shooting."

Besides the cockroaches and rats, there were other visitors. Sand crabs, black flies, and mosquitoes were ever present. Disease was a constant companion. Malaria, dengue, dysentery, trench foot, tropical fever, and elephantiasis had sailors frequently coming and going to the infirmary. The only way to prevent the dreaded "jungle rot," a fungus infection that appeared almost anywhere on the body, was to stay dry. That was nearly impossible in the humid climate.

Some sailors slept on the ship to escape the animal life on land, but that meant clothes and mattresses were permeated by sweat and stank from the thick tropical heat and humidity.

Jack respected and trusted his squadron commander, Alvin Cluster. Not only did they develop an affinity for each other, but bonded over common and important views. Both were dissatisfied with certain administrators and the Navy bureaucracy.

"My opinion is that some of these people dragging us down ought to be in line for medals from Hirohito," Cluster said one day as they stood on the dock.

Jack laughed. "Yes, some of them are very deserving."

PT-109 was ready. From the reinforced cockpit behind the bridge, Jack viewed his boat, now largely refreshed with new camouflage paint. On his right and left were four Mark 8 torpedoes, one behind the other. Ahead of them were depth charges that could be used against enemy submarines. A life raft was secured just beyond the bridge. A few feet ahead and to his right was a twin .50-caliber anti-aircraft machine gun. An identical gun was behind him at the opposite corner. Jack left the cockpit and walked to the back. He stood behind the single 20-millimeter anti-aircraft cannon. Behind that was a smoke screen generator.

Next, he went below to review the crew's cramped sleeping quarters at the rear. Two sleeping cubby holes for him and Lennie Thom and a desk and chair comprised the executive officers' quarters. The small galley had a two-burner stove, oven, sink, and refrigerator.

"Wind her up!" shouted Jack, spinning his index finger in a circular motion as he headed out that night for his first patrol. It turned out to be a dark, quiet evening. When they returned, Jack sat at his desk. In his log, he wrote:

> *Visibility nearly zero May 23. Red light seen on surface of water—bearing 30 degrees—distance 4 miles PT 109 investigated. Results negative.*

That was the way it went on subsequent forays. The uneventful patrols gave him a chance to become familiar with the 109, his crew, and life aboard the boat. He became adept at maneuvering, receiving a perfect 4.0 in handling and a 3.9 for command ability.

When it came to sustenance, nearly everything came out of cans.

BECOMING JFK

Corn beef, cheese, stew, and plenty of Spam. Their diet improved when they received the occasional emergency rations from luxury aircraft: chocolate, hard candy, bouillon cubes, dehydrated cheese, crackers, sugar, instant coffee, and gum. Coffee and cigarettes were staples along with aspirin. Everybody was required to take vitamin A, which was believed to increase night vision. To augment their diet, sailors fired a rifle or dropped a hand grenade into a school of fish and grabbed a few stunned groupers.

Jack did everything he could to keep his crew's spirits up, trying to make their lives hospitable in the difficult and hazardous environment. Sooner or later, Jack guessed, they'd find themselves in dangerous circumstances that demanded everybody's full cooperation. If they didn't have faith in their skipper or their fellow crewmen, lives would almost surely be lost. When Jack saw a supply ship come in, he sped out, seeking to get meat, milk, butter, eggs, and vegetables for his men. Although his privileged background was far different from that of his crew, Jack strived to treat them as equals and worked alongside them, pitching in wherever needed.

One morning as Jack, Lennie, and Johnny relaxed in their hut, a Melanesian youth wandered inside as if it was his home. He had an infectious smile and playful manner. His name was Lani, and he kept coming back. One night he fell asleep on the floor next to Jack. The agile youth was a pleasant diversion, and they allowed him to stay.

Jack learned basic pidgin English and struck up conversations with the boy, asking about life when the British Empire was in control of the island.

"English we no like." The boy's eyes grew fierce. "I hate the padre."

"Why did you hate the padre?" asked Jack.

"He no good. Treat me bad. Beat me. And others." He made a whipping motion. "I hate him."

"I would hate him too," Jack said. Lani shook his head, bared his teeth, and made a chewing motion. "No. I *ate* him."

Johnny and Lennie stopped their card game, and the three men stared at each other.

When Lani wandered off, Lennie said, "I don't like the idea of waking up to find him gnawing on my leg."

"As long as you don't offend him, you'll be safe," Jack replied. "Besides, you probably taste better than the stuff the navy feeds us."

Soon after, New Zealand authorities took the boy away.

Jack's conversations with Alvin Cluster and others convinced him that the war wouldn't be ending anytime soon. Reason: the Allies' strategy.

"Our stuff is better than theirs," Jack said to Johnny and Lennie one night. "Our pilots and planes—everything considered—is way ahead of theirs, and our resources are inexhaustible, but this island-to-island thing isn't the answer. If they keep doing what they're doing, even that motto 'Golden Gate by '48' won't come true."

"I'm with you on that," agreed Lennie.

Jack felt it was a good opportunity to discuss morale and teamwork. "I think we're working pretty well together so far. I'm glad to have Pappy McMahon along. Good to have an older guy. The rest are on it. I'm a little worried about Ray Albert. Rubs people the wrong way. Always knows what's best. Complains a lot."

"I've noticed."

"Let's keep an eye on him. Make sure he doesn't do anything stupid. War is heating up out there. It's important that we stick together," Jack said.

BECOMING JFK

When Lennie suggested a card game, they went over to join three other officers in a tent. They used a crate as a table for the poker game. Although Jack found the game boring, preferring the intricacies of bridge, he enjoyed the camaraderie and the discussions during or after a hand.

"Damn!" said Jack, when he saw the others' hands. He would have won had he not folded. "Not again," he said, exasperated.

"You could learn a lesson from this guy in Guadalcanal I played with, Jack," said one officer. "Not that he'd ever give you one. He cleaned up. Hixson, I think his name was. Played it close to the vest. I heard he's made nearly enough playing poker to buy a house when the war is over. No, not Hixson. Nixon, that's it. Smart guy. Not a lot of fun though."

After the game, Jack brought up an issue he knew was on everybody's mind. What to do in a battle if they faced insurmountable odds. "There's folding in cards and there's folding if it ever comes to that out there, or here. What happens if the enemy has the advantage? A hundred of them against a couple of us. Shipwrecked on some island or they've sunk your boat. What do you do?"

Stories of Japanese atrocities at Bataan after the surrender in the Philippines had filtered down the American ranks. "Better to go down fighting than to have them torture you for their pleasure," said one man.

Another echoed that sentiment. "As long as I can take a few with me, I'll die happy. What about you?"

"I'd wait and see before making that decision," said Jack. "If there's a chance of survival, I like the idea of seeing another day—even if it's in an enemy pokey. But I recognize there may not be a choice at the moment. They may not be taking prisoners."

Chapter 26

At the end of May 1943, a day after his twenty-sixth birthday, Jack's squadron was ordered up to the Russell Islands to replace other units moving on. The mission: to cover the next major assault on New Georgia.

Following one uneventful night, Jack was ready for a change of scenery. "Let's head back!" he said to his crew after receiving word their patrol was over. Now he had another mission—to get back before anybody else. The boats that got back fastest could refuel without having to wait long. That meant more rest before the next patrol. The 109 got there first more than most.

Jack throttled up again, but the engines sputtered. It wasn't the first time. PT boats were notoriously cranky. After a few seconds, all three engines engaged, and Jack deadheaded for the refueling dock. He loved to go full throttle and encouraged Pappy to "see what you can do to give us a little more juice. We might need it out there at some point."

From the cockpit, Jack had the 109 going full tilt towards the tool shed, which was located above a rickety wooden dock. Jack had previously ignored a warning from Pappy that going full speed before shifting to reverse at the last moment was ill advised. "One of these times an engine might not do what you want it to do," Pappy cautioned Jack. "Then we got trouble."

As usual, Jack took his chances. Throttles wide open, a water tail of a cock behind, the 109 was neck and neck with another PT. Taking a peek at his competitor, Jack gave a friendly wave. He was reminded of racing the *Victura* back home, but this was different. It had become a game of chicken—whoever waited the longest before shifting into reverse would win. Now, so close to the dock, Jack could make out the figures of men outside the tool shed.

When the other skipper backed off, the 109 won. His crew cheered, and Jack signaled Pappy to reverse the engines. But the engines died. The 109 bore in on the dock. Oblivious to the growing danger, a crew on the dock was busy getting out refueling tools.

This isn't going to be good, thought Jack, trying to steer away from a head-on collision. He clenched the wooden steering wheel as the 109 plowed into a section of the dock. Several of his own crewmen were knocked flat. Dock workers were thrown into the water. Wrenches, jacks, and screwdrivers scattered into the water. As well Men inside the shed thought they were under attack and came outside, only to find out their invader was a PT boat.

The 109 finally came to a stop.

The warrant officer, whom Jack outranked, cursed him. "What the hell's the matter with you, Kennedy? Are you a fucking lunatic?"

"Well, uh, I'm sorry," Jack muttered. "Engines failed. I'll have them looked at."

Jack made the situation worse when he tried to back the boat out; additional tools fell into the water.

Due to the crash, several PT boats had broken loose from their mooring, and sailors scrambled to retrieve them. Jack used the distraction to maneuver the 109 into a hidden inlet. Having embarrassed himself, put others in danger, and possibly damaged his engines, Jack wondered what the consequences would be. Certainly, higher-ups would hear about it. Who knows what they might do? He worried he might be relieved of his command or face a court martial.

"Men, I'm sorry for all the commotion," said Jack, addressing his crew. "I guess being the first to refuel is not going to be a priority from now on. Unfortunately, that means less rest for you. Anyway, we're going to hang out here for a little while until things quiet down."

Jack was also concerned that he'd lost the respect of his men, that they'd lost confidence in him after the fiasco. He might have to do something to gain it back. Right now, he was disgusted with himself and ashamed of his foolhardiness.

After tying up, the warrant officer told him Cluster wanted to see him immediately.

"Don't bother to sit down because I'm going to make this short and sweet," said Cluster, getting up from his desk. He planted himself in front of Jack and glared. "You fucked up, Jack. Don't let something like that happen again, or I'll take your boat from you. Or worse. I like you, Jack. You're a good skipper." He pointed at Jack. "But you got your warning. Now get out of here."

Jack had earned a new nickname. When he entered his tent, his mates mocked him. "Get out of the way! Here comes Crash Kennedy!"

Jack managed a wan smile. Hoping to avoid further kidding, he cranked his Victrola and played one of his favorite tunes, Frank Sinatra's "All or Nothing at All."

After the song, the sing-song tune of geckos and the piercing cry of a faraway bird provided the background score. Jack read a copy of *Life* magazine. Three PT boat officers in full dress adorned the cover. Inside was a story entitled "PT Boats in the Pacific" in which John Hersey interviewed three skippers. The story covered the daily lives of the men and recounted several of their battle stories. Hersey provided a more balanced, if heroic, depiction of life on a PT boat as opposed to the recruitment puffery of *They Were Expendable*.

The scream from a Japanese plane interrupted Jack's reading. While others in the house dove for the slit trench outside, Jack became entangled in mosquito netting and thought he might die ignominiously. Finally able to break free, Jack dove for the trench.

"That came out of nowhere," said another skipper afterwards. The aerial attacks continued for a week as the Japanese tried to target fuel depots and engineering installations. Some couldn't handle the psychological trauma of the relentless bombardment. Several times, Jack saw sailors propping up gaunt servicemen as they were removed from the island.

Jack and the other PTs continued to patrol The Slot, a geographic area of the Solomon Islands that Japanese forces used to resupply the islands they still controlled. Hoping to make his mark, Jack was eager to do some damage on the enemy supply barges. So far, he hadn't fired any of his weapons. As he patrolled one night, he wondered if he ever would. The only interruption was the squawk of birds and some occasional radio communication between PTs.

Until the sky lit up.

A Japanese floatplane had detected them and lit a flare. The 109 was illuminated like a bug under a flashlight in a darkened room.

Jack throttled up while sneaking a look at the night sky. There was nothing to see—but he knew what was coming.

Boom!

A bomb hit the water, exploding a good distance from the boat.

Boom!

When this one detonated, Jack ducked low in the cockpit while everybody else dove for cover. With a sound like breaking glass, small pieces of hot metal fragments from the bomb raked the boat. Jack took evasive action and zig-zagged until the threat was over.

"Lennie," Jack instructed, "check to see that everybody is okay." Lennie reported back that there were no injuries.

As they arrived back at the dock that morning, Jack, like the rest of his crew, was exhausted and shaken. It was his first battle action as skipper, and it had been a close call. This work, once dull, had now turned dangerous.

After a restless sleep, Jack took an early afternoon walk, seeking to relieve the stress of the night's events. He passed two shirtless servicemen comparing tattoos on their arms—one of an eagle and the other of a scantily-clad woman.

Jack continued walking away from camp, his thoughts clouded by the events of the previous night. Coming toward him was a Melanesian woman with short, sun-bleached hair, wearing a simple Western-style dress. She stopped and smiled warmly.

"Push-pushy in the bushy? Bring me pipe," she said in accented English.

Jack, still groggy, blinked in confusion. "Pipe?" Then he remembered what the officer had mentioned about the local custom of trading pipes. He hesitated but continued walking past her. However, a thought tugged at him. This was wartime, and life felt fleeting—he could have been killed the night before.

Turning back, he called to her, "I'll get a pipe."

She nodded. "I wait for you."

A few minutes later, Jack returned with a pipe and handed it to her. She gestured for him to follow, leading him to a small village not far from the camp. Inside a modest hut, she turned to him, her gaze steady and kind.

Their connection was quiet, unspoken. Jack felt an unfamiliar sense of comfort in the simplicity of the moment. Over the following days, he visited her several times, each time bringing a small gift or accessory. They shared conversations in a mix of pidgin English and gestures, exchanging fragments of their lives. The woman spoke of her family—a husband and son—while Jack told her about his large family back home.

On his final visit, she surprised him by refusing his offering, instead handing him a freshly caught fish. "No need, Mr. Jack," she said, smiling warmly. "I like you. Share this with your men."

The simplicity of her words struck him. Their encounters weren't transactional, as he'd initially thought. There was a generosity and cultural openness in her approach, one that he hadn't experienced before. She gently touched his arm and said softly, "Take time, American boy. No hurry."

Jack couldn't help but remember Inga's advice about patience and connection. He nodded, taking her words to heart as he reflected on how profoundly different this experience felt.

In mid-July, Jack learned he'd been reassigned to another squadron on the recently captured island of Rendova. The United States was gradually taking control of the Solomon Islands. They would be tasked with interrupting Japanese barge shipments between islands, stalking the Tokyo Express supply convoys, and defending against attacks in the area. So far, U.S. efforts to halt Japanese resupplying operations had been unsuccessful.

Before he left for Rendova, Jack paid a final visit to the native woman. "Be safe, Mr. Jack," she said when he told her of his imminent departure. He would miss her warm, engaging manner and their enjoyable coupling.

As he packed his gear, Jack thought about the ever-present threat of death amidst the frequent reports of ships sunk. He'd become aware that many had renewed their interest in religion, or turned to it for the first time. But for him, it didn't seem to be of much help.

"Some are becoming more religious out here, but I'm not," he observed to a fellow officer. "God doesn't take sides in wars. Or he takes both sides. Maybe when all this is over, I'll find there is something to pray for."

Still, Jack continued to go to church, more out of habit than anything else.

As he boarded his boat, Jack stared at his four pitiful Mark 8 torpedoes. Would he ever launch even one of them? He was learning they were more decorative than anything else.

"Half the time when we push the button to fire, nothing happens," one skipper had complained. "The torpedoman has to hit the firing pins with a hammer."

Since the torpedoes weren't accurate at ranges beyond a thousand yards, PTs had to sneak within a few hundred yards of a ship, well within range of a destroyers' big guns, to score a hit. Too risky. Hundreds of torpedoes had been fired, and once in a blue moon a torpedo hit something. Often, they didn't explode on impact.

After first arriving at Rendova, Jack shared quarters with Bud Liebenow. At twenty-three, Liebenow was the youngest skipper in the fleet, having distinguished himself in previous operations. Jack knew Liebenow from Melville, they regarded each other with friendliness and mutual respect, and they enjoyed exchanging views on how they ran their boats.

"In our squadron, nobody sleeps when we are on patrol," Liebenow said.

Jack nodded. "That's one way. I think the men could use a break sometimes." Jack wasn't a strict captain. He allowed the men a couple of off-duty hours to relax during patrols. He believed it was good for morale to take a break, and the practice kept his crew fresher, especially when days off were infrequent.

They both expressed doubts about their new boss, Lieutenant Commander Thomas Warfield. When he'd taken command, he immediately built a brig at the end of the dock to imprison two men he had detained at sea. Warfield said the men would stay in the brig, even during an air raid. He had a bunker constructed on Rendova from which he controlled PT operations. He never went out on a PT, which didn't sit well with the other skippers. Shortly after Jack arrived, Warfield suffered two disastrous operations.

Jack's first interaction with him hadn't been pleasant, either.

"You may be the ambassador's son, but you'll get no special treatment here," Warfield said after introductions.

Jack replied, "And I don't want any."

Jack and his crew continued their patrols from Rendova. On the night of July 19, the 109 had been on patrol for several hours. No sighting of the Tokyo Express. Jack idled with all three engines engaged.

Hearing something that sounded like an engine different from enemy floatplanes, Jack peered upwards. "It looks like one of our new ones," he said to Lennie, who was standing just outside of the cockpit.

It wasn't. The Japanese floatplane had seen the 109's V-shaped phosphorescent wake and was after them. The floatplane dropped its payload of two bombs at the convergence of the Vs. Both missed, but the explosions sent Jack flat on his back across the deck. Machine gun fire peppered the 109. Chunks of plywood ricocheted, hitting Jack in the face. He got back on his feet, grabbed the wheel, and took evasive action.

"You all right?" asked Lennie, after the attack.

"Yeah." Jack had a few scrapes but no blood. "Check on everybody else."

The enemy was desperate to hold off the American advance. The war was coming closer.

When they returned to Rendova, Lennie said, "Going to eat?"

"All in all, what happened out there makes for a loss of appetite," Jack said dryly, as they walked together on the dock.

Less than a week later, the 109 was escorting another PT back to Rendova. It had been hit and its executive officer killed. But then his own 109 became the target. After a flare, the floatplane dropped a bomb that exploded perilously close, sending up plumes of water. A second bomb resulted in a bright orange explosion. Once again, shrapnel fragments rained down upon Jack's men.

"I'm hit!" one of them yelled. Jack tried to engage his engines, but they stalled. The 109 was a sitting duck. Finally, McMahon managed to engage all three engines, and Jack zig-zagged to safety. Two crewmen had been struck by shrapnel, and the deck was so littered with various sizes of metal, it looked like a junkyard. Back at Rendova, the injured men received medical care, but they never returned to the 109.

Jack began thinking of a new strategy. Weary of being targeted by the floatplanes, he questioned the practice of having all three engines engaged. More engines meant a bigger wake for the floatplanes to see. There were different rules for different squadrons regarding how many engines to have in gear. Some patrolled at minimal speed, running with their engines muffled. Others put two engines in idle, engaging only the center engine. Fewer engines equaled less wake, but that approach also meant a delay in getting up to full speed. All options presented a risk.

His boat had been attacked several times by floatplanes seeing his wake, Jack reasoned, but he'd yet to see a Japanese battleship.

BECOMING JFK

Discussing the recent Japanese attack with another skipper, Jack said, "The goddamn planes can see our wake when we have all three engines running. It's like we're saying to them, 'Here we are! Come and get us!' Keeping the center engine activated might be the safest option." If there was trouble, he'd activate the other engines.

"But what if you encounter a nearby enemy ship?" the skipper countered. "You've only got one engine running. How are you going to get away?"

"That's right. But from what I've seen, it's just the planes that are after us. Haven't seen any destroyers. Have you?"

"No."

"There's another advantage," Jack continued. "With only one engine going, you can better hear the planes up in the sky. With three going, it's nearly impossible until the planes are right on top of you. Seems to me the chance of a destroyer sneaking up on us is pretty slim."

On patrol that night, after throttling down to one engine, Jack had Lennie take over. He walked to the stern to study the wake. The phosphorescent backwash was minimal. So there wouldn't be any surprises, Jack alerted his motormacs to the new strategy, and for the next few nights, Jack frequently throttled down to one engine. No floatplane attacks. So far so good. But the previous close calls had affected the crew. Jack saw worry etched across his men's faces.

At dinner before patrol, Jack noticed Kirksey's hands shaking so badly he couldn't bring his coffee cup to his mouth … until he added another hand to hold his coffee steady.

"You all right, Kirk?" Jack asked, taking him aside later. He recalled meeting Kirksey for the first time. They both had protruding ears, although the torpedoman's jutted out farther than Jack's.

"I don't have a good feeling about this," said Kirksey, looking down.

"I won't be around much longer. My time is up."

"Ah, you'll be all right," Jack said, patting Kirksey's slumped shoulders. "Just a rough couple of nights. For all of us. We'll get through it."

But Kirksey became more morose. It was nearly impossible to get a word out of him.

Jack approached Lennie with his concern. "Kirksey hasn't gotten over the last attack. He's certain something is going to happen to him."

"Haven't we all thought that?" said Lennie. "We've been in a number of recent scrapes."

Jack nodded. "It's on everybody's mind that something could happen. But when a fellow gets the feeling that he's in for it, the only thing to do is to get him off the boat."

"He might do something to endanger the crew and himself," Lennie said.

"Right." Jack reiterated his belief that those who think their time is up are the ones that get it. "When we get back to Tulagi, I'll have him replaced. Best for everybody."

Chapter 27

"Anybody using that?" Jack said, pointing to the formidable 37-millimeter anti-tank gun.

"No, not at the moment," said the supply clerk.

"Mind if I borrow it? I'll put it to good use."

Jack wanted more firepower. A few nights previous, the 109's rudder had failed, and they had been forced to cut short their patrol and return to Rendova. When Jack learned that the remaining boats had used bigger guns to attack and sink a Japanese barge, he figured more firepower would improve his chances of also making a kill, not to mention better defending themselves

Jack and several of his crewmen brought the weapon aboard. "Look what we got," Jack said.

"Nice job, Skipper," said Lennie. "We could do some damage with that. Where we gonna put it?"

Because of its size, there was only one place it could go—the forward deck.

"We can do without that," said Jack, pointing to the life raft.

"But what happens if we get hit?" said Motormac Gerard Zinser, the only career navy man on the boat. "Might need it."

"We'll be all right," Jack said confidently. "If something happens, other boats will pick us up." Jack addressed his crew. "Men, it's time we went on the offensive. The other PTs took down a barge the other night. We can too. From now on, we're a gunboat. Help me take off the raft," he said, walking to the forward position.

Jack had no luck finding a carpenter to help them mount the gun, so he opted for a temporary solution. The gun's wheels were bolted to the deck, and lengths of coconut trees were lashed to the legs. There'd be no protective armor or turret for the gunner, and the shells would have to be manually loaded.

"That's the best we can do until we can get a carpenter to get this thing on right," Jack said.

In the early afternoon, Jack noticed a flurry of officers going in and out of Warfield's tent. There were rumors that a big operation was in the making.

"Something's up," said one skipper to Jack as he exited the mess hall and headed for his tent. "The brass is jumpy. And so am I."

Command had issued a Code Red, which meant that the Japanese supply fleet was close by. An American attack could be ordered at any time.

"Dive bombers!" somebody yelled minutes later, followed by an ear-splitting air raid siren.

Jack bolted out of the tent to see more than a dozen Japanese fighter planes roaring over Rendova Peak and puffs of smoke emerge from enemy machine guns. He flung himself into a fox hole, but he couldn't stay long. He had to get his boat out of the harbor. During a momentary lull, he bolted for the 109.

As he climbed into the cockpit, he pointed to the 20-millimeter gun and shouted, "Kirksey! Harris! Shoot!"

Kirksey loaded an ammunition drum and Harris began firing at the planes.

"Marney! Go!" Jack said, directing Gunner's Mate William Marney to the .50-caliber gun.

Spumes of water flared in the harbor as planes unloaded bombs on the PTs. Jack saw a plane headed their way, a bomb underneath its wing. It passed him, but seconds later Jack glimpsed the dive bomber crash into a group of moored PTs. Then another PT was obliterated, and several sailors were thrown overboard, splashing helplessly amid the wreckage of floating debris. He had to get the hell out of here. Or that would be his fate, too.

"Cast off!" Jack bellowed from the cockpit. Throttling up, Jack sped out of the harbor, his bow above the water. He looked up only briefly as he zig-zagged ferociously, turning the wheel in the opposite direction every few seconds to avoid the bombers.

"Jack! Look out!" shouted Lennie, pointing to an escaping PT barreling in on his port side.

To avoid a collision, Jack veered quickly away and exchanged a brief frozen stare with the other skipper. After that, he was in the clear, a safe distance away from the island. Jack took a deep breath. "I don't know which was worse," he said to Lennie. "Dodging our boats or escaping enemy planes. I'm relieved we did both."

Jack worried the enemy would return for another pass. They usually did, but not this time. The raid was over in what felt like a never-ending minute. The "all-clear" sounded. A one-pass, the Japanese attack was meant to limit their exposure to Allied anti-aircraft fire, but also reduced their ability to inflict damage.

Jack returned to base and saw the destruction. The crashed Japanese plane lay smoldering, its nose buried in the side of a PT. A small fire raged in the PT nest as sailors hosed down the wreckage. Several soldiers carried a lifeless body out of the rubble.

We're in the middle of it now, thought Jack. The war was intensifying here as Japan desperately tried to hang on to its diminishing territory.

Later that day, Jack was ordered to a meeting with the other skippers. "It looks like the enemy means business," Warfield barked in the crowded tent.

BECOMING JFK

Jack sat on the floor with some others; early arrivals had found chairs. Behind Warfield, a chalkboard listed PT boat numbers and their readiness, categorized by fueling status, operational condition, repair level, and special mission.

"They tried to hurt us so we can't hurt them tonight. We've learned there's a big convoy headed tonight to their camp at Villa Plantation on southern Kolombangara Island." Pointing to a position on the map, Warfield continued, "We're going after them. We'll use everything we have. The plan is to disable or sink Tokyo Express ships south of Kolombangara before they unload."

He went on to explain that the Japanese convoy would head south toward Blackett Strait, a small body of water bounded on the west by Gizo Island and the northeast by Kolombangara Island, where it would drop off fresh troops and supplies.

"Our destroyers won't be able to get them all. Some will get through. That's where you come in. It's up to you guys to do damage to the ones that do. This is going to be a really big night," Warfield went on, his eyes gleaming. This was Jack's chance to make a big splash.

Warfield made it sound like tonight was going to be a Broadway opening and he was the producer, Jack thought. He didn't have much admiration or respect for Warfield. Jack thought the way he organized the unit, coupled with his short temper and condescending manner hadn't helped morale. So far, his battle plans hadn't been successful. And Jack had heard from other skippers that Warfield referred to him as that "poor little rich kid."

Fifteen boats would be going out. Jack was assigned to Group B, a group of four boats commanded by a veteran of combat, Hank Brantingham, in PT-159, with Bud Liebenow in 157, and John Lowrey at the helm of 162.

Each unit would have a radar-equipped lead boat. When the radar revealed an enemy vessel, the lead boat would get out of the way and let the three others move in to attack.

"Any questions?" Warfield waited an instant, but it was clear he didn't want any. "Good. Those of you who are scheduled to be going out tonight will have to get ready in a hurry. Get right to it."

Jack was tired. He and many others had been on patrol almost every night for the past two weeks. He made a quick detour to the bathroom, made an incision, inserted a pellet, and then made his way to his boat. He thought about what lay ahead of him. This would be his first battle. He'd be part of a large-scale battle plan, and it was all happening on the fly. Tonight, he might fire torpedoes and perhaps take down a Japanese ship. He'd been on the defensive until now, mostly dodging floatplanes. A few weeks earlier, he'd had his gunner fire at an unmanned Japanese barge. That had been the extent of his offensive effort.

In theory, Warfield's plan sounded sensible, but Jack had his concerns. "How are you feeling about tonight?" Jack asked, falling in step with Bud on their way to their boats. "You've been through this before. Any tips on hitting something and staying alive?"

Liebenow laughed darkly. "Warfield seems pretty confident, but he's not coming out there with us. He hasn't put up great marks so far."

"That's not good," Jack said. "But there's something else I'm worried about."

"What's that?"

"There hasn't been any talk about what to do if a boat gets in trouble. What are we supposed to do if another boat gets lost or sunk or damaged? What kind of search and rescue procedures do we follow? Or what if we get stranded on an island? I don't recall any training on how to survive."

"If you get in trouble, you gotta get yourself out of it. We're on our own. Be safe out there," Liebenow said, peeling off towards PT-157.

On his way to inform his crew of the plan, Jack was intercepted by Ensign Barney Ross. Ten days ago, Ross had been executive officer of the PT-166. Mistaken identification had resulted in disaster. While he was trying to help another PT with engine trouble, his vessel was misidentified as the enemy and attacked by American B-25s. The PT fired back in self-defense. One sailor died when the boat sank, and three of a B-25's crew drowned when the plane crashed.

"Mind if I join you tonight, Jack?" Ross asked.

Another experienced officer would be welcome. Jack had a feeling it was probably going to be a dangerous night. "Not at all, Barney. Come right along. I'm short of men anyway."

Jack knew his crew wouldn't be happy about the evening's assignment. This was supposed to be their night off. "We're going out tonight, men," said Jack, addressing his crew, then briefly discussing the mission. "Let's get ready."

Heads drooped and some swore at the change of plans. The men were tired, and like Jack, many had lost weight due to lack of sleep, tension, and frequent bouts with disease.

"Don't get us killed tonight, Skipper," muttered Albert, as they passed one another on the foredeck.

"I'll do my best," said Jack, hiding his annoyance. "And I'm sure you will too."

Pointing to the new gun, Jack said to Barney, "Know anything about these?"

"No, I'm afraid I don't."

"I don't think any of us are too well informed on it either. Not sure how the damn thing works. We may need it tonight."

After they figured it out, Jack breathed easier. "She's all yours,

Barney. You'll also be the forward lookout."

Dinner was a silent affair that evening in the galley as everybody anticipated the night ahead. Kirksey was especially morose. He never looked up. He had told Harris to take care of his things because he "wouldn't be going home."

After Harris relayed the conversation to Jack, he cornered Kirksey and suggested he stay ashore that night. There'd be no punishment.

"Sorry, Skipper," said Kirksey, looking away. "I've got to go. They'd say I'm yellow." He put on his life jacket.

"Okay," said Jack. "You'll be all right."

With preparations complete, Jack shouted, "Wind her up!" He pushed the throttles forward, the signal for Motormac Zinser below to activate the engines. "Cast off!"

The rumbling of fifteen PTs heading out from Rendova Harbor into the dusk was deafening. Forty miles in the distance, they were through Ferguson Passage to their ambush point at Blackett Strait.

The picket line of boats waiting for the Tokyo Express spread out over six miles. Jack followed Brantingham's orders to fan out. The 109 was paired with Lowrey's 162. He would have preferred the more experienced Liebenow.

Watching and waiting in the warm, humid evening, Jack had only his center engine in gear, motoring at low speed. The steroid had kicked in, and Jack felt a surge of energy.

There was nothing to see on the moonless night. Not a star in the sky. Blackout. Like being in a closet with the door shut, Jack thought. Only a gray outline of the 162 was visible, and he could just barely make out the shores of Japanese-occupied Kolombangara.

A search light lit up the boat, and seconds later a heavy gun targeted them. The 109 was sprayed by a spume of water from an errant shell.

BECOMING JFK

"General quarters!" shouted Jack, believing the attack had come from Kolombangara Island. The crew rushed to battle stations and Jack throttled up. He spun the wheel, zigging and zagging. The evasive action worked. The lights went out and the firing stopped.

"Where's Lowrey?" asked Jack.

"I don't know," said Lennie. "We lost him."

The 109 was all alone.

Jack held his position northwest of Kolombangara, waiting for the Tokyo Express, hoping to rejoin the others later. He contemplated what to do if he sighted a destroyer. It would be foolhardy to attack on his own. He'd have little or no chance to do any damage and would no doubt put his boat and men in peril.

In the distance, Jack heard the sound of gunfire and assumed it originated on the island battery that had targeted him. He was flying blind. At midnight, Jack received a radio report that Japanese destroyers were in the area. He considered making adjustments. He could put the entire crew on alert and engage the other two engines. But he still believed his foremost enemy were floatplanes. Despite the report, he believed his rotating watch was sufficient. Moreover, if he encountered an enemy battleship, he'd have time to get up to full speed. Status quo for now.

For the next couple of hours, garbled voices on the radio were almost impossible to understand.

The Tokyo Express, having repulsed the PT attack and evaded the American destroyers due to its early start, continued on to Kolombangara Island. The attempts to hit the Japanese fleet had not been successful. Twenty torpedoes had been fired. None had hit their mark. The enemy ships had unloaded supplies and debarked nine hundred men to fortify the island. Their mission complete, the convoy of destroyers—*Amagiri, Shigure, Arashi,* and *Hagikaze*—headed back.

Out of the mist, a boat was sighted. Jack let out a small breath of relief when it turned out to be Lowrey's 162 and then later PT-169 from another division. However, staying together again proved impossible. The 109 several times lost sight of and contact with the other two boats. They were here and then gone, swallowed up by the moonless night. Jack was reminded of playing with toy boats in the bathtub as a child; the boats continually drifted away, and it was impossible to stay in contact.

Thinking it would be advantageous to reconnect with the others—both for safety and to increase their chances of hitting a Japanese ship—Jack decided it was worth the risk to use his radio, although he was aware Brantingham believed radio silence was safer. It was true that the radio was often inaudible. The engine noise either masked what was being said, or the radioman might be off doing something else.

"Take over," Jack told Lennie. Jack went below and talked on VHF radio. "Suggest we try to form up and join forces with the other boats still out here."

The others agreed, and the three boats motored southeast, where they reunited but once again drifted apart in the blackness.

Jack throttled down to one engine. He couldn't see anything. Now 2:15 a.m., the 109 was several thousand feet from the nearest boat. From the cockpit, Jack swore at Warfield. "This is a dumbass operation. There's no coordination. It's impossible. Warfield doesn't know what he's doing. I don't know what the hell is going on. No idea where the enemy is." In the chaos of war, Warfield's PT boat picket line strategy was a long-ago memory.

Chapter 28

A mist now developed, and the gentle moisture offered cooling relief. It had been late afternoon when Warfield first ordered the mission, but that seemed like a couple of days ago. His hands on the wheel, Jack recalled rushing his crew to get ready. Dealing with Kirksey. The Japanese big guns narrowly missing him. The frequent, harrowing separations from his division.

Jack's thoughts drifted to Inga and her visage appeared. Sexy. Tender. Maternal. And unavailable. He refocused on staying alert, on engaging all his senses.

A few men were on break, sleeping or dozing. Next to him, Lennie was sprawled on the deck. So was Motormac William Johnston. Gunner Bucky Harris had nodded off and was using his life jacket for a pillow.

A gentle wave rocked the boat. It was 2:27 a.m.

"Ship at two o'clock!" cried Marney from the forward turret.

One of ours, Jack thought. Another PT drifting like the rest of us. "Lennie, take a look at this," Jack said matter-of-factly.

Lennie scrambled to his feet.

It was coming.

The massive hull of a warship barreled toward them, and now was less than a thousand yards away. It's turning into us, going like hell, Jack thought. He had seconds to escape catastrophe.

Throttling up to engage his two other engines, Jack frantically turned the wheel. His instinct was to attack and fire torpedoes, but there was no time even if the 109 hadn't sputtered, drifting on a single motor. *Where are my other engines?*

Jack spun the wheel to the left, hoping to escape the path of the warship. Again, the 109 responded sluggishly on the single engine.

"Sound general quarters!" Jack barked at Radioman Maguire at his side, who shouted out the order.

The warship was so close Jack could make out agitated Japanese voices. Every second, the ship seemed to enlarge exponentially, a dark cloud hell-bent on consuming the 109. Crewmen froze, gripped by fear and what was coming for them.

With an ear-splitting, thunderous crunch, the sharp bow of the *Amagiri* plowed into the 109's wooden hull and steel segments. It pierced the boat close to its front starboard torpedo tube, only yards from Jack. A sharp pain tore through his weakened back as he was slammed backward into a steel bulkhead. Knocked flat, he anticipated a final onslaught. This is what it feels like to die, he thought. He looked up to see the massive shape slicing diagonally through his boat—just behind him.

There was a flash of brilliant yellow-red light. A gas tank exploded with a terrific roar, sending a plume of fire skyward one hundred feet. The sky lit up, illuminating the destroyer's strange, inverted Y-stack. The *Amagiri* completed its work, shearing off a large section of the right rear portion of the 109. But Jack's section stayed afloat. The destroyer raked cannon shots at what was left of the boat before disappearing into the dark.

Surprised to find himself alive, Jack felt a surge of life energy course through his body. He got to his feet and called out, "Who's aboard?" Only Maguire and Mauer responded. That meant everybody else was either dead or flailing in the ocean among blazing waves, gas, sharks, and barracuda. The three survivors clung to the bow—the only section above water. Burning gasoline crept within a few feet of a gas tank.

"Over the side!" Jack commanded.

They swam away from the wreckage, treading water for fifteen minutes. When the flames died down, Jack ordered them back to the wreck.

"Anybody out there?!" he called. No response.

"Swing your blinker," he ordered Mauer, as he flung off his shirt and shoes and dove in to search for survivors. Gaseous fumes made him retch as he navigated through the flaming waters.

"Mr. Kennedy! Mr. Kennedy!" Jack heard Harris scream from about a hundred yards away. "McMahon is badly hurt!"

Jack swam in their direction. "Is that you, Pops? How are you, Mac?"

"I'm all right. Kind of burnt." He'd been engulfed by a wave of fire below the deck and pulled underwater, then emerged five hundred feet away from the boat's remains—but in a patch of fire.

"How are the others?" asked Jack.

"I hurt my leg," Harris said. An airborne object had struck him as he dove into the water when the 109 was hit.

"Let's get to the boat," Jack said. He grabbed the strap of McMahon's life jacket and began towing him. But the current and wind were drawing them away from the wreck.

After a half hour, Harris moaned. "I can't go any further."

"For a guy from Boston, Harris, you're certainly putting up a great exhibition out here."

"Go to hell," retorted Harris, flailing in the water.

"C'mon, let's get you out of that sweater and jacket so you can show us how you swam on the Navy swim team. I'll be right back, Mac."

Jack helped free Harris of his clothes, who then was able to swim back to the boat on his own. Jack returned to McMahon. A breeze had caught the wreck. It was only a hundred yards away, but they weren't getting any closer. Jack strained to make progress, but his arms were weakening. Would the remains of his ship be carried away, or sink? It took an hour for Jack to tow McMahon to the remaining section of the bow and get him aboard. Jack stood up and looked out over the blackness. He couldn't see anything.

"Mr. Thom is drowning!" screamed Zinser. He'd forgotten that Jack had traded the lifeboat for the gun. Zinser and Ross slapped Thom, trying to wake him from his stupor. "Bring the boat!"

"God damn it, there is no boat!" Maguire shouted, swimming out to help.

Jack dove back in.

"Please, God, don't let me pass out!" Zinser screamed when Jack reached him. The saltwater was torturing his burns.

Jack shook him by the shoulder. "I will not allow you to die!"

They returned to the wreck where the survivors huddled on the remains of the bow. There was nothing behind them—the stern was gone. His back aching, Jack grimly observed ten battered, shivering sailors huddled together. He called the names of his crew. Two didn't answer. Kirksey, who had been behind Jack, and Marney, who had first spotted the warship. For the remainder of the still dark morning, the crew took turns calling their names.

"Keep swinging the blinker," Jack ordered. Surely, he thought, one of the remaining PT boats who had witnessed the fireball would see the blinker and save them. But no one came.

Jack considered shooting his flare gun, but feared the Japanese would see it.

Exhausted, the crew drifted to sleep. Jack, Thom, and Ross took turns resting while keeping watch for Japanese ships. What remained of the 109 drifted south toward the open sea.

As the sun began to rise, Jack realized nobody was coming to rescue them. They were on their own. He allowed himself a moment of anger.

The other PT boats had to have seen the fiery explosion. Why had they not come over to help? Or alerted Warfield to send a rescue operation when they returned?

Jack stared at the enormous cone of Kolombangara, where ten thousand enemy soldiers were stationed. He could also see a Japanese outpost on Gizo Island. Easy for the enemy to send out a vessel to finish them off.

Jack surveyed his bedraggled crew strewn across the deck. McMahon was flat on his back, his groans constant. Two crewmen slumped, their mouths open and eyes closed. Harris was in a fetal position. Others looked dead but were sleeping. Jack checked on each man, trying to gauge their physical and psychological condition. The next challenge was figuring out what to do if they were spotted and attacked. Fight or surrender? He flashed on the Bataan Death March.

Needing to reestablish his authority as well as get a sense of morale, Jack said, "There's nothing in the book about a situation like this. Seems to me we're not a military organization anymore. The question is whether we should continue to operate as a unit. Or is it every man for himself?" He didn't believe what he was saying, deliberating engaging in a bit of gamesmanship, attempting to make sure the crew stuck together. He didn't think anybody wanted to go it alone. Fortunately, nobody did.

"What do you want to do if they come out? Fight or surrender?" Jack asked.

"Fight?" Albert said. "With what?"

Their arms were limited. They'd have to defend themselves using six .45-caliber automatic pistols, a .38-caliber handgun, a machine gun, and three knives.

There was silence as the men pondered the possibility of an enemy follow-up attack. Jack knew some would say they'd fight to the death, although they didn't mean it, believing only cowards surrendered. Others might want to surrender immediately. A scenario where some fought and others surrendered ensured they'd all die. Once the shooting started, the Japanese would kill them all.

"Anything you decide, Mr. Kennedy," a crewman said. "You're the boss."

Yes, he was. But he wasn't sure what to do. His training hadn't included a plan for what to do if you were stranded in the open ocean within sight of the enemy.

"Let's just talk this over." Jack was buying time.

"Some of you have wives and some have children. What do you want to do? I have nothing to lose."

Mauer spoke up. "If they do come out, we'll see them before they get here. If it seems that we have any chance at all, let's fight. But if they send out three or four barges with enough men to overwhelm us, I say give up. We're no good to anybody dead." He paused. "But I'll go along with what you think is right."

"I'm with Mauer," agreed Zinser.

Jack now realized they had another problem. The tilting hulk was making a gurgling sound and sinking inch-by-inch into the sea. A few hours later, they were only fifteen feet above water. By mid-morning, the bow was gradually turning upside down. Johnston retched while he was moved along with McMahon to the upturned hull.

"For now, I want everybody to stay as low as possible on the deck so we avoid enemy lookouts."

"If I ever get out of this, I'll never ride a PT boat again!" said a crewman. With nothing else to do, the men raged.

"Why haven't they come for us?" wailed Albert. "We're done for."

Albert's defeatist attitude bothered Jack, and he worried it would affect the others. Jack scanned the skies hoping to see signal search and rescue planes. He could see Rendova Peak. Surely a lookout would see them and send help.

By 1:00 p.m., the bow was turning. Only the slippery section of the keel was above water. There wasn't much to hold on to. Most of the men were half in the water. Without food or water, they had to leave now if they were going to make it somewhere by dark.

But where?

A fairly large island that was close, but Jack worried it was more likely to be occupied by Japanese troops. A small island would be safer. He sighted a speck of land he guessed was between three and four miles away.

No time for discussion. The keel was only a foot above water. Pointing to the sliver of land, Jack said, "We will swim to that small island."

"But there are closer ones," Albert grumbled. "Better to go there."

"It's further away than some of these other islands here," Jack said, "but there's less chance the enemy will be there."

Jack decided he'd carry McMahon on his back while holding the wounded man's life jacket strap in his teeth. "I'll take McMahon with me. The rest will swim together. Make a raft. Thom will be in charge."

A life raft was constructed from the wooden planks used to house the 37-millimeter anti-tank gun. A lantern wrapped in a life jacket would help keep it buoyant.

"Will we ever get out of this alive?" somebody asked with a moan.

"It can be done," Jack said firmly. "We'll do it."

Lying on the keel, the only part of the boat above water, McMahon said, "Go on without me, Skipper. I've had it."

"Mac, you and I will go together. That's an order."

"I'll just hold you back," protested McMahon. "You go on with the other men—don't worry about me."

"What in the hell are you talking about?" challenged Jack. "Get your butt in the water! You're coming, Pappy." He drew on an ancient Greek proverb to poke fun at McMahon and get him moving. "Only the good die young."

"Telling me I'm not one of the good?"

"No. I'm saying you're not young. Get in the water."

Somebody said, "Anybody see our lifeboat? Oh yeah, it's back at Rendova. I knew we forgot something."

Jack pretended not to hear, but guilt over that decision hit him hard.

"Hang on," called Thom. "Especially you two," he said, pointing to Johnston and Mauer, who couldn't swim. "Everybody make sure your life jackets are secure."

Jack whispered to Thom that he and Ross would need to exhort the rest of the crew. Some of them would give up or want to go to the nearest island. "Don't let them stop, Lennie."

Jack turned to McMahon. "Pappy, normally I don't like people on my back, but I'm going to make an exception for you. Get on top of me and give me your strap."

With McMahon on his back and facing the sky, Jack clenched the injured crewman's life jacket strap in his teeth. They set off for the island, breast stroking while the others kicked and paddled. Jack swam for about fifteen minutes, rested, then resumed stroking. It was impossible not to gulp saltwater.

Like an impatient child, McMahon asked, "How far do we have to go now?"

"It won't be long."

But it was.

After struggling for more than two hours, Jack overheard

discouragement. "If we go on like this, we'll all be lost," said Albert. "I'm going to swim on my own. Going to that bigger island. Who wants to join me?" Not waiting for an answer, Albert let go of the raft.

"I'm in charge here," said Lennie. "Get back on the raft. We all stick together." Reluctantly, Albert reattached himself to the raft.

His back hurting, dehydrated, and his arms tiring, Jack tried to ignore his discomfort. Could he continue for a couple more hours?

"How do you feel, Mac?" Jack asked while he rested.

"I'm okay, Mr. Kennedy. How about you?"

"I'm all right." But he wasn't. His breathing was becoming increasingly labored, and his arms felt like dead weights. He gagged as saltwater seeped into his open mouth. He had to rest more often now.

But after another hour, they were almost there. They'd make it. Ahead of the raft, Jack anticipated the obstacle of the coral, which could rip them to shreds. One problem at a time.

"We're almost home, Mac," Jack said.

Jack maneuvered his human cargo through the sharp coral edges of Plum Pudding Island, but it was impossible to avoid scrapes and cuts in the shallow waters. McMahon screamed as he brushed against a sharp edge.

Jack reached land first, spat out the strap, and collapsed after releasing McMahon. His legs in the water and his face in the sand, he tried to stand up. *Must hide from enemy eyes*. Jack vomited violently from ingesting all that saltwater.

"Let's give ourselves a minute, Mac," Jack said. With pauses to stop and take a breath, they crawled ten feet to the bushes and crumpled beneath the foliage. Jack willed himself to sit up. He was heartened to see the others nearing the beach. Albert had let go of the raft and arrived next. But when he began shouting at the remaining rafters, the men were furious, fearing he would alert any Japanese on the island.

When the remaining men came ashore, there were back slaps along with grim smiles.

"God, it's great to touch land," swooned a crewman. "Wasn't sure if I ever would again."

"It ain't Miami Beach, Skipper, but I'll take it," said Ross to Jack.

"Yeah, but the enemy isn't far away," Jack said, pointing to the large outline of Japanese-held Kolombangara Island. "We need to lay low."

While they rested, Jack pondered a plan for survival and rescue, probably in that order.

Chapter 29

"Men," Jack said, "we're safe for now but—" Hearing the hum of engines, he put his finger to his lips.

The eleven men peered through the bushes and held their breath as a Japanese barge carrying troops cruised within a hundred yards of the beach. Jack wondered if they had been seen. The barge could have been part of a Japanese operation hatched after the PT boat explosion, and thus the Japanese military might land, but to the men's relief, the barge continued in the direction of Japanese-held Gizo. Had the enemy come a few minutes earlier, they would have seen Jack and his men. No chance of escape on this small spit of land.

"A few of you take a look around," Jack said. "See if there's anything to eat. Or water. I've got to rest for a few minutes." Jack vomited and collapsed in the bushes.

The scouts reported the island was about a hundred yards long and about seventy yards in diameter. At first, sustenance seemed plentiful. There were coconuts in the trees, white wading birds on the shore, fish in the sea, and hermit crabs. But the coconuts weren't ripe and were inedible, the crew lacked the tools to catch the birds or trap fish, and there was no fresh water. Nobody had eaten since Sunday, which seemed like a week ago. The castaways couldn't survive here for long.

In the late afternoon, they heard the roar of airplanes. "Stay down," ordered Jack. They couldn't go out in the open. Since these were Japanese-controlled islands, most likely those were enemy aircraft.

Jack surveyed his crew. McMahon was in the worst shape. Burns covered his face, arms, and body. Scabs formed over his burned eyelids. Zinser's burns were also painful but not nearly as severe. Johnston was out of it, silently staring at the water. Harris yowled in pain when he walked on his bad leg. They needed food and water. The men had taken to licking the dew off the leaves, even though it was coated with bird crap. They named their temporary home Bird Island.

Jack motioned for Ross and Thom to join him behind a bush. "How are we going to get out of here?" he asked. They discussed the two chief options: try to hail passing planes overhead or go to a different island closer to where PT boats patrolled. Even though it had only been a few hours since he had completed an exhausting journey, Jack leaned toward swimming out into Ferguson Passage that night, hoping to hail a patrolling PT.

"Jack, that would be suicidal," Ross protested. "The Japanese or the sharks will get you. And you'd probably lose your bearings out there."

Thom agreed with Ross. "If you do see a PT, that could be the worst thing of all. PTs going out into the passage are on full alert. No doubt there will be trigger-happy guys on board."

Although he realized his chances of success were slim, Jack believed immediate action was necessary. Several of his men were in such bad shape that they couldn't wait to be rescued. But there was another reason for doing something now. Jack felt responsibility and blame for the decimation of the 109. It had happened under his watch. He'd come up short avoiding the disaster and two of his men had lost their lives. For now, he had to take all risks to save the survivors.

"All right, that's all. I'm going out tonight. One more thing: While I'm gone, you guys watch Albert. I'm afraid he's losing it. He might do something crazy and make things worse for all of us." Since they had landed, Albert had continued to say, over and over, that they were all going to die.

The island they inhabited was part of a reef of sandbars. Jack planned to get to the end bar where it intersected with Ferguson Passage, then swim out in hopes of hailing a passing PT.

After informing his crew, Jack ordered a watch for the night. "I'll take the light with me," he said. "If I find a boat, I'll flash the lantern twice. The password when I return is 'Roger'; your answer is 'Wilco.'"

At dusk, Jack stripped to his pants and secured his rubber life belt. He wore shoes for protection from the coral. His .38 hung from a lanyard around his neck. He grabbed the heavy lantern, still wrapped in the kapok jacket.

"Be careful out there, Skipper," a crewman said. "Those barracuda might come up under you and eat your testicles."

"Thanks for the warning."

Alternately walking and swimming along the reef depending on the depth of the water, Jack made his way. The reef was teeming with fish. His lantern illuminated a massive school of fish that passed close by. He aimed his light at it. The fish splashed and kicked until they disappeared.

For a mile and a half, Jack cautiously navigated the passage. Slipping and flailing on the smooth coral bottom, Jack sank several times into gaps in the reef. When he reached the end of the sandbar, he stopped to rest for a few minutes. Then, after taking off his shoes and tying them to his life jacket so he could tread water more easily, Jack swam out into the passage. For several hours, he slowly treaded water, stopping occasionally to rest. He hoped to hear a wake or the sound of a PT. But he heard nothing in the darkness. He guessed the PTs had chosen to go around Gizo instead of through Ferguson Passage. His solitude was interrupted by a flare, dropped by a Japanese floatplane near Gizo Island.

After several hours, Jack decided he'd have to head back. But now the swirling current had become his foe. Jack was helpless as it shoved him back into Blackett Strait, and then into a wide arc back out to Ferguson

Passage. The sea was calm here. Lulled by the warm, lapping water and weak from hunger and the effects of the crash, Jack dozed.

A gush of sea water splashed into his mouth and jarred him awake. Jack spat and coughed. He had lost his bearings and wasn't sure how many hours he'd been in the water. If he swam the wrong way, he'd find himself stranded in the vast passage and wouldn't have the energy to find his way back.

As he treaded water, he swiveled his head, searching for the outline of land. He saw something. Was it their island? It was. He got closer and shouted, "Roger! Roger!" But he was helpless, drifting past the island as the current pulled him back out to sea.

Holding firm to the kapok around the lantern, Jack floated in a dreamlike stupor. He couldn't swim anymore. He had to get back to his men, he thought. But he couldn't manage it. His mind seemed to exist apart from his body. Exhausted and weak from hunger, he floated in and out of consciousness. Images of the destroyer bearing down on him, his mother and father watching him, and his men waiting for him flashed in his mind in his dream-state.

Throughout the night, he drifted until a hint of light brought him to life and his eyes fluttered open. It was now August 3. He had no idea where he was, and he was worried he had lost touch with reality. Hearing only the whooshing of waves, Jack cried out. He had washed up on the sandbar where he had started. He struggled onto the spit of land and fell dead asleep. When he awoke, he found himself the sole inhabitant, along with one tree and a couple of bushes. He gathered his strength and started his swim back. It was late afternoon before he staggered over the reefs back to Bird Island.

The men had figured he was a goner. Seeing a figure making its way out of the water, Maguire shouted, "It's Kirksey!"

The men rushed out from the bushes to haul him in. They guided him to the bushes, where he collapsed.

"Sorry to disappoint you, John," said Jack. "It's only me."

After resting, Jack considered what to do next. Somebody had to go out, but he knew he was too weak to do it himself on consecutive nights. He'd been in the water almost continuously since the *Amagiri* had plowed through the 109.

"Barney, you try it tonight," Jack said.

While Ross went out that night, Jack tried to sleep, but he was cold and sick from his ordeal. Barney had no better luck.

Nourishment was almost nonexistent as Wednesday, August 4 rolled around. The men gathered rainwater, but each man was able only to get a few drops. They stared hungrily at the hermit crabs but weren't desperate enough yet to try them. Survival training would have come in handy about now, thought Jack.

"We're going to get back if I have to tow this island," Jack cracked, doing his best to keep spirits up.

To increase their chances of finding help and food, Jack determined they had to get closer to Ferguson Passage, where there was a better chance to contact American boats. From their island, he could see a larger island and what appeared to be abundant coconut trees. Some of the coconuts might be edible, and there was more chance of finding fresh water. But it would be a long open-water voyage. They'd be visible to Japanese troops while they swam.

Addressing his men, Jack pointed to the island. "We're going to that one."

"Hope they aren't waiting for us to swim ashore so they can mow us down," said a crewman.

"It's possible," acknowledged Jack, "but we'll have to take that chance. Everybody on the raft. I'll take McMahon."

They quickly gathered their belongings and checked the raft. Jack sprang from the bushes, took a look around to make sure the coast was clear, and then waved everybody forward.

Once more, Jack put McMahon on his back. It took three hours to make the journey to the island of Olasana. Finally ashore, Jack grimaced at the pain in his feet, which were festered and bulbous from coral cuts. They sheltered in the bushes.

"Hey, these are pretty good," said Thom, after he hacked open a coconut. He was surprised to find them ripe enough to eat and the juice drinkable. Soon, everybody was eating the white fiber and slurping the juice, but both made Jack and McMahon sick.

Ross wanted more. "I'm going to try one of these," Ross said, picking up a small snail. The men watched as Ross extracted the insides and put it in his mouth. "Pew!" He spat it out. "Can't do it." The coconuts would have to suffice.

As evening neared, Jack considered swimming out to Ferguson Passage, but a hard rain nixed the plan.

There was a burst of excitement when a lookout reported he'd seen an Allied plane fire its guns at an island about a half mile away before flying off. It had happened so quickly that there was no chance to signal the aircraft.

Albert still was without any hope. "Let's face it, we're all going to die."

"Aw shut up," countered Johnston.

Prayer sessions were becoming frequent. Guys in small groups bowed their heads and asked to be rescued. Johnston mocked them. "You guys make me sore. You didn't spend ten cents in church in ten years, then all of a sudden you're in trouble and you see the light."

Overhearing the discussion, Jack could relate to both points of view. He hadn't prayed so far during the ordeal, but if the situation got worse, he probably would. When you're down to your last hope, praying comes easily to everybody—maybe even those who don't believe in God or a superior being.

"I've got to do something," Jack said to Barney and Lennie. "Even if it turns into nothing. It's important for the men to see that we're doing something. Give them hope." He pointed to the island that looked to be about a half mile away. "Barney and I will go there. See what we find. It's not far."

"You haven't forgotten that our guys were strafing that island, have you, Jack?" said Thom. "Doesn't that mean the bad guys are there?"

"Could be any number of things," said Jack. "Maybe a barge was near the island. Or they were testing guns. Perhaps it was just a practice run. Or, as you say, they were shooting at soldiers on the island. Let's get ready, Barney."

"I've got a good feeling about this island. We're due for some good luck. Luck of the Irish," Jack said as they swam ashore at Naru and hustled for cover.

"I hope so," Barney said, "because any more bad luck and we won't make it out of here alive."

They crossed the island to the Ferguson Passage side. "Look!" Barney said, pointing to the wreckage of a small barge on the reef, about a quarter of a mile from where they stood.

"That's probably what the plane was attacking," Jack said.

More promising was the sight of a crate that had washed ashore. It was secured by rope and had Japanese writing on the side. They dragged it into the bushes. Like a kid opening Christmas presents, Jack cut the rope and broke open the crate.

Candy. A crate of hard, teardrop-shaped candy.

They sucked on the treat. "Best candy I ever had," said Jack. "Even if it is Japanese. We have to get this back to the others."

"Jack, look!" Barney shouted, pointing to the outline of a canoe hidden in the bushes. They ran to the canoe, which was damaged, but inside it they discovered a large tin of rainwater. It was about a quarter full. They were overjoyed.

"Our luck is getting better," Jack said, as they took turns sipping from the container. Another box contained about thirty small bags of Japanese crackers and more candy.

They gorged on the candy and water. Then Jack said, "Take a look, Barney." They were astonished to see two men atop the wrecked barge. At this distance, it was impossible to tell who they were. "What do you make of that?"

"I don't know," Barney said.

"Probably not Japanese," said Jack. Their skin appeared dark, and they weren't dressed in military gear. Jack bolted from the bushes, shouting and waving at the two natives. The four men stared at each other, neither pair sure if the other was friend or foe. Suddenly, the barge-men became agitated and fled in their canoe.

"No, God damn it!" swore Jack, throwing a rock in the water as he watched the two men paddle away. Jack puzzled over what he could have done to let them know they weren't Japanese. He could have waved his shirt in surrender. Or made a joke and climbed on Barney's shoulders to show they were peaceful. As with the collision with the *Amagiri*, Jack again second-guessed himself. He'd missed a chance to contact friendly natives who might have led them to safety.

Chapter 30

Using the damaged canoe as a float, Jack paddled out into the passage. When he returned after another unsuccessful foray, he told Barney, "You stay here overnight. I'm going back to bring the guys some food. Those fellas we saw today might realize we are on their side and send help. If nobody's here, another opportunity is gone."

Jack packed the canoe with the snacks and the water drum. Towing the canoe made for slow going because of the weight of the water. But at least he didn't have somebody on his back.

Jack was treated to one of the best homecomings of his life. Even before he'd made it to shore, he heard shouts. "We're saved! Two locals have found us!"

Jack rushed to the scouts and threw his arms around them. His pidgin English came in handy. The locals were the two men he'd seen the day before who probably thought he and Barney were Japanese. It was a fluke the scouts were there. Biuku had become thirsty, so he and Eroni stopped for coconuts on their way to Sepo. Jack was told a standoff had occurred as the scouts waded ashore and encountered the men. Believing they were Japanese, the scouts prepared to push off from the canoe until Lennie emerged. His white skin and blonde hair saved the day.

The scouts shared their yams, and after feasting on the snacks and drinking from the tin, Jack's crew was in good spirits. "Let's save some water," said Jack. "Help will be on the way, but we need to be careful."

For the first time in a long time, the crew slept on full stomachs.

The next morning, Lennie tapped Jack awake. "Jack, I've got bad news. During the night, Albert drank the rest of the water."

Jack slammed his fist. "What? Why would he do that? Has he lost it?"

By then, others had found out what happened and cornered Albert in front of a palm tree. Several of the crew got in the guilty man's face, and Jack was worried they were going to beat him to death.

"Go ahead, kill me," Albert said defiantly. "Doesn't matter. We're all going to die anyway. Might as well get it over with."

"Hold it, everybody," Jack said. The men turned towards him. "Get away from the bastard. I don't know how he could do something like this. But he did. For now, we leave him alone. Our only concern now is getting off this island. What happens when we get back is another matter."

Jack got into the canoe and covered himself in leaves for the ride back to the island where Barney was. When Biuku told him they saw a swimmer coming their way, Jack knew it was Ross.

"I'm sorry you swam all this way for nothing," Jack said, as Ross climbed aboard, "but we're going back. These are our two friends who thought we were the enemy yesterday. Forgive them, Barney."

Back on Naru, the scouts led them to a hidden canoe. If they were going to make a try for Rendova, they could fit four in each canoe. Five men would be left behind to fend for themselves. It was a long trip to Rendova, and they were still forty miles deep in enemy waters. If they were seen by the enemy, it would be all over for them … and for the scouts too. Better to get a message to friendly allies who could send a boat for everybody. Jack could send the scouts, but he worried they might not be believed. Or understood. He couldn't take that chance. But there was nothing to write on and nothing to write with. "Biuku, there's no paper to write a message."

Eroni scampered up a tree, returning with a coconut, which he gave to Biuku.

"We have lots of papers," said Biuku. "Write message on this coconut."

"How did you think of this?" Jack said with admiration. Then, using his knife, he scribbled on the husk:

NAURO ISL
NATIVE KNOWS POS'IT
HE CAN PILOT
11 ALIVE
NEED SMAL BOAT
KENNEDY

Biuku and Eroni, with their precious coconut, paddled away for Rendova.

When they disappeared into the horizon, Barney sat on a rock. "I guess all we can do now is wait."

"No, I don't think so," said Jack, vowing to continue seeking help until they were saved. "We're going out tonight."

It was now August 6. He couldn't solely count on the scouts finding help. Who knows what might happen on their journey? The enemy might kill them or take them captive.

"Barney, help me with this canoe," Jack said later that night. He pointed to the canoe Biuku and Eroni had given them.

"Gee, I think we'll tip over if we go out," Barney said, pointing to the wild seas.

"Oh, no, it'll be all right. We'll go out."

After shaping paddles from the Japanese box and carrying a coconut shell to bail with, they pushed off. When they got out into the passage, the weather became unmerciful. Struck by strong winds, drenching rain, and five-foot waves, the canoe became waterlogged and unwieldy. A burst of wind tipped it over, throwing Jack and Barney into the water.

"Sorry I got you out here, Barney!" Jack yelled as they climbed back aboard the canoe.

"This would be a great time for me to say I told you so, but I won't. I'll wait and tell you later. If we ever make it back."

"We will."

For the next few hours, the swirling water amid the white foam played havoc with their direction. They paddled toward the faint outline of an island, but the reef blocked their path. The waves tossed the canoe like it was a toy. All they could do was hold on. And then they couldn't even do that. They became airborne as a large wave swung the entire canoe, ripping them away and sending the canoe flying. Jack was pulled under and forced into a round of somersaults. Which way was up? For the third time since the 109 had gone down, Jack thought this was the end.

Finally, his feet touched the reef, and he held firm against it before coming up for air. "Barney!" shouted Jack. "Barney!"

Had his risky decision to go out in the awful weather cost Barney's life? He yelled Barney's name until he was hoarse. No answer.

"I'm over here," said a weak voice finally heard.

Barney was partially submerged on top of a reef outcropping. The big wave had thrown him against the coral, which had gashed his right shoulder and arm. He already had infected and swollen feet.

"Barney, we'll leave the boat and make our way back. I'll put the oars over the coral so you won't have to touch it."

The arduous step-by-step trek back to Olasana took almost two hours, but it was good to be back with his men.

"Helluva night," Jack said the next morning.

"I've had better," Barney said, wincing at his wounded shoulder.

"Well, maybe you'll feel better when you see what I see."

Coming toward them was a long native canoe with a crew of six paddling. The message had gotten through!

One of the scouts handed Jack a letter, and in accented King's English said, "I have a letter for you." The letterhead was entitled: "On His Majesty's Service."

"You've got to hand it to the British," cracked Jack, amused at the pomposity.

The natives had brought with them a stove and plenty of water. The crew feasted on yams, potatoes, fish, and roast beef hash.

McMahon received a basic covering to keep him out of the elements and make him as comfortable as possible. Still, arrangements were needed to have the crew picked up. They would go to Komu Island, where a scout watcher was stationed. Once more, Jack covered himself up with palm fronds for another journey. From beneath the dark green leaves, he glimpsed the blue sky. They rowed with a peculiar rhythm, slapping paddles on the gunwales between strokes.

Suddenly, Jack heard the hum of plane engines. "What's going on?"

"Bad planes. Stay down!"

Jack saw a paddler stand up and wave. The Japanese planes flew off.

In the late afternoon, the canoe pulled up to Komu Island and the headquarters of scout watcher Reginald Evans.

Jack emerged from underneath the palm fronds. Resembling a modern-day Robinson Crusoe, he was deeply sun-burned, his pants were torn, he was shoeless, and his legs and feet were mottled with coral wounds. And that's not all. His face bristled with six days of unshaven growth, and his hair was matted.

"Hello, I'm Kennedy," he said to the approaching Evans, offering a handshake.

"Come and have a cup of tea," Evans said warmly.

After a few sips, Evans told Jack that Warfield wanted the natives to take him back to Rendova. A boat would be dispatched to bring the rest of the crew back.

Jack objected. He didn't trust Warfield to plan the tricky rescue. "No, that won't do. I'm not going to live the high life while the rest of the guys remain shipwrecked. I'm going."

Arrangements were made for a PT to pick Jack up first that night at Komu Island. When Liebenow shot four rounds as a signal, Jack paddled out in a canoe, pulled out his snub-nosed .38, and replied with three shots. The gun clicked empty. Jack grabbed a captured Japanese rifle, stood up in the canoe, and fired off the remaining round. The recoil nearly knocked him into the water.

"Hey, Jack!" a voice called out.

"Where the hell have you been?" Jack replied as he crawled up the ladder and boarded Liebenow's boat. It was a wisecrack, but it was also his truth. He aimed his anger at Liebenow, but his target was all those who had abandoned him and his men. Where had they been for the last week while he and his men struggled against long odds to survive?

"Hey, Jack, we've got some food for you!" said Liebenow to his former bunkmate.

"Just what I need," Jack said sarcastically. He was still so mad he couldn't eat. "No thanks. I just had a coconut."

It was after midnight before they approached Olasana. Once the PT got close to shore, a dinghy was put over the side, and Jack joined another man in the small boat.

When they got close, Jack shouted, "Lennie! Hey Lennie! Lennie, where are you?"

"Here we are," a sleepy voice replied. Although a watch had been set, nobody had been able to stay awake.

"The boats are here!" somebody shouted.

Men came straggling out of the bushes. Jack could see the silhouettes of their arms raised in jubilation.

One by one they transported the crew members to the boat and then to PT-157. Jack stood next to Liebenow at the wheel while they motored back. After a few minutes, Liebenow asked, "So, what did you do with your boat?"

It was a strange question, and Jack wasn't sure what to make of it. Not "what happened," but "what did you do with your boat?"

"Gone," replied Jack. "Just one of those things."

Liebenow pressed him. "Jack, how in the world could you let a destroyer run you down? How were you not able to get out of the before getting cut in two?"

"Lieb, to tell you the truth, I don't know. It all happened so quickly. I just don't know how it happened."

"Did you have all your engines activated?"

Jack told him he had only one engaged and the reasons why he'd decided not to activate the others.

Liebenow snorted. "In my squadron, if Commander Kelly came aboard and found you had only one engine going, he'd have killed you."

Jack had had enough of Liebenow's questioning. "Well, I wasn't in Kelly's squadron," Jack retorted and looked away. But he worried: If the well-respected Liebenow had doubts about Jack's inability to escape the destroyer, then the higher-ups might have serious questions about his actions—or lack thereof.

The survivors arrived back on Rendova at 5:15 a.m., Sunday, August 8, 1943—eight days after getting rammed.

Chapter 31

Jack spent a week recovering in the sick bay at Tulagi, but it would take a lot longer to recover emotionally. Sitting on a cot outside the makeshift hospital tent, Jack vented to Cluster. "It was a bad night."

"Total fuck-up," agreed Cluster. "I hope we can survive Warfield. He doesn't know what the hell he's doing. Did you know that he ordered Brantingham to return to Rendova. The only boat with radar. Put you and the others at quite a disadvantage."

"I didn't."

Overcome with the enormity of everything that had happened in the last eight days, tears began streaming down Jack's face. "Kennedys don't cry," his father liked to remind his children. This was an exception.

Jack had kept his emotions in check for a week, but now there was no stopping the avalanche of grief. He raged at the other skippers who had abandoned him. Given the same circumstances, he would have searched for survivors. The faces of Marney and Kirksey were etched in his memory.

"At least one of the other boats must have seen the explosion and the fire," he said to Cluster. "They had to know something had happened, yet they made no effort to go over and find out. I'm very bitter about it."

When a crewman told Jack the priest had said masses for him and the crew after they went missing, he was furious. "I don't like that at all. I wasn't ready to die. Why the hell had those at headquarters given up hope?"

Others stopped by to see how he was doing, and Jack alternated between resentment and cynical humor.

"Jack, what went through your mind when you saw that destroyer coming straight at you and you thought you might be killed?" PT Skipper Joe Kernell asked.

"You really want to know?"

Kernell leaned in.

"I thought, my God, I still owe Joe Kernell two-hundred and fifty dollars in bridge debts!"

Kernell's mouth gaped open as Jack rummaged around in his belongings for a few seconds before finding a check. He wrote out the amount with a wicked smile and handed it to Kernell.

"Now we're even, Joe."

A few days later, Jack was ordered to Warfield's tent. When he entered, his commanding officer pointed to a chair. Scowling, Warfield said, "I don't know what happened out there, Kennedy, but I know one thing: That's the first time one of our PTs has been sliced in half without defending itself or escaping. You had torpedoes, deck guns, and three engines that, if engaged properly, could have taken you out of harm's way. From what I understand, none of those options were used. Is that correct?"

"Sir—" Jack should have known better than to try to answer.

"I'm not the only one who wonders what happened out there. General MacArthur heard about it, and he isn't happy. The United States Navy doesn't like it when one of its ships goes down without a fight."

Jack hid his surprise at hearing the mention of MacArthur's name.

"From what I understand, you had a hand in getting your men to safety," Warfield continued. "That's all well and good, but if you hadn't gotten your boat sunk, none of that would have been necessary. And two of your crewmen wouldn't be dead." He let that sink in. "What is certain is that you were the commanding officer, so all responsibility for what happened falls on your shoulders, doesn't it, Lieutenant?"

Jack nodded.

"Kennedy, in my opinion, you're not a particularly good boat commander. I think you and your crew got kind of sleepy out there. Weren't alert. You knew the destroyers were in the area. Why couldn't you get out of the way? I think you saw this thing coming at you, and you got bugged a little bit. Shoved the throttles forward too fast. Killed your engines."

Shoved the throttles forward too fast? Should have taken my sweet time while a destroyer was coming after me. This from a guy who never went out on a PT boat. "Sir—"

Warfield put up his hand. "Kennedy, I don't think you realize how lucky you are."

"Lucky?"

"Lucky that you're not British. Had you been in the British Navy, you most certainly would have been court-martialed, which is the standard practice for captains whose vessels are sunk."

Jack held his breath.

"Nevertheless, there is going to be a review of the events."

Jack was stunned, then he fumed. Should be a review of that fucked-up battle plan, he wanted to say. And for not sending a rescue mission. But he held his tongue.

"Dismissed."

Jack left the tent and walked to a lagoon where he could be alone.

If the inquiry led to serious consequences—a court-martial perhaps—that would put an end to an otherwise promising political future. It would be ludicrous to consider running for office if that black mark was on his record.

Jack sat on a rock overlooking the lagoon and considered his responses before being interviewed—or was it *interrogated*? He thought back to the moments before the destroyer emerged, and to Marney's warning. He asked himself: If the same event occurred again, would he have altered his command operations? The answer was yes. Once he learned of nearby destroyers, he would have activated the other two engines and increased the number of men on watch. In the end, it had been a freakish event—a one in a million catastrophe. But the 109 had been that one.

On the other hand, Jack was satisfied with his efforts to get his men to safety. He had taken great risks to do so, but he wondered if he would have done so had he not felt somewhat responsible for the debacle. Would he have jeopardized his life to go out in the Blackett Strait several times to seek help? He couldn't be sure. He thought he might die two consecutive nights. A sense of culpability had forced him to take more chances than he normally would have.

Jack took a deep breath, then walked into the tent. He wondered if MacArthur would send over one of his officers to interrogate him. He sighed in relief when he saw two junior grade lieutenants behind a makeshift desk. One of them was Warfield's intelligence officer, Byron White!

White motioned for Jack to sit in the chair facing him and the other investigating officer.

Giving no indication that he knew White, Jack wondered if Warfield knew that he and White were friends.

"Lieutenant Kennedy," said White, "I'm going to ask you about the events of August first and second. Everything that happened just before the collision."

White asked Jack to give him a summary of the events before the collision, wanting to know where everyone was stationed just before it happened.

Jack recounted where everybody was, beginning with Maguire on his right.

"How many engines did you have engaged when you were struck?" White asked.

"One."

"Why was only one engine engaged?"

"The other two were idling."

"Why were the other two idling?"

"Less of a wake for floatplanes to see."

White nodded but didn't follow up.

Then the key question came: "Before the collision, did you know that enemy destroyers were in the area?" Jack said he had received a midnight report indicating they were. Since he had done nothing to alter his tactics, Jack fretted that his answer may have doomed his career, and perhaps his life.

"Then what happened?" asked White.

Jack described how the *Amagiri* was on the 109's starboard bow, 200 to 300 yards away, going about 40 knots and closing fast. "I turned the boat," Jack said.

"Which way?"

"Starboard. To get out of the way of the destroyer."

"Did you plan to fire torpedoes?"

"It happened very quickly. There was very little time."

"So a torpedo run was a possibility," White said.

Jack didn't answer. He recalled Maguire taking the initial step of turning on the keys to begin the process. It would look better in the report if it said he was trying to make a torpedo run, even though he knew there wasn't time for one in those few seconds.

Thankfully, White moved on. "Was there an attempt to use the lifeboat?"

He didn't want to admit he'd replaced it with the anti-tank gun—a gun now at the bottom of the sea. His choice of firepower over safety had been wrong. True, they had been able to make it to the island by makeshift raft, but it still was an error in judgment.

"The lifeboat was unavailable," Jack said, hoping White would assume it had been destroyed or lost during the collision.

The other officer asked questions about events after the collision.

"Okay, Lieutenant, I think that covers it," said White.

Jack walked out of the tent. *They're either going to kick me out or give me a medal*, he thought.

For several nights, Jack slept fitfully, brooding as he waited for the report to be finalized. There were several ways it could go. One, the report could criticize him for ineptitude that led to the collision. A second result could be a military discharge. A third possibility would be a court-martial.

Jack hoped for a fourth conclusion: that in the chaos of the collision, he had acted decisively to get the survivors back on the remains of the boat. And afterwards, he had performed admirably and courageously, his efforts critical to having the crew rescued.

On August 21, the five-page report was issued. Only the first page and a half were about events prior to the collision and noted the attempt at a torpedo run. (Later, the report was amended, eliminating mention of a possible torpedo firing, deeming it an impossibility given the time constraints.) There was no reference to the missing lifeboat. There was no mention of the report he'd received warning him that enemy ships were nearby.

Jack was ordered to sign off on a story for *Mosquito Bites*, the newsletter written for PT boat servicemen. It read, "Lt.(jg) Jack Kennedy believes that the reason he was unable to get out of the way of the Jap destroyer which rammed him was because only one of his engines was in gear. He strongly advises that, whenever enemy destroyers are known to be in a patrol area, all engines should be in gear."

Incredibly, what might have been devastating to his career had become something positive. Jack was surprised to learn the event had garnered quite a bit of national coverage back home. The military was eager to build morale to counter losses in the Pacific. He guessed that was why any negative circumstances regarding the event had been omitted. A headline in the *New York Times* read: "Kennedy's Son Is Hero in Pacific as Destroyer Splits His Boat."

A celebration was underway. Jack sat with Biuku and Eroni and his crew in the mess hall. Jack stood up, and the room, which contained about a hundred people, quieted. After thanking his crew for sticking together and applauding their courage during the ordeal, Jack said, pointing to Biuku and Eroni, "I want to thank these two fellows. Biuku, I want to thank you for being thirsty and most of all for choosing our island for a coconut. It was an excellent choice. Your parched throat may have saved our lives."

Jack felt a strong bond to his men. Without that bond, he didn't think the crew of the PT-109 would have survived. They were young men, but very mature and proud. The best he could do was give Biuku a gold coin. Seven color ribbons were also given to the two island natives. "If I don't have any more accidents," Jack said, "I will try to come and see you again."

Seeing them off in their canoe, Jack once again thanked them for their efforts. "I'll never forget you. I hope you won't forget me."

As he walked back, Cluster intercepted him. "Jack, that was a good way to go out."

BECOMING JFK

Jack halted. "What do you mean, *go out*?"

"When your boat goes down under you, you are eligible to go home. I'm writing a report saying you deserve a Silver Star. That's the highest honor. Plenty to do at Melville."

Jack was stunned that Cluster thought he deserved a medal. Only a few weeks before, Jack had been worried about being disciplined. He felt an immense sense of guilt over the way the mission had gone and the loss of his men. It could have been a disaster, but now he was being rewarded.

Jack was haunted by the specter of the *Amagiri* advancing toward his boat as he waited helplessly for the collision. Every time—just as the destroyer loomed above him, and he heard the familiar Japanese sailors' voices—he awoke, blanketed in sweat.

Jack felt that this recurring nightmare indicated his unfinished business with the enemy. He decided that the best way to get rid of the nightmares was to do something. Take action. Sink an enemy ship, blow away an enemy barge, or perform a daring rescue of marines. He needed success. And revenge. The loss of Kirksey, Marney, and his boat demanded payback. He couldn't stomach being the only PT skipper whose boat was rammed and sunk by the Japanese. He wanted to get back at the enemy in any way possible.

"No, that's all right," Jack said. "I don't plan on going anywhere for the time being. Thanks, but no thanks. I want another boat."

Now it was Cluster's turn to be shocked. "Are you sure?"

"I am," Jack said. He'd made it clear he wasn't done.

Chapter 32

While he waited for a new assignment, Jack held informal debates in his tent. Six men sat around a makeshift table. He used *The Saturday Evening Post*, *Life,* and *Collier's* to kick off discussions regarding world affairs.

"Why the hell are we out here?" asked Jack. "I think it's important to think about our role now but also our role in the future. So I'm all for everybody to read, come up with your own ideas, and take part when we get back. At least that's what I intend to do. I think it's an obligation."

An opportunity presented itself when Cluster told him the ineffective PT boats were going to be converted to and recommissioned as gunboats. "We're removing the torpedoes and depth charges, putting in new armor plating, and packing them with heavy guns," said Cluster. "Going after the barges. If you want to stick around, I'll see that you get a gunboat. Interested?"

"Yeah. I'm in." Jack liked the idea of commanding something closer to a warship.

Jack was assigned to PT-59 and worked tirelessly to help convert it. When he was promoted to full lieutenant, Jack began putting a crew together. One day as he was assisting some machinists with the placement of the new guns, he was interrupted by familiar voices. Jack turned to see Maurer and Maguire.

"What are you doing here?" said Jack. He figured they'd been assigned to another boat or sent stateside.

"What kind of a guy are you?" Maguire said. "Forget about us?"

"What?"

"You got a boat and didn't come get us?" said Mauer.

BECOMING JFK

Jack turned away, his eyes welling up. "Well, uh, I was just on my way. Thanks for coming by. Saved me time."

In September, after five weeks, the 59 was remade. Jack became the first gunboat skipper to command the new kind of small warship, now known as Gunboat 1. Bristling with armaments, these small vessels had 40-millimeter guns in the fore and aft, six .50-caliber machine guns positioned on each side, and four more machine guns behind and forward of the cockpit. He'd command a crew of nineteen.

Several other former members of the 109 joined his crew when the boat moved to a new island, Vella Lavella.

Jack itched for battle. He volunteered for dangerous missions, hoping for a chance to retaliate and extract a measure of revenge. Hate had found its way into his being. He hadn't hated the Japanese before they sank his boat—they'd been a faceless enemy—but his fury had escalated. He'd put faces to the Japanese sailors' voices he'd heard moments before the collision. He was haunted by images of the laughing enemy pointing gleefully at the prospect of plowing into his boat. Time to return the favor. Even things up. Or more. "God damn bastards," he found himself muttering as he walked around the base.

"I'll do it," Jack said, when a senior commander said he needed a gunboat as a decoy to draw enemy fire. But the operation was scuttled.

Now running a tighter ship, Jack eliminated off-duty breaks and cut down on joking around with the crew. He was dead serious this time around.

Jack was assigned to patrol the nearby island of Choiseul, where five thousand Japanese troops awaited evacuation. The Japanese were phasing barges out as they prepared to abandon the island. Frustrated, Jack's only action had been firing at three barges before they disappeared unharmed into the night.

"Lieutenant!" said the temporary commanding officer at the dock while Jack refueled. "I need your help!" The officer said eighty-seven marines were trapped at Choiseul and surrounded by enemy troops.

"Sure," said Jack. "But my tank is less than half full. Won't be enough to get there and back."

"That's okay. I'm sending two other boats. One of the others can tow you home."

Jack gritted his teeth, not liking the idea of relying on others to get back to base. "All right."

"Stranded marines on the island!" he shouted to his crew. "Let's go get them! Wind her up!"

Three gunboats sped toward the entry of the Warrior River at Choiseul. When they arrived at its mouth in the early evening, the weather had turned sour, rainy, and cloudy. Visibility was dim as they motored down the river toward the beach. As he maneuvered closer, Jack could hear the screams of men and the crackle of gunfire. Frantic marines waded toward a landing craft as Japanese fire rained down on them. Jack saw the shadows of several marines throwing their arms up, then falling into the water. One landing craft loaded up and headed for safety, but another had hit a coral reef. About 250 yards from shore, it began to sink.

"I'm going after them," Jack said. He maneuvered his boat between the shore and the sinking ship, then yelled, "Get those guys aboard!"

Japanese fire increased as the men fled the ship. Jack considered returning fire, but feared he'd hit some of his own men.

His crew grabbed ten men, one of them wounded. Blood spurted from that man's chest as he was lifted aboard.

"Lieutenant, I've got a man in bad shape here," the medic said.

"We'll find a place for him," Jack said.

Once he was given the all-clear, Jack gunned the boat back to safety.

BECOMING JFK

A few minutes later, he handed the wheel to his second in command and went below to check on the wounded man. He lay on Jack's bunk. The medic was readying a plasma bottle and sutures.

"Am I all right, Doc?" the man said weakly.

"Jimmy, don't worry about it," the medic said gently. "You're going to be okay." The medic held his hand, but a few minutes later, Corporal Edward Schnell died.

Jack returned to the cockpit, shaken at seeing a man die on his bunk.

Two hours later, Jack's gunboat sputtered and conked out. As another PT slowly towed it back, Jack heard the sound of Japanese aircraft. They were sitting ducks. Fortunately, four Australian P-40s suddenly appeared to provide cover, and the gunboat made it safely back.

After the conflict, Jack hatched his own plan. He was tired of responding to enemy attacks. He wanted to go on the offensive for once.

"What would you think about going back there?" he said to Chief Petty Officer Glen Christiansen. "Taking it to them. Go after those sons of bitches."

"What do you mean, Skipper?"

Kneeling, Jack used a stick to carve Choiseul Island and the Warrior River in the dirt. He drew a rough outline of his plan. "The three gunboats go up the river. We'd have a lot of firepower." Jack paused. "And we'd go during the day."

Christiansen took a step back. It was rare for any American vessels, gunboats or not, to go out during the day. "Sounds pretty dangerous, Mr. Kennedy."

"I think we could do it. In and out. Let them have it."

"But we don't know what's up there. Jesus Christ. There's no way."

Disappointed that Christiansen didn't share his enthusiasm, Jack hoped the higher-ups would approve.

A few days later, he was intercepted by Cluster on the way to the mess hall. "Jack, you did a good job there back on Choiseul. I understand you want to go back and do some damage."

Jack huffed up, optimistic that Cluster would be on his side. "Yes, I think we could hit them. Hurt them badly."

"We might. But we might also get hurt too."

"That's a chance I think we should take."

"We tried that on Kolombangara. You know what happened? Warfield hadn't figured out that once the boats got inside the river, it would be a bitch to turn them around. A lot of people got killed."

"I wouldn't want that," Jack replied, dispirited.

"No, I'm sure you don't."

Jack wondered whether he'd become consumed by retribution and redemption. Perhaps that was clouding his judgment. There would be other opportunities.

Then one night, after he was given permission to head home following an uneventful patrol south of Choiseul Bay, Jack said to Christiansen, "Let's stay out a little longer. Might find something."

The dawn light was widening, which put his boat at risk. A lookout sighted three Japanese barges beached and abandoned on Moli Island.

Jack maneuvered Gunboat 1 close.

"What are you going to do?" somebody asked, "Nobody there."

"And nobody will ever be once we're done with them," Jack said matter-of-factly. He ordered all guns trained on the vessels. "I want those barges in pieces. Commence firing!"

For several minutes, machine guns puffed smoke and rat-a-tat-tatted rounds into the barges. Jack smiled grimly as he watched them being decimated. Chunks of wood flew into the air, and gaping holes now made it possible to see through the barge. One barge was nearly cut in half by the fusillade. Jack felt a tap on his shoulder. It was Christiansen, bewildered by the excess. Jack nodded and gave the order to hold fire.

"You got them, Skipper," said Christiansen.

Jack was still fixated on what remained of the barges. A few seconds later, he snapped out of his stupor and said, "I feel better. Now we can go back."

He might never sink a Japanese warship or take down a working Japanese barge. But at least he'd decimated something—even if it was a couple of abandoned barges.

Walking on the dock after the patrol, Jack gritted his teeth. His stomach and back pain had worsened since the crash. He had frequent headaches and often felt feverish. His weight was dangerously low. He'd lost 25 pounds during the previous three months. Back to skin and bones. But that had happened before. He'd gain it back as he always did. Unless the trials of the last few months had caught up with him.

An exam revealed he had malaria, for which he was prescribed atabrine. He also had colitis—or as Jack called it, "gut ache," which was something he'd had as far back as he could remember.

Cluster ordered him to Tulagi for further hospital observation. Jack thought it likely that his time in the Pacific was coming to an end. So did others. His men came to see him off. Standing at the dock, he shook everybody's hand and said he was proud to have led them as his crew.

"If there's ever anything I can do for you," Jack said, his voice cracking, "ask me. You will always know where you can get in touch with me." Then he gave a brief wave, turned, and got on the boat.

At Tulagi, Jack used a cane to hobble around and wore a sacroiliac belt to aid his back.

"How are you doing?" asked a red-headed sailor. "Paul Fay is my name," he said, introducing himself. "But everybody calls me *Red* for obvious reasons. I'm glad you and most of your men made it back. I just wish more had been done to help you and your crew after you got hit."

"You're not the only one."

X-rays indicated chronic disc disease of the lower back and an ulcerated crater. Jack had also acquired another nickname—"Yellow Man"—due to his skin color.

"Is that it?" Jack said wryly after an exam. "Could have been worse, right, Doc?"

"I suppose so. Anyway, you're done here. You're too beat up to do the navy any good without getting yourself killed."

Jack nodded. He'd had it.

In December, Cluster took him off the active duty rolls. Jack knew it was only a matter of time before he'd be sent home. He had wanted to do more, have a kill under his belt, or make his mark in some other way. The bittersweet events at Blackett Straight were forever woven into the fabric of his soul. He had lost two men and his ship, but he had helped save the rest. It didn't even out and never would. He said his goodbyes and told Red, whom he'd become friendly with, to stay in touch.

On December 23, 1943, Jack boarded the escort carrier USS *Breton* for the return trip to the United States. As the Golden Gate Bridge came into view twelve days later, Jack thought about the past few years. War was a dirty, dangerous, and unpredictable business. He'd survived, just as he had predicted, even as others he fought beside hadn't made it.

But his life would never be the same.

PART FIVE
WRITER/EDITOR

Chapter 33
January 1944

After returning to the United States, Jack went straight to Inga's apartment in Beverly Hills. It was the beginning of his thirty-day leave. He wanted nothing more than Inga's tender affection after the horrors of his wartime experiences. Though they had kept up a written correspondence, it had been close to three years since he'd seen her. He hoped the magic would still be there.

The door opened, and there was Inga, beautiful as ever. But his enthusiasm dimmed. Behind her was a man.

"Hello there, sailor boy." She gave him a brief hug and introduced a Navy doctor. Inga served coffee and sat close to the doctor, who casually draped his arm around her.

What am I doing here? thought Jack.

"I don't know if you've heard, Jack, but I've taken over Sheila Graham's society column. I'm quite enjoying it. Meeting so many interesting people. Including this one." She gave the doctor a loving glance. "Tell me about this business with your boat. And how you saved your men."

"Well, I didn't save my men. Just tried to keep everybody alive long enough so our guys could find us. Most of us returned. A few didn't."

"Yes, I'm sorry about that. I'm sure there was nothing more you could do. Tell me what it was like when you saw the Japanese ship coming at you." She picked up a pad and pen. "You don't mind if I take notes."

So, what he hoped would be a loving reunion was going to be a sterile interview about something he'd rather forget. The doctor put his hand on Inga's leg. It wasn't what Jack had come for. But he wanted to help her.

BECOMING JFK

Jack nodded.

After an hour of questioning, Inga put down her pad, her eyes shining. "This will be quite interesting to my readers. Thank you for putting up with my questions. Do you remember the first time I interviewed you?"

"Vaguely," he said with a wry smile.

At the door, Inga kissed him on the cheek. "Take care of yourself," she said, and waved goodbye.

The result of the interview was widespread coverage, which included *The Boston Globe*. His front-page picture there was bigger than Churchill's or Eisenhower's. The headline read: "Tells Story of PT Epic: Kennedy Lauds Men, Disdains Hero Stuff."

Several weeks later, Jack met his father at the Mayo Clinic to discuss his health with the doctors. Then he flew to Palm Beach on January 11, 1944, to spend the last two weeks of his leave. A friend of his from Hyannis Port, Chuck Spalding, picked him up. Spalding was nearing the completion of his naval air training. His book *Love at First Flight*, a humorous novel about the training process for naval aviators, had been a hit the year before.

"Congratulations," said Jack after learning of the book's success. "Maybe I'll write something entertaining about my time in the Pacific. But right now, I can't think of much."

When Jack arrived home, he was greeted by his family in the foyer. "It's good to have you back," said his mother, offering a plate of oatmeal molasses cookies.

"Thank you, Mother," he said. "These are good."

"Jack, you are quite bronzed. But so thin and drawn."

"Yes, Mother," said Jack. It was an observation, not an empathetic response.

Twelve-year-old Teddy said, "Want to play some football, Jack?"

The three of them tossed the football around for a few minutes, then Jack said, "Chuck, let's hit that supper club tonight, the one we used to go to."

Jack put on white linen pants and a blazer. It had been a long time since he'd dressed up. They pulled up to the club, and Chuck tossed his keys to the valet. The club's roof had been pulled back and the dance floor was packed. But Jack was surprised to discover that he didn't feel any desire to mingle, let alone dance. What's wrong with me? he wondered. There are some beautiful women here. They took a table and ordered a beer.

"I see a gal who deserves my company," said Chuck.

"You go ahead. I'm going to wait a bit."

Several women gave him flirty glances, but Jack looked away. He didn't know what he was doing there. He certainly wasn't ready to have a good time. He flashed on the Japanese warship bearing down on him. And the faces of Kirksey and Marney. Maybe he shouldn't be celebrating his return. He couldn't with those images haunting him.

"What's the matter? Sitting here all alone. Nobody good enough for you to take a spin with? Not even me?"

Standing before him was a beautiful, raven-haired woman wearing bright red lipstick, but she might as well have been a Martian. Jack smiled anemically. He didn't feel like dancing, but he realized if he didn't get up soon, he'd stay rooted to his seat the entire night.

They waltzed, but the woman failed to arouse his interest, though he hadn't danced with a woman since first shipping out. In mid-song, he said sadly, "I can't. I'm sorry." Then he returned to his seat, where he stayed the rest of the evening.

BECOMING JFK

After a few days at home, Jack knew something was wrong, but it didn't have anything to do with his physical condition. He wasn't himself, and he didn't know why. It didn't make sense. Here he was in beautiful Palm Beach, back with his family, and removed from the horrors of war. But he was despondent. It was hard to get up in the morning. Many days he sequestered himself in his room and read. He rarely cracked a smile and made no attempt to engage with people. He barely ate. As he wandered through the kitchen, the family cook asked if Jack wanted a snack. "Don't worry about me, Margaret. Never hungry."

Hyperactive and unable to relax, Jack incessantly tapped his foot or thumped his hand on his knee. He withdrew. He was unable to enjoy the everyday pleasures of playing tennis, swimming, or nightlife. The activities seemed so mundane and worthless after the life-and-death events of war.

Jack was no longer a PT skipper, but he couldn't completely escape the war. The Miami area was a hotbed of PT boat activity. Since Teddy had been hounding him for bits of information about his war years, Jack might as well show him what he had been doing. With Joe overseas the last couple of years, their younger brother shadowed Jack. After making arrangements with the officer in charge, the two of them drove one morning to Bayfront Park, where the boats were tested before being sent abroad. Jack considered how many men would survive the brutal war still raging in the Pacific. He recalled the adage "They were expendable." He hoped not too many more would be.

Assembled there were nine PTs in rows of three. After Jack identified himself at the office, he pointed to a PT. "Let's get on this one, Teddy."

They climbed aboard and Teddy was thrilled. War was a game to him. "Wow, Jack! You had one of these!"

"I did until the Japanese decided I wouldn't and rammed my boat."

"I wish you could have got out of the way, Jack. Then you'd still be a captain."

"Well, the Japanese had other ideas. Let me show you around." Using his flashlight, Jack took his brother below to see the narrow quarters and let him sit in the cockpit and pretend he was steering.

Scampering to the torpedoes, Teddy tapped the tubes. "I hope someday I can be a captain like you and shoot these at the bad guys. Is it all right if I go there?" Teddy said, pointing to a machine gun turret.

"Okay," said Jack. It was locked and unloaded.

Teddy clambered into the turret and grabbed the gun handles. "Rat-a-tat-tat-tat! Rat-a-tat-tat-tat!" he shouted. "I got 'em, Jack!"

"I'm sure you did." I hope you never get that chance, thought Jack, but he didn't want to quash his brother's enthusiasm. He'd been the same way.

The day brought back the not-so-distant memories of his last patrol on Gunboat 1 and before that the foray to save marines at Choiseul. He'd had enough of PTs and war, and he wondered whether it had been a mistake to bring Teddy here and see him thrilled with the weapons of combat.

Even though it was 85 degrees, Jack felt cold. "Let's go, Teddy."

But the chills didn't go away. Twice, Jack had to be rushed to St. Mary's Hospital, his thin yellow frame shaking uncontrollably.

In early February, and just starting to feel like his old self, Jack flew to New York City. The foursome at New York City's Café Society included John Hersey and Frances Cannon. Jack's date was Flo Pritchett, the attractive fashion editor of the *New York Journal-American*. Hersey had written *A Bell for Adano*, a top-selling novel about World War II.

"There was a bit of coverage about your boat mishap out there, Jack," said Hersey. After taking a sip from his drink, Hersey lit up a Lucky Strike and asked for more details.

Jack was reticent; he didn't want the incident to dominate the evening's conversation. But as he summarized the events, Hersey became captivated. "Fascinating," he said more than once.

They were interrupted by William Shawn, then the assistant editor of *The New Yorker*. "Hello," said Hersey, and after introductions, briefly mentioned Jack's experience.

"Well, I'm glad you made it back safe and sound," Shawn said, before excusing himself.

"Jack, I'd like to write about it," said Hersey. "With your cooperation, it would make one hell of a story. And I don't mean a newspaper story. I think *Life* magazine might be interested."

"Let me think about it."

His father was over the top with excitement when Jack called to get his opinion. "Do it, Jack. Great publicity. Can't go wrong!" His father had tried to get *Reader's Digest* to write a story but had been rejected.

Jack told Hersey he was agreeable but suggested first contacting four of his crew members now back at the training facility in Melville.

The next day, Jack attended his grandfather's eighty-first birthday celebration in Boston at the Parker House and spoke at a war bond fundraising event. He looked out at the crowd of over a thousand people who had given him a fervent welcome when introduced. He sensed they were eager to hear his views, but he was cautious. "I have read accounts of action since I came back. And things seem to be going fast. Then I look at a map and think how long it took us to get from Guadalcanal to Bougainville, and I realize it's going to be a long war."

Afterwards, Jack wished he hadn't been so pessimistic. He could tell the audience wanted more optimism and bravado. But that's how he saw things, and he just didn't have it in him to pretend the war would be over soon.

The large crowd nonetheless cheered him like he was a pop idol. As he walked out, he cracked, "Now I know how Sinatra feels." Jack had helped sell a half-million dollars' worth of war bonds.

A few days later, he checked himself into New England Baptist Hospital to deal with his continuing stomach problems and to determine what to do about the degeneration of his spine. He'd also scheduled his interview with Hersey, to take place while he remained in the hospital.

That day arrived and Jack propped himself up in the hospital bed.

"Let's get started," said Hersey. Starting in the afternoon, they talked at length about the events of that week in August 1943.

Jack's brow furrowed when recounting the night he'd spent in the water after drifting off the reef. Hersey probed. "Was something different that night—I mean besides spending the entire night in the water?"

"After a few hours, I got cold, and I lost track of time." Jack smiled sheepishly. "I think I also lost my mind for a while out there. It was somewhere else—like it was detached from my body. Maybe that's why I didn't try to get back to the island. I wanted to, but I couldn't. It was the strangest feeling."

Hersey gave him a pencil and paper and said, "Jack, would you mind drawing me a map of where you got off the reef and spent the night in the water. Help me pin it down."

"Sure," said Jack, looking skyward for a moment to bring back the memory, then drawing rough outlines of the islands and Ferguson Passage.

They then went through the entire ordeal. After several hours, a nurse came in to take his vitals. The sun had nearly set, but the interview continued.

Finally, Hersey put down his pad. "I think I've got what I need."

Uncertain how Hersey's story would differ from those that had already appeared in the newspapers, Jack asked, "Do you think there's anything that hasn't already been said?"

"I think there is, and I think people would be interested in getting a deeper understanding of the events and what you and your crew went through. I intend to write it in a different way."

"What do you mean?"

"Well, it won't be just the facts. It'll be the truth as I see it, but I'm going to use techniques fiction writers use to make it more interesting."

Talking about the dangers he had faced triggered concern about family and friends. Jack had seen too much death, and he didn't want it coming any closer. He worried about Lem, who wanted to get into combat, and wrote to him trying to dissuade him. Joe was in Europe flying bombing missions and had reported there had been heavy casualties in his squadron. I hope he gets through, Jack thought.

Worried about Bobby's enlistment, Jack tried to discourage him from going into aviation. Of course, he'd been like them at one time—eager to get in the fight, to be where the action was. And now he could see the same thing happening to Lem, Bobby, and Joe, who all seemed eager to put themselves in harm's way.

That's what led to more killing and more wars. A never-ending cycle. He guessed everybody had to find out for themselves—sometimes the hard way.

If he wanted to walk like a normal person again, the doctors told Jack it was necessary to have the operation he'd avoided in South Carolina. On June 11, a battery of photographers awaited Jack when he arrived in full dress black at the Chelsea Naval Hospital for further tests.

"Where do you want me?" said Jack. His father had pressured his friend—the new secretary of the Navy, James Forrestal, to approve the medal application. He'd also alerted the press to the ceremony.

Standing in front of the brick building, Joe Sr. posed with the chief surgeon as he pointed to the Navy and Marine Corps Medals on Jack's uniform.

"Here's your magazine," said an attractive nurse, putting a copy of the June 17 edition of *The New Yorker* on his bed. "Your father sent it over."

Life had rejected the story, but the chance encounter with Shawn at the party had paid dividends. Jack opened the magazine to the one-word headline: "Survival."

"Well, let's see what Hersey has to say about how we survived."

"Enjoy your reading," said the nurse, preparing to leave.

"Would you mind if I read some of it to you?" he joked. "I think it would be good for my health."

"Sure." She smiled. "Anything I can do to make a patient feel better. Well, almost anything."

"Good. Make yourself comfortable," he said, pointing to the foot of the bed.

It was peculiar to read about oneself, but Jack became entranced with Hersey's prose. "At about ten o'clock, the hulk heaved a moist sigh and turned turtle." Jack put down the magazine. "This guy really knows how to write," he said to the nurse.

"He does have a way with words," she agreed.

Jack found it peculiar to have Hersey tell the story as though he—Jack—was going through the ordeal in the present. "Listen to this. 'He stopped trying to swim. He seemed to stop caring. His body drifted through the wet hours, and he was very cold. His mind was a jumble. A few hours before, he had wanted to get to the base at Rendova. Now he only wanted to get back to the little island he had left that night, but he didn't try to get there; he just wanted to.'"

"Is that right?" said the nurse. "You felt powerless."

"Yes," said Jack, for a moment transported back to the watery darkness of that night. After he finished reading the article, he thanked her for listening. "I feel much better."

"Anytime," said the nurse, getting up and fluffing his pillow. "Now you get some rest."

A few days later, he was transferred to New England Baptist Hospital, and on June 23, the operation took place. Though surgeons expected to find ruptured or herniated discs in his spine that would be easily repairable, none were found. They did excise some abnormally soft cartilage. Basically, though, they could do nothing about the degenerative condition of his back. He'd have to live with it.

Jack was transferred back to the Chelsea Naval Hospital to recover. "Well, look who's back?" said the nurse he'd read Hersey's story to. "It's nice to see you again."

"Yes, although I wish it was under different circumstances." Jack winced at the severe muscle spasms in his lower back.

He was prescribed large doses of narcotics to ease the pain, and his back was strapped tightly in the hopes it would help him heal. Again, he'd lost a considerable amount of weight.

Visitors helped to ease his psychological and physical pain. Besides his family, friends came by. Jack offered a weak wave of his bony wrist when Torby, back from the South Pacific, entered.

"How do you feel?" Torby asked.

Jack had trouble raising his head, and Torby couldn't hear him, so he moved closer.

"I feel great," Jack said.

"Great?"

With a lopsided smile, he added, "Well, great considering the shape I'm in."

Lennie and his new wife stopped by, but it wasn't long before the nurse, seeing Jack's fatigue, came in and said they'd have to leave.

"Sorry. I hope you can come back in a few weeks. By then, I'll be up and at 'em," Jack said.

After more than a month at the hospital, Jack began to feel better and decided he could use a night out.

"That's quite out of the ordinary," said the nurse when Jack suggested a visit to the roof garden of the Ritz-Carlton. "But I would love to see it. I'm off at five."

They slipped out of the hospital and drove his father's car to the hotel. "This evening will certainly help speed along my recovery," said Jack. He hobbled through a couple of dances. Then they cuddled in the rooftop garden. Between kisses, Jack said, "I can't think of anything that could be more beneficial to my health than this."

As they exited the hotel, Jack realized he was missing something. His keys. And something else. "Where's the car?" It was gone. He'd left his keys in the car, and somebody had stolen it. "Dad won't be happy."

They took a taxi back to the hospital. Jack turned to the nurse. "We'll just add the fare to the hospital bill... under the category of 'rest and recuperation.'"

Chapter 34

"Jack, you have a visitor!" his mother called, interrupting his reading in the sun room. He was in Hyannis recovering from the operation. His mother brought the young woman in along with a tray of deviled eggs, cottage cheese, butter sandwiches, and lemonade. He was surprised to see it was a woman Joe had dated. They had met briefly, and he remembered thinking her nice-looking and intelligent.

"I've got a million things to do," his mother said and left Jack alone with his visitor.

"Welcome back, Jack," the young lady said, coming over to him on the couch and touching his hand. "I know you had quite a time over there, and I'm just glad you got back safely. Hopefully Joe will too."

"Yes, I'm worried about him." He thought of his brother and the large number of men in Joe's squadron who had been shot down piloting B-24 bombers on anti-submarine patrols over the English Channel and the North Sea. Eligible to come home after flying his quota of missions, Joe, like Jack, instead recruited a crew to volunteer for another ten missions.

They talked a while longer, then as she was leaving, she gave him a kiss on the cheek. "I'd like to welcome you home properly some other time—if you know what I mean. You did a lot for our country. Saving your men and everything. I'd like to give back something in return." She winked. "Give me a call."

Two days later, Jack did just that, and the result, despite his tender back, was an enjoyable romp at her house.

BECOMING JFK

In early August, Jack received a letter from Joe. He had learned of the encounter.

> *I understood that we had an unwritten agreement event sent since the affaire Cawley, that we would not meddle. How about it?*

Jack considered whether he had violated the brothers' agreement not to pursue women who Joe dated. After Joe had made moves on Olive Cawley several years earlier, they'd argued, and Joe had agreed to back off. But he hadn't gone after this woman, Jack rationalized. She had offered herself. That was different.

Jack read on. His brother had read Hersey's story and complimented his bravery but questioned his decision-making before the collision.

> *Where the hell were you when the destroyer came into sight, what exactly were your moves then, and where the hell was your radar?*

Like everybody who wasn't there, it was easy for Joe to question Jack's actions, but it stung. Jack thought about defending himself, but he didn't want to get into a back-and-forth in letters. Perhaps they'd talk about it when Joe returned.

He never got the chance.

A few days later, while convalescing at Chelsea Hospital, Jack received word that Joe's plane had exploded during a bombing mission. Jack rushed back to Hyannis Port to be with his grieving family.

His mother greeted him with a distant smile. Affection and warmth, even in times of tragedy, was not in her DNA. "Hello, Jack."

They never got closer than five yards.

"Hello, Mother."

His brothers and sisters sat forlornly in the sun room. They rushed to him for a group hug. His sister Jean, sixteen, dried her tears on his jacket and said, "Jack, why did it have to happen?"

"I don't know, Jean. It just did."

His father was upstairs, secluded since hearing the news. He'd made only a brief appearance to tell his children of the tragedy.

"Joe wouldn't want us to sit here crying," Jack said to Teddy. "Let's go sailing."

Jack and Ted walked to the Hyannis Port Yacht Club. They silently prepared the *Victura*, and then swung it out into the Sound. Jack thought about the many times he and Joe had sailed this same boat competing in the Edgartown Regatta, among many others. They'd been a good team, cooperating for the most part, enjoying the challenge of taking on more experienced sailors. Now, Joe was gone forever.

"Do you think Joe will come back?" asked Teddy.

Jack wasn't sure if Teddy had digested the news about Joe being presumed lost and was perhaps thinking there was a glimmer of hope.

"No, he's gone, Teddy. We might as well get used to it."

After an abbreviated sail, they docked and made the short walk home. "I'll see you later, Teddy," Jack said when they arrived. He veered towards the water. A flood of memories came back to him, some bittersweet.

Once, when they were very young, he and Joe had bicycled around the block in opposite directions, slamming into each other when neither yielded. Jack needed twenty-eight stitches, but Joe didn't have a scratch.

Joe was the standard to which he had compared himself during their early years. With girls, with athletics, and with academics. Most of the time he didn't think he could measure up, so he went his own lazy, ineffectual way. Nothing bugged him more than being compared to Joe, the Golden Boy.

BECOMING JFK

He picked up a small rock and heaved it into the water. His father had wanted Joe to be the first Catholic president. When their father wasn't home, which was often, Joe became a surrogate father. Jack remembered Joe's wide grin that could quickly turn ugly. Hot-tempered, Joe was only too happy to engage in fisticuffs, and could even be a bully sometimes.

Jack sat on the sand and faced the water. In the last few years, Jack knew he had surpassed Joe. There was his globe-trotting journey compiling information for the ambassador, and his father choosing his counsel, not Joe's, on how to remake his reputation after resigning. There was also his book. He'd eclipsed Joe in military rank and in stature based on medals awarded and national acclaim he'd received after the PT-109 episode.

A few days later, Jack drove to Boston's Logan Airport to pick up Kick, who'd flown in from England. In May, she'd defied her parents and married a Protestant Englishman in London, and Joe had been the only Kennedy in attendance.

Jack saw her coming down the runway. She was wearing a robin's egg blue American Red Cross summer uniform.

She flew into his arms. "Oh, Jack," she cried, and wept on his shoulder.

Jack held her tight.

After Kick composed herself, they walked arm in arm to the car, ignoring the crowd of onlookers and media. They stopped at a church in Hyannis Port before going home.

"Jack, are you all right?" Kick blurted out as he drove home. She was shocked at how gaunt he looked—his cheek and jaw points were sticking out. She also noticed how yellow his skin was. "Has the navy been starving you? What do you weigh—a hundred and twenty-five pounds?"

"Oh, more than that, Kick." But not much more. "It's been a rough couple of years."

"Do me a favor, Jack? Do it for me."

"What's that?"

"Take care of yourself. I couldn't handle losing another brother."

"Okay," Jack said solemnly. "I'll do my best."

As he was walking by his father's office a few days later, Jack heard his father wailing. He couldn't help but listen. "He didn't have to go on that last mission!" he heard Joe Sr. say on the telephone. "He was eligible to come home," his father sobbed. "Oh, God: Why!"

I guess sometimes Kennedys do cry, thought Jack.

Jack sought further details about what had happened. He telephoned his old contacts at navy intelligence and found out Joe had volunteered for a near-suicidal mission. He was piloting an aircraft packed with explosives. He was supposed to bail out, after which the flying bomb would be guided to German V-rocket sites in Calais that were targeting London. But a malfunction occurred before he was able to parachute to safety, and the plane exploded.

Jack wondered why Joe had volunteered for such a dangerous mission. Perhaps, jealous of Jack's status as a war hero, he wanted to outdo Jack. If he hadn't received all that fame for his PT-109 adventure, Jack figured, Joe might still be alive.

More grief was to come less than a month later. Kick's husband was killed by a sniper.

While at the hospital for a check-up, Jack jotted down his recollections of Joe. Now that Joe was dead, he was just a memory, but Jack decided he wanted to do something to memorialize his brother. Perhaps some sort of scrapbook or written work to honor Joe. But he didn't want it to be only his recollections. Jack began contacting and interviewing Joe's old roommates, his valet, his former teachers and professors, his chaplain and commanding officer—even his last mistress.

Chapter 35

Jack sat outside by the pool enjoying the balmy Palm Beach weather. Although the war wasn't over quite yet, Jack was eager to begin a new chapter of his life. It had been three and a half years since he'd enlisted, then served in military intelligence. There had been Inga. Then the PT-109 catastrophe and aftermath. On March 1, 1945, he detached from military service due to injuries sustained during the war. Now he had the freedom of choice, although he wasn't sure what to do with it. But his father had plans.

"Jack," his father said, sitting down opposite him, "there's an opportunity that I think you'll want to take advantage of. It's not immediate, but I want you to start preparing. Curley isn't going to run for re-election in the Eleventh District."

"He won't?"

"No. He'll be running for mayor again next year. It's in his best interests."

Jack recalled the then-mayor's appearance at the Old Howard during his Harvard days a decade earlier. Since then, Curley had been found guilty of fraud charges. and required to pay $42,000 in penalties.

"I've helped him with his financial problems," Kennedy Sr. said. "In return, he'll vacate his Congressional seat and run for mayor again. That means an opening for you. There will be a special election for the congressional seat."

Jack was stunned by his father's machinations but decided it was best not to know too many of the details. As a Cambridge resident at Harvard, Jack at least had lived in the district. "So," he said, mulling over the possibility, "if I decided to make a go for it, I'd be running in '46."

"That's right. Gives you time to get healthy, do other things to improve your chances. For now, let's keep this between us." He stood up and walked back into the house.

You had to give it to Dad, Jack thought. He didn't waste any time. Jack had been thinking about his next move, but he hadn't expected to seek public office so soon. He wrote to Red Fay:

> *I can feel Pappy's eyes on the back of my neck. I'll be back here with Dad trying to parlay a lost PT boat and a bad back into a political advantage. I tell you, Dad is ready right now and can't understand why Johnny boy isn't all engines ahead full.*

Jack was still adjusting to civilian life, but he began warming to his father's idea for him. When there was an opportunity, you had to grab it. If you didn't, it would almost certainly disappear. He took pen to paper and hinted at his plans to Lem, who was now stationed in the Pacific and headed for Iwo Jima.

> *As I may have told you, I'll go to law school in the fall, and then if something good turns up while I am there, I will run for it. I have my eye on something pretty good now if it comes through.*

Hoping mineral springs would help his back and general health, Jack holed up at Castle Hot Springs. Tucked into the mountains about an hour north of Phoenix, Arizona, it was a semi-private club converted from an air force installation. He shared a bathroom and the phone down the hall.

Feeling unwell, his skin the color of saffron, Jack stumbled down the hallway to use the pay phone outside the bath. Somebody was using it—a guy he'd seen before. He looked about forty, blue-eyed and solidly built.

"I'll be done in a minute," said Pat Lannan.

After Lannan finished his call, he said, "You're Jack Kennedy, aren't you? Heard about your book and the excitement in the Pacific."

"Yes," said Jack, not anxious to talk about himself. "What about you?"

"I'm in business in Chicago, but I'm here recuperating from a bronchial ailment. Hope the desert air does me good."

"Yeah, me too."

The two became friendly over the next couple of days.

"This place is kind of a hole, isn't it?" Lannan said.

"I think we could do better."

For the next several weeks, Jack and his new friend rented a cottage together. Jack busied himself working on his book about Joe, riding horses, and swimming.

They were sitting around the cottage's fireplace late one night when Jack said, "I don't know about you, but I'm ready for something different."

There wasn't much to do at the resort. They packed up for Phoenix and the swanky Biltmore Hotel. But it felt too dressy, so they moved to the Camelback Inn for a few weeks. Every day they rode horses.

"Let's race to that shed," said Jack. He thirsted for competition. They sped off, and Jack had a slight lead when they came to a rocky ravine. Pat slowed down, but Jack took it at full gallop and increased his lead. He couldn't resist going fast.

"Good race, Pat," said Jack, when Pat pulled up a few seconds later. "I enjoyed that."

Later that day, April 12, they received word that President Roosevelt had died. "My father and Roosevelt didn't get along that well," he said to Pat, "but I think Roosevelt was good for the country."

"What would you think of going to Hollywood?" Jack said the next night at dinner. "I could use a little more excitement."

The way Jack looked at it, if things weren't all that good where he was, it was time to go someplace else. No time to waste. Perhaps the feeling had something to do with his ill health. Sometimes he wondered how many days he had left. It occurred to him, before he dismissed the thought, that one of these times he wouldn't recover as he had so many times before. He was never healthy for long. One day his luck might run out.

"I know a few people there," said Pat. "We could have some fun."

They flew to Los Angeles and checked into the Beverly Hills Hotel.

"Look who's here?" said Jack, surprised to see Chuck Spalding when they arrived in the lobby. "What brings you to Hollywood?"

"I've sold my book to Gary Cooper." Cooper was a well-known actor, famous for his roles in *The Pride of the Yankees* and *For Whom the Bell Tolls*. "It's going to be a movie!"

"Congratulations," said Jack.

Pat knew the actor Walter Huston, who was staying in a cottage on the hotel grounds. At lunch, Huston invited them to a daytime cocktail party at the home of the famed British and American actress Olivia de Havilland. Huston mentioned that his son, John, had just broken up with the actress. Maybe I can catch her on the rebound, thought Jack. He'd become enamored of de Havilland after seeing her in *The Adventures of Robin Hood* and *Gone With the Wind*. He couldn't wait to meet her.

At the party, Jack was introduced to the actress and was immediately captivated. Her lips were orange-red, and she was elegantly dressed in a sequin-collared shirt and skirt ensemble. After they'd talked for a while, Jack realized she was smart as well as beautiful.

"I understand you are a free agent," said Jack in something of a double entendre. De Havilland had gone to court in a landmark case and won freedom from her contract with Warner Brothers.

"Yes, I am," she said, not sure if Jack was referring to her relationship with the younger Huston or her contractual status as a film star.

They continued talking, and Jack leaned toward her, fixing her with a stare. Boldly, he asked her out to dinner that evening.

"Well, thank you, but I already have plans," she replied.

"Perhaps you'd like to reschedule them," Jack persisted. "You don't want to miss out on a wonderful evening."

De Havilland looked at him in disbelief. "No, I don't think so." She walked away.

Jack made a final overture, but she refused again. When he and his friends got up to leave, Jack still couldn't take his eyes off de Havilland. Jack bid her goodbye and opened the door to leave. But he'd mistakenly opened a hall closet. Tennis racquets, balls, and clothes came crashing down on him. As he picked himself off the floor, Jack held up a racquet and said to the tittering crowd, "Tennis anyone?"

At dinner that night at the Beverly Hills Hotel, Jack was surprised to see de Havilland dining with the frumpy, middle-aged writer Ludwig Bemelmans, famous for the *Madeline* children's picture book series. Jack made eye contact with de Havilland, but all she offered was a half-hearted wave. Jack was bewildered.

"I just can't understand it," he remarked to his buddies. "Just look at that guy! I know he's talented. I know he's got great ability, but really! Do you think it was my walking into the closet that did it?" He couldn't fathom losing out to this old guy.

"Maybe you'll have better luck tomorrow," said Chuck. "You can come along to Cooper's party."

Cooper's house was protected by wrought iron gates. An electric eye opened the entryway and simultaneously illuminated the grounds, pool, and house.

"Coop has rolled out the red carpet for you," Jack quipped. Soon he noticed a familiar face. "It's nice to see you again."

"Yes, we didn't have much chance to chat last time," said Sonja Henie. "At the Stork Club, wasn't it?"

"Yes. We had a dance."

When Sonja raised her pencil-thin eyebrows and asked if he knew she'd met his father during his movie business days, Jack had little doubt the two had crossed paths in more ways than one. He didn't need to make the first move—she made it for him, suggesting they continue their conversation back at her place.

"My husband won't be back for a while," she said casually.

Jack remembered her husband was Dan Topping, owner of the New York Yankees. "Oh, that's convenient. How long do we have? A couple of hours?"

"More than that," she replied with a sly smile. "He's on duty in the Pacific."

When they arrived at Henie's home, Jack wasted no time. He unhooked her bra, admiring her toned, athletic figure.

Afterward, as they lay together, Jack broke the silence. "Tell me about Hitler. I heard you gave him the Nazi salute. What was he like?"

As with Inga, Jack found himself entangled with yet another Scandinavian woman who'd raised her arm to Hitler. Sonja nodded, unperturbed by the question.

"Oh, so you know about that. Yes, I saluted him during the 1936 Olympics—the same ones where he hosted Inga in his private box. I even had lunch with him at his retreat in the Bavarian Alps. He was quite the gentleman. Never laid a hand on me."

Jack smirked inwardly. Hitler seemed to have a thing for stunning women, but clearly lacked interest in taking things further.

"Of course," Sonja added, her tone sharpening, "once he invaded Norway, my feelings changed. I want him to burn in hell."

Jack nodded. "Hopefully, he will."

Jack's father learned about his tryst with Henie. He seemed to have eyes everywhere. During a nightly chat on the telephone, Joe Sr. said quietly, "Jack, I suggest you drop her at once. It's the Nazi thing. It can't be good for you. Or the family." There was a pause. "What do you think?"

"I was going to." That wasn't true. He had no timetable to end the affair. But he didn't want his father to know that. Or that he was right. "She's not my type of gal."

Chapter 36

On the way home from California in late April 1945, Jack flew to the Mayo Clinic to see whether another back operation was necessary. He had barely checked into his room when he was handed a cable. At the behest of Jack's father, Louis Ruppel, the executive editor of the Hearst-owned *Chicago Herald-American*, wanted Jack to go back to San Francisco and report on the impending creation of the United Nations.

Jack realized this would be a fantastic opportunity to mix with high-ranking officials and see first-hand how the fledgling United Nations would work, or if it could work. He had his doubts that the world's leaders would apply themselves to limit conflict.

"I want your dispatches to come from the point of view of the ordinary GI," said Ruppel by phone.

"I wasn't a GI, but if you'll accept the copy of a navy man, then I'm ready to go."

Relieved that another back operation wasn't immediately necessary, Jack flew to San Francisco and checked into the Palace Hotel on Market Street on April 25. He also secured a room at the hotel for Chuck Spalding and his new wife.

San Francisco had been invaded by five thousand people, including delegates from forty-six countries, advisors, dignitaries, and more than twenty-six hundred media. In addition, returning GIs were everywhere.

The next morning, after breakfast in the hotel's historic glass-domed atrium, Jack walked west on Market Street. He was eager to get to work, but first he needed to acquire his journalist's credentials. Jack headed to the press room at the Fairmont Hotel on Nob Hill, but he could see some sort of commotion ahead. A pack of brawny, mean-looking bodyguards coming in the opposite direction forced him to get out of the way. They were guarding the grim-faced Soviet foreign minister Vyacheslav Molotov, who ignored reporters trying to get a comment.

To Jack, the incident hinted at further tension between Russia and the United States. Already Molotov had ignited a controversy by objecting to a motion naming U.S. Secretary of State Edward Stettinius as president of the conference. Molotov demanded that the four sponsors of the conference (United States, USSR, United Kingdom, and China) be named rotating co-presidents. A compromise was reached.

After walking a couple of blocks and enjoying the cool spring air, Jack boarded the cable car at the Powell and Market turnaround. He stood on the running board and held onto the pole. The conductor rang the bell, and the cable car lurched forward. After passing Union Square, it began its ascent toward Nob Hill. Jack hopped off at California Street and made his way into the hotel.

The press room on the fourth floor was jammed with newspapermen filing stories. The air was thick with tobacco smoke, but through it he was surprised to see the portly director of *Citizen Kane*, Orson Welles, and actors Lana Turner and Rita Hayworth sporting press credentials. While receiving his full access badge, the press coordinator warned him that reporters could talk to decision-makers, but they were prohibited from attribution.

Jack returned to the Palace Hotel and attended an off-the-record talk with the U.S. Ambassador to the USSR, Averill Harriman. Harriman was worried U.S. journalists were not being tough enough on the Soviets for violating the Yalta accords and their intention to control Eastern Europe.

"We must recognize that our objectives and the Kremlin's objectives are irreconcilable," said Harriman, adding that the two countries would have to find ways of mediating differences in order to "live without war on this small planet."

Jack's first story ran in the April 28 edition. Above it was his picture, byline, and identification as "a PT-boat hero of the South Pacific and son of former Ambassador Joseph P. Kennedy." When he got a copy, Jack ran over to Spalding's suite and pounded on the door.

"Hey, Charlie, I got something to show you! Open up!" When Spalding opened the door, Jack thrust the newspaper at him. "Hey, what do you think?"

"You got quite a spread there, Jack."

Even though Jack was excited about seeing his name in print, his commentary about the conference was less enthusiastic. "There is an impression that this is the conference to end wars and introduce peace on earth and good-will towards nations—excluding, of course, Germany and Japan. Well, it's not going to do that," he wrote.

He went on to warn of coming friction with the Soviets. Citing the Molotov controversy, Jack wrote: "The Russians are going to make a fight on all of the little issues in the hope that they can write their own terms on the big ones."

San Francisco was awash in cocktail parties and press soirées, and Jack made a point of going to as many as he could. But he took the mornings off to rally his health before heading out to attend briefings and press conferences, and to interview sources.

After writing and filing his stories, Jack was eager to pursue the nightlife. Dressed for a black-tie evening, he relaxed on his bed, shoes off, propped up by three pillows, a drink in one hand and phone in the other. He was talking with Ruppel about his assignments when Spalding entered.

After hanging up, Jack said, "Charlie, I've been thinking a lot about what I'm going to do. I've made up my mind—I'm going into politics."

"Geez, Jack, that's terrific! You can go all the way!"

"Really?"

"All the way!"

Jack was pleased and energized by Spalding's fervent support. It was important to Jack that somebody besides his father believed in him. Here was a friend, yes, but also a man whose judgment and character he respected.

That evening, Jack didn't have to go far to find entertainment. The Palace was hosting a cocktail party. Jack stood by a fountain banked by a mass of vivid red flowers while he renewed acquaintances with Arthur Krock. He noticed an attractive young woman waltzing with the much older Anthony Eden, Britain's chief delegate.

When the dance ended, Jack said, "Pardon me, Arthur, but I think Eden's gal could use a different partner."

He tapped Eden on his shoulder, put his arm around the woman's waist, and waltzed her away from a perturbed Eden.

"I hope I didn't interrupt anything," said Jack.

"You did," she said. "He's a very important person that I'd like to get to know."

When their dance ended, Jack felt a tap on his shoulder. "Sorry, old boy." He was surprised to see the mustachioed Eden cutting in on him. The woman was happy to see Eden return. Cutting in on the person who had cut in on you was poor etiquette, and they both knew it, but Eden didn't like being topped.

Later that night, Jack brought Red Fay, who lived nearby, to dinner with Harriman and Charles (Chip) Bohlen, special assistant to the U.S. secretary of state. The talk revolved almost completely around how the United States would counteract Soviet efforts in Eastern Europe. Jack found it stimulating to converse with high-level politicians. Afterwards, they gathered in Jack's suite. He had invited a woman he'd met at the cocktail party to join them. He was heartily engaged in political discussion with Bohlen and Fay, until he saw Harriman, twenty-five years Jack's senior, wrap his arms around that same woman out on the balcony.

"I don't care if he is the ambassador," Jack said to Red. "He's not going to get away with this." He bolted for the balcony. "Excuse me, Ambassador. C'mon in," Jack said, motioning to the woman.

"It's all right, Jack," said Harriman.

"No, I want you to hear this. I'm finding Ambassador Harriman quite interesting," said the woman, who turned back to Harriman. He smiled triumphantly.

Jack now understood. Harriman, and Eden earlier, had higher political status than he did. He was just a lowly reporter. This wasn't Hollywood, where he'd found success among women. Looks and personality didn't count that much here. Women were drawn to political power—of which he had none.

It was becoming clear that the United States and the Soviet Union were going to be the world's new superpowers. The Russian delegation, led by Molotov and Andrei Gromyko, the Soviet ambassador to the United States, dug in their heels over any negotiation with the West. Based on his talks with Harriman, Bohlen, and others, Jack wrote, "There is growing discouragement among people concerning our chances of winning any lasting peace from this war. There is talk of fighting the Russians in the next ten or fifteen years."

Jack was dismayed by the veto power granted to the five major powers on the Security Council. In a commentary, he said, "Thus, any of the Big Five can effectively veto assistance to an attacked nation. With this grave weakness, it is little wonder that the smaller countries have attempted to make treaties with their neighbors for protection against aggressors."

At the midway point of the conference, Jack again considered the prospects of the United Nations. When he returned to his hotel after a busy day, Jack took out his notebook and jotted this down:

> *Danger of too great a build-up. Mustn't expect too much. A truly just solution will leave every nation somewhat disappointed. There is no cure-all.*

He went to his typewriter and started writing a commentary that would say the United Nations would be "merely a skeleton. Its powers will be limited."

By the close of the conference, he'd completed sixteen commentaries. Jack was generally pleased with his journalistic effort, despite a note from Bobby. He laughed when he read his younger brother's comment:

> *Everyone thinks you're doing a simply fine job out there except Mother, who was a little upset that you still mixed 'who' and 'whom' up.*

The conference ended June 26, with fifty nations signing a charter formally creating the United Nations. On the same day, Jack boarded a flight back east. The Hearst conglomerate was pleased with his work and assigned him to cover the elections in Britain. Prime Minister Winston Churchill was in the midst of a fierce fight to hold on to power. But first, Jack planned to spend a few days in Hyannis.

On the flight home, Jack considered his satisfaction with journalism and writing. He enjoyed writing because it helped him determine his views. At the conference, he valued having intense and educational discussions with people from all walks of life. But he didn't want to be a full-time observer. In San Francisco, he hadn't been the one making decisions, offering suggestions, debating the issues—and that ultimately was what he wanted to do. But writing could be an important adjunct to a public life and add substance to his views.

He looked forward to writing his memoir about Joe. He'd never before written anything so personal for publication.

After greeting his family, Jack stared at the 360 maroon boxes laid out before him in the sun room. Inside each box was a copy of his seventy-five-page book, *As We Remember Joe*. He had written the foreword and lead essay, plus edited contributors' recollections. His father planned to distribute the book to friends, colleagues, and those who had served with Joe in the military.

Jack took one copy out of a box and opened it to his concluding observation: "If the Kennedy children amount to anything, now or ever, it will be due more to Joe's behavior and constant example than to any other factor."

His father entered the room. "You did a nice job on this, Jack," he said, picking up the book. He glanced at a few pages. "You'll forgive me if I don't read it immediately." His voice wavered, and he looked down. "Too soon."

Jack nodded. Rarely had he seen his father show his emotions. They had that in common.

The elder Kennedy put down the book. "Jack, I'm proud of your work in San Francisco. I think people will be interested in hearing and seeing you talk about it. I've arranged for you to give a short address at the State House here. Just a few remarks, but the papers will certainly cover it."

The wheels were turning. But while he was grateful for his father's support, Jack began to think about how he'd manage his political future. His father had his back, but Jack sensed there'd be times ahead when he'd have to tell his father to back off. He didn't want him pulling all the strings.

The occasion at the State House was Jack's first time speaking before a chamber of elected officials. He ran a hand through his hair, smiled, and thanked the body for the opportunity to address it. Yet he wasn't the least bit nervous.

In his speech, he hinted at his doubts about the San Francisco conference. "It was the best we can get and deserves the support we can give." The stimulation of making direct contact with a political audience had been satisfying; he had noticed nods of agreement and enthusiastic applause. You could move people in different ways, he reflected afterwards, but speaking, rather than writing, was the most direct way to be influential.

He would do his best to become adept at both.

Chapter 37

It was July 4, 1945, and they were on the way to a Churchill campaign stop at Walthamstow Greyhound Stadium in East London, where Churchill would launch his re-election campaign. The war in Europe had ended the previous month. It had begun to rain in London, and the wipers, among other things, worked only intermittently. Jack, Pat Lannan, and Kick were crammed into her small Austin-Healey.

Jack had been following events from San Francisco and in his last report cautioned: "The British Labor Party is out for blood. They are going all the way: Public ownership of the Bank of England, government control of rents and prices, gradual government ownership of mines, transportation, planned farming—the works. While everybody knows Churchill's strengths, they are not sure that he can buck the recent strong surge to the left."

Between the words "Walthamstow" and "Stadium," a huge black greyhound in full sprint embellished the entrance. There were betting buildings everywhere, but Jack didn't think he'd bet on Churchill. The previous month he'd made a speech comparing the Labour Party to the Gestapo. The trio took seats in the grandstand. Jack guessed there were about twenty thousand in attendance.

It soon became apparent that many were opposed to Churchill. Using his hat as a shield from the sun, Churchill tried his best to deal with a restive crowd, which booed him relentlessly. Jack was appalled at the treatment that Britons gave Churchill, this man who had heroically guided his country through the war. Next to him, several young people shook their fists and took up the chant, "We want Labour!"

Churchill was unperturbed and showed no anger. But he couldn't resist calling them the "booing party." How quickly people forget, mused Jack, or at least want something different. Politics was a strange business.

Jack wrote in his diary each night. Then, using a small manual typewriter, he put down his observations and thoughts and assembled them in a loose-leaf binder. Concluding that Britons wanted something different than "toil and sweat" after the hardships of the war, Jack was convinced that its citizens wanted no part of tightening their belts.

While covering the short British election, Jack was surprised to be contacted by his brother's former mistress, Patricia Wilson. She lived about an hour from London. They'd never met, but Kick had told Jack about Joe's affair with her.

"Jack," she said by phone, "I have some things of Joe's I'd like to give back to you. Besides, I'd like to meet the brother of the man I loved. I think Joe would have wanted us to. Would you be able to stop by?"

After tea and sharing stories about Joe, Wilson moved closer to Jack on the couch. "Thank you for coming, Jack. It means a lot to me."

They locked eyes.

"Well?" said Wilson. She put her hand on his leg.

Minutes later, they were in Wilson's bedroom.

Afterward, Jack wondered why two of Joe's women had tried to seduce him. Both times, it had been totally unexpected. Since they couldn't have Joe, they'd take him. He was the next closest thing.

While England was in the process of determining its future leadership, Jack made for Ireland on July 24 for a two-day visit. He stayed at the

American Legation property on the grounds of Dublin's vast Phoenix Park. After stowing his trunk in his suite on the upper floor, Jack headed for downtown. He stopped at the venerable Bewley's Grafton Street café for tea, then wandered around Dublin. He noticed there were few cars and that most people here either walked or rode their bicycles. Petrol was hard to get. The streets were scrupulously clean. The famous Irish doors were freshly painted and the brass shining.

The next day, Jack arrived at the neoclassical white mansion called President's Residence. He was there to interview the Irish prime minister

"Nice to see you again, Jack," said Eamon de Valera. He came out from behind a large wooden desk to shake hands. The stern de Valera wore glasses and had a protruding nose. He was a friend of Jack's father, whom Jack had met in 1938 in Italy at the investiture of Pope Pius XII.

In 1921, De Valera had declared Ireland a republic, but if it was, how could it also be a member of the British Commonwealth? Ireland's neutrality during the war and its refusal to allow the Commonwealth to use bases in Ireland for military purposes had exacerbated the situation.

"Jack," said de Valera in response to his question regarding the future of Ireland, "we are fighting the same battle we fought during the uprising of 1916 in the war of independence and later in the civil war. The only settlement we will accept is a free and independent Ireland, free to go where it will be the master of its own destiny."

Jack nodded. "In the north, Sir Basil Brooke, head of the government of Ulster, has said that he will not give up an inch of the six counties to unite Ireland. How do you respond to his position?"

"Quite simply, Jack." He pounded his fist on the desk. "From our present position, we will not retreat an inch."

In his dispatch, Jack noted that the government of the north in Ulster "roared down to the gentlemen in Dublin that 'not an inch' will be given up of the six counties. And in the south, de Valera hurled back the challenge that from his present position he will retreat 'not an inch.' As of this weekend, the problem of partition seems very far from being solved."

The visit to Ireland, although short, made a strong impression on Jack. It was the land of his ancestors and so a part of him. Jack compiled nine pages of notes regarding his visit. The words poured out of him.

The next day, David Gray, the American minister to Ireland, announced what Jack had predicted. "Churchill is finished," he said at a meeting of the legation that Jack attended. "Labour has won a resounding victory."

Jack continued to file reports, but he realized American interest in the British election wasn't as strong as his. His last story went unpublished, but he had other plans. He'd been invited by Navy Secretary James Forrestal to tour Germany.

Jack joined Forrestal on his C-54 plane on July 28 for a trip to Berlin for the Potsdam Conference. There, the heads of the big three allies—the English, the Americans, and the Soviets—would attempt to stamp their imprint on the fate of Europe. Berlin was now divided into four separate zones—English, American, French, and Soviet.

Forrestal was a small, fierce, thin-lipped man who rarely smiled. Fingering his bow tie, he said, "Consider the navy, Jack. I see a bright future for you. You served your country and the navy with distinction in the Pacific. You did a great job helping to save your crew." Forrestal leaned forward and tapped Jack's shoulder. "I was very impressed when I heard about that."

"Thank you, sir," said Jack. "The navy is certainly one of the options I'm thinking about."

"You're going to see a country that has been totally devastated," he warned Jack before touching down in Germany. "And you'll see it up close. You may find it shocking."

Jack looked down on the bombed-out landscape. The rural areas appeared unscathed, but all German cities all had the same ash gray color—the color of churned-up powdered stone and brick. There were endless gaping plots of land, buildings of which only a skeleton remained. The railroad centers were especially badly hit, but the rural areas had been spared, and the fields appeared to be fully worked.

"They are desperate people," said Forrestal. "Especially the women. They are just trying to survive. The cities are almost completely made up of women—either young or old. Only a few old men."

After landing in Berlin, they drove to Potsdam for a conference that would decide the fate of Germany. Truman would be joined by Stalin, and by Clement Atlee, who had replaced Churchill. For miles on both sides of the road, Russian soldiers were stationed at 40-yard intervals. The green-hatted and green-epauletted soldiers were Soviet Premier Joseph Stalin's personal handpicked guards. Rugged and tough-looking, the unsmiling troops appeared perfectly disciplined.

As they passed, the Russians presented arms in robot-like fashion, ending with their rifles to the center of their chests. The Russians were here, they weren't going anywhere, and they wanted you to know it.

The convoy arrived at President Truman's elegant villa in Babelsberg, surrounded by MPs standing at attention. Immaculate grounds separated it from the Havel River. Plain-clothes Secret Service guarded the immediate exterior.

The bespectacled Truman came down the steps and greeted Forrestal. As they talked, Jack was astonished to see Forrestal stiffen, then cross his arms. The short conversation ended, and Forrestal stalked back to the car and slammed the door.

"Son of a bitch," he sneered. "Apparently, the secretary of the navy and head of the largest navy in the world isn't worthy of participating in the conference. Screw Truman. We'll do our own tour to see what's happened. You up for it, Jack?"

"Of course," said Jack, surprised at the vitriol Forrestal had unleashed on the president.

They hopped back into the car. Forrestal muttered and swore intermittently. He told the driver to go to Berlin. An hour later, they passed the Excelsior Hotel. Jack remembered staying there only a week before war broke out in 1939. Now, it was in ruins.

Jack got out of the car and joined an examination of Hitler's Reich Chancellery. He imagined the German dictator presiding over military meetings at which plans were hatched to disrupt the entire world. How do you stop the madmen of the future? Jack wondered.

Two guides, one a Russian captain and the other a Russian-speaking American first lieutenant, led the tour of the Chancellery.

"Do you ever have political conversations with the Russian captain?" Jack asked.

"No," the American said. "There had been a few incidents where Americans began explaining what our democratic republic system was, but after the Russians in the higher echelon discovered it, such conversations ceased."

Only a shell of the Chancellery remained. The walls were chipped and seared by bullets and scorched by fire, an indication of the fierce fighting before the Russians had captured it. Jack walked down about 120 feet to Hitler's air raid shelter. A basement full of junk and discarded furniture, it resembled a shelter he'd seen at a friend's house in Hyannis. Electronic equipment and overturned chairs littered the floor. Stuffing protruded from a dilapidated couch. The dictator was supposed to have met his death here, but the Russian captain said there is no complete evidence proving that the body found was Hitler's. According to him, the Russians believe Hitler is still alive. Was it possible, wondered Jack, that Hitler had escaped? The Russian army had been the first to arrive in Berlin.

Emerging into the sunlight, Jack put on his sunglasses, straightened his pinstriped suit, and linked up behind Forrestal to tour the ravaged city. Forrestal, in hat, bow tie, and jacket, led the procession of military brass that also included Averill Harriman and Charles Bohlen.

They walked the completely devastated Unter den Linden. Jack recalled the government buildings, hotels, the Reichstag, and Imperial Theatre from previous visits. All of that was gone now. The Allied bombing had been very effective. Little remained, and every building was gutted. Mounds of rubble were everywhere. Bodies lay strewn on the street. Jack was forced to cover his nose—the stench from the corpses, sweet and sickish, was overwhelming.

Jack was close enough to see the survivors' yellow-tinged faces and pale tan lips. Most were children under fifteen or older women, and almost all were carrying bundles of their belongings. He wondered where they had been going. Did they even know?

Farther down the street, Jack chatted with an American officer. He learned the survivors slept in cellars and that the women would do anything for food. Rape was commonplace. Only a few women wore lipstick, Jack noted. Maybe they didn't have any, or maybe they were trying to make themselves as unattractive as possible to the Russian soldiers.

As they walked, Jack noticed a dark-haired, grim-faced young woman in a shabby gray coat watching the procession. He peeled away and put his sunglasses in his jacket pocket. "*Entschuldigen Sie, bitte,*" he said.

Her face was gaunt and her hair unkempt, but she gave him a hint of a smile. "Yes, hallo. Are you American?"

BECOMING JFK

Pleasantly surprised to find an English-speaker, he chatted with her for a few minutes before Forrestal and his party began to move on. "I will come back later today and bring you food."

"Thank you," she said appreciatively. "I will be here. Where else would I go?"

After the tour, Jack visited the military store, claiming Forrestal and his aides were hungry. He stuffed as much as he could into a knapsack. When he returned to the place where he'd met the woman, she was sitting on a crag of rubble. He handed everything to her and sat down. He remained silent as she ate ravenously. When she was done, he asked what it was like at the beginning of the war.

"I thought our country was going to win the war, but the first victories were just shiny," she said.

"What about during the war?" Jack asked. "What were you doing?"

"I had just finished my secondary school education. So I could go to university, I had to do the Reich Labor Service for six months." She said she assisted frontline troops with food and ammunition and helped repair damaged roads. "The work was very hard. We worked about seventy or eighty hours a week."

"I don't know how you did it. After you finished your service, what happened?"

"I returned to university, but as the war turned worse, I was sent to the Western front. I was part of a crew that would shine a big search light at night," she said, pointing to the sky. "Show the enemy planes so they could be shot down."

Jack wasn't surprised that Germany had used all its available resources to stem the tide. "When did you think the war was turning against Germany?"

"One day in 1942, I saw American planes coming over. I knew then that the war was lost. My brother was killed on the Eastern front, and my fiancé is a prisoner of war in Italy." She looked down. "I don't know if I'll ever see him again."

"I hope you'll be together again. What happened when the Russians took over Berlin? How have you survived?"

The woman's hands shook. "I was scared because I'd seen them shoot women who refused to hand over their jewelry or lie down for them. They came for us. I thought I was dead when they took my two sisters and me down to the cellar. My clothes were taken off. We gave them all our rings. We cried and pleaded for them not to kill us."

When she began to sob, Jack put his arm around her. He felt the urge to lie with her, but was ashamed, torn between offering solace and a sexual urge.

"What happened then?" he said.

The woman stood up. "I waved a bottle of wine," she continued, violently swinging a bottle at Jack as though he was Russian. "They let us go untouched."

He could believe that no Russian would want to rape her after her demonstration. "You're very lucky. Why do you think they let you go?"

"They saw the Holy Mother's picture and the crucifix. One of them said, 'You must be against Nazis if you're Catholic.'"

Jack was astonished that her Roman Catholic religion had saved her life.

"I think Russia and the United States will fight soon. But only when Russia is ready. They know your equipment is far superior. And it will be the ruin of Germany, for it would be the common battleground," she said.

"I hope you are wrong, but you may be right," Jack said. "What will you do now?"

"Try to stay alive. I sleep in a cellar over there," she said, pointing to a bombed-out building. "My sisters are with Russian soldiers. I do not see them much. It is a choice they made. Perhaps it is the right one. I could not do that—not yet."

Jack didn't know what to say. "Good luck to you. I'll bring you more food tomorrow."

"*Danke.*"

Jack returned the next day to the cellar. A mattress was tucked away in a corner. Clothes were arranged neatly in piles on wooden slats. A lone pansy drooped from a broken bottle. They sat on crates.

The woman devoured the army rations, eating more slowly than the day before. She wore the same coat, but had on a different skirt. Her hair had been brushed, and she had applied lipstick. In between bites, she offered a shy smile.

"What will you do after you leave and go back to America?" she asked.

"I'm going to work in government. Next year, I plan to run for office." It felt good to say it.

"Why?"

"My older brother was going to try to be president of the United States. My father, who was ambassador to England, had it all planned. But Joe was killed last year in a bombing mission."

"I'm sorry. We both have lost brothers. It's terrible." After a long silence, she asked, "So you are going to be—how do you say—*a politiker*?"

"Yes. Now, it's up to me."

"Is it something you want to do?"

"Yes."

"Why?"

"It's interesting work, and I think I can make a contribution."

As Jack emerged into the sunlight, he saw three American soldiers watching a Russian soldier stroll by with his arm around a German woman.

Before Jack left this part of Germany, he interviewed the chief of the American military government in Berlin, who said the Russians had denied American entry for several days so they could continue looting the city. Pierre Russ, chief of the International News Service bureau of Berlin, told him the Russians moved in with such violence at the beginning—stripping factories and raping women—that they alienated German members of the Communist Party, which had strength in German factories.

There was no doubt that the Russians had gained an advantage over the United States in terms of political indoctrination in their sector. They had opened schools and published papers—none of which the United States had accomplished. The United States didn't seem to have a definitive policy, but Jack felt that the Russians had a long way to go before they could erase the first terrible impressions they had made on Berliners. Maybe the Russians didn't care. They just wanted to get even.

Although Jack had plenty to write about, he was prohibited from sending dispatches on behalf of the Hearst newspapers because he was Forrestal's guest. His diary would have to be his personal report.

On July 30, he joined Forrestal and his staff for a tour of German ports and cities, including Bremen, Bremerhaven, and Frankfurt. In Frankfurt, Jack followed behind Forrestal on the tarmac as he met with Supreme Commander General Eisenhower.

They drove to Eisenhower's command center, where the general gave a summary of the situation regarding the Soviets. Impressed by Eisenhower, Jack wrote in his notes, "It was obvious why he is an outstanding figure. He has an easy personality, immense self-assurance, and gave an excellent presentation of the situation in Germany."

From Frankfurt, they flew to Salzburg on August 1 and then drove to the mountain town of Berchtesgaden in southern Germany. Jack noted the people in the town seemed well-fed and healthy and that there was no bomb damage.

When they arrived at the elegant inn where they'd stay before visiting Hitler's Eagle's Nest mountain retreat the next day, Forrestal said, "Jack, since this is the end of the trip and we're going back tomorrow, I've arranged for a special dinner tonight. We're going to enjoy ourselves."

The large party dined at the former headquarters of a German general. Underneath it, he was told, were six miles of corridors.

"Come join us," said Forrestal, motioning for Jack to sit down with several others. "I hope you have found the trip interesting as well as informative. I know I have. Any thoughts you might have about the post-war world?"

"There is no doubt in my mind that we can expect a long and difficult struggle with the Russians and Communism as a whole. I think the challenges of that will dominate our foreign affairs for many years to come."

"I agree," said Forrestal.

"Regarding the situation here, I don't think the Russians are ever going to pull out of their zone of occupation, and they plan to make their part of Germany a Soviet Socialist Republic. If we don't withdraw and allow the Germans to administer their own affairs, we will be confronted with an extremely difficult administrative problem. Yet, if we pull out, we may leave a political vacuum that the Russians will only be glad to fill."

Accompanied by Rhine wines and champagne, platters of gourmet dishes arrived. First, cured meats, followed by potato soup, various sausage and schnitzel dishes, boiled beef in a broth of vegetables and spices, flavored dumplings, cheesy noodles, and potato salad. The feast ended with a Sachertorte dessert.

Cigars were passed out after dinner. An occasional cigar smoker, Jack plucked one from the box. The inside cover said "Reichsmarschall Hermann Göring." A military attaché said, "These were in Göring's railcar when we caught him. He won't be needing them."

Jack unwrapped the cigar, bit off the end, and lit up. "These are quite good," he said, sounding a bit surprised.

They drove up to the Eagle's Nest on the morning of August 2. The road was covered with solid rock and cleverly camouflaged. On arrival at the top, they drove through a long tunnel carved through the rocks. The party got out of the cars and entered a double-decked elevator—the lower deck had been reserved for the SS.

Hitler's mountain chalet was completely gutted, the result of an air attack by the Royal Air Force in an attempt on Hitler's life. The building was cavernous and empty. It had been stripped of its rugs, pictures, and tapestries. Jack toured the lair, imagining Hitler conducting war operations here. He walked into the living room, which faced out on all sides of the valley below. As he took in the wondrous view, Jack momentarily forgot where he was—the former home of the man who had plunged the world into darkness.

In his room back at the inn, Jack reflected on what he'd seen that day and what history would say about Hitler. The war had only ended for Germany a few months earlier, and information was trickling in about the horrors committed by the regime.

"Hitler will emerge from the hatred that surrounds him now as one of the most significant figures who ever lived," Jack wrote. "He had boundless ambition for his country which rendered him a menace to the peace of the world, but he had a mystery about him in the way that he lived and in the manner of his death that will live and grow after him. He had in him the stuff of which legends are made." Pride before a fall, Jack concluded.

The next day, the party drove back to Salzburg, where Jack joined Forrestal for the flight to London.

"I hope you'll think seriously about a career in the navy," said Forrestal. "There's no doubt you'd be a valuable addition, and I would do everything I could to help you succeed. Will you think about it, Jack?"

"I will." But he had already made up his mind.

Pat Lannan was waiting in the lobby when Jack arrived back at the Grosvenor Hotel in London. "Welcome back, Jack."

"Thanks," said Jack, suddenly feeling weak. "Pat, do me a favor and help get me to my room. It's been a long trip. Feeling a bit feverish."

"Sure, Jack," Lannan said, grabbing Jack's arm. Jack went limp. They barely made it to his room before he collapsed.

"Must be malaria," Jack said, smiling feebly. "Same thing happened in the Pacific."

The fever continued to rise along with shaking and the chills. His clothes were wringing with sweat. Jack spent the next couple of days at the U.S. Naval Dispensary in London.

By August 6, Jack was well enough to fly home aboard Forrestal's plane. While he was in the air, the atomic bomb was dropped on Hiroshima. He'd written an article at the beginning of the year that hadn't been published called "Let's Try an Experiment in Peace" in which he predicted that weapons of mass destruction would soon be in production.

He hadn't thought they'd be used so quickly.

PART SIX
CANDIDATE

Chapter 38

October 1945

In the sun room in Hyannis, Jack read *The Cape Cod Times* review of a speech he had given to the Hyannis Rotary Club. "Listen to what the paper said about my speech," he said to his brother Bobby, now twenty, and recently discharged from the navy.

"The writer said my voice was somewhat scratchy and tensely high-pitched. And that I have an appealing waif-like quality. Just what I need. I've got to fatten up. But it does say the general feeling in the meeting room that day was that Jack Kennedy was going places."

"You will, Jack. And I'll help in any way I can," Bobby said.

"Thanks. Let's throw the ball around." Jack picked up a football, and they went outside. Preparing to pass, Jack said, "Go long."

Bobby took off, sprinting across the lawn toward the Sound. Jack floated a decent spiral, and Bobby caught it on the run, raising the ball exultantly.

"Hey, we're a good team!" Bobby yelled.

Later that night, Jack stared at a map of the Eleventh Congressional District. It meandered all over greater Boston like the diagram of a spreading disease. It took in Italian East Boston and the North End, but also consisted of solidly Irish Charlestown and a bit of Brighton. Then it wandered across the Charles River and added the cities of Cambridge and the three-deckers of Somerville. It looked like a half-moon braced against the coastline.

Jack had doubts about the predominantly blue-collar, working-class district electing a guy who came from a wealthy family. He'd have to find a way to reach them. He wouldn't be the typical back-slapping, baby-kissing mingler that Boston was used to. That just wasn't him.

Still, his family had a history in the district, which could help. His late fraternal grandfather, P.J., had owned bars in East Boston and had represented it in the state legislature. And Honey Fitz had been elected to Congress in the district and twice been mayor of Boston. The Kennedy name was well known.

However, Jack didn't live in the district now and had only resided there as a student at Harvard. A legitimate charge of carpetbagging could be leveled against him.

No announcement had been made, and papers didn't need to be filed until April for the June 18 special Democratic primary election. In the Democratic stronghold, the winner of the primary was guaranteed election in November.

Jack decided to start campaigning in January and began lining up people in each part of the district who could help him. He was told about Dave Powers of Charlestown. Powers had sold newspapers in the Charlestown Navy Yard and knew thousands of voters. He ushered at five masses every Sunday, and coached local youth athletic teams. There was only one problem—he supported another candidate who lived in Charlestown.

On a bone-chilling, late January evening in 1945, Jack cold-visited Powers. He climbed the stairs to the top of his three-decker home in Charlestown and knocked. When Powers opened the door, Jack put out his hand and said, "My name is Jack Kennedy, and I'm running for Congress."

"Good for you," said Powers, who had recently been discharged from the air force. Unmarried at thirty-four, he lived with his sister and her eight children. Behind Powers, Jack saw several children peering curiously at him.

"I've been told you would be a good person to help me in Charlestown."

"If I help anybody, it would be John Cotter," replied Powers.

"I understand." They talked further, and as he was leaving, Jack said he'd be speaking at a meeting of Gold Star Mothers in Charlestown. "Would you come to the meeting and watch me?"

Powers hesitated. "Well, all right. But that's all."

They met two days later and boarded the subway together. After their car emerged from the tunnel, and they made their way on foot to the American Legion Hall, Powers pointed out neighborhood highlights and key markers of the congressional district. The Bunker Hill Monument was in front of them, the obelisk commemorating one of the first battles of the Revolutionary War. Somerville and Cambridge were to his left, and behind them the North End and East Boston. Below them, longshoremen and freight handlers were working on the docks. "Those are the kind of people you'd represent if you win," said Powers.

Jack had no doubt he'd be interacting with a different set of people than he normally did here in Charlestown. Many came from hardscrabble neighborhoods a world away from his privileged upbringing.

They climbed the elevated tracks across the bridge to the American Legion Hall. Jack entered the hall and looked out over the sea of women before him. Each one had lost a son in the war. While he waited to be introduced, Jack put his hand in his jacket's side pocket. Sometimes he didn't know what to do with his hands. He spoke for ten minutes and then concluded his speech with "My mother is a Gold Star Mother too."

When it was over, Jack was surprised to see the women descend on him. It was half an hour before he could leave. Jack reminded the mothers of their own sons, many of them about Jack's age. Some wept, dabbing their eyes as they shook hands with him or patted him on the back.

BECOMING JFK

On their way out, Jack asked Powers how he had done. "You were terrific," said Powers. "I've never seen such a reaction from a crowd in my whole life."

Jack smiled. "Then you'll be with me?"

Powers said he'd be lambasted in town for supporting a millionaire's son over the local favorite. "They're going to give me hell over here." But he agreed anyway.

In April, Jack officially announced his candidacy and opened a headquarters in Boston near the historic Public Garden. Smaller satellite offices would be opened in each of the district's key communities. He also rented a lightly furnished two-room apartment at the Bellevue in Boston's toney Beacon Hill. Honey Fitz lived just down the hall. The apartment would serve as a place for Jack to sleep and to hold campaign meetings.

Jack's first speeches weren't so much a disaster as they were unsuccessful. In speeches given on international issues before the campaign began, he always felt confident. But whenever the subject was local or state issues, he wasn't in his element and, knowing this, ran through this part of his remarks, rarely looking up to make eye contact with his audience. His voice was a high-pitched monotone.

While making his way out of one event, Jack overheard a woman comment that he looked like "a little boy dressed up in his father's clothes." Another woman said, "Why is his skin so yellow?"

When a woman thrust her baby at him for a kiss, Jack held it away. "That's a cute baby," he said and made his way quickly through the crowd. He wasn't a baby-kisser.

Then after one campaign event in which his speech had failed to generate excitement, Jack sat with his father, feeling uncharacteristically blue. They were talking over what could be improved about his speech. Sitting in the living room of his apartment, sheaths of paper of his speech spread before them, they read through it from beginning to end.

"Jack, right here," his father said, pointing to the beginning. "You've got to look at those folks in front of you and give 'em a smile. You can't just start reading. Folks want to see you, not your hair."

"All right."

"And slow down. It looked to me like you wanted to get the hell out of there. That's no good. You have to do better."

Jack and his father talked about the campaign team and set about assembling a staff with a variety of old and young pols. The campaign slogan became "The New Generation Offers a Leader—John F. Kennedy."

Jack's father had hired John Dowd, an advertising firm owner, as a publicity consultant for the campaign. One afternoon, Dowd visited Jack's campaign office, accompanied by his attractive secretary, who took notes during the meeting.

A week later, as Jack left the office, he caught sight of Dowd's secretary and flashed her a charming smile. "Would you mind taking a memo?" he asked.

"Not at all, Mr. Kennedy," she replied brightly, grabbing a notepad and following him into his office.

Once inside, Jack closed the door behind them. She was simply too pretty to resist, and judging by the look she had been giving him, the feeling seemed mutual.

"All right," he said, moving closer. "Let's get started."

"Anytime you're ready, Mr. Kennedy," she replied with a playful tone. "What would you like me to do?"

Jack smiled. "You don't have to do anything. I'll take care of everything." He began unbuttoning her blouse, and within moments, they were entangled on the desk.

The sound of the door clicking open startled them both. Jack looked up to find a campaign aide standing awkwardly in the doorway.

"Oh, sorry," the staffer mumbled before quickly shutting the door.

Later that day, Jack ran into the same aide in the hallway. With a grin, he quipped, "If I don't have sex once a day, I get a headache."

The aide raised an eyebrow. "Have you considered taking an aspirin—or handling it yourself?"

Jack smirked. "Sure, but I've found this particular method of prevention works best—for everyone involved."

Jack appointed Powers to head the Charlestown campaign headquarters on Main Street. Several of Jack's friends arrived to help out, including Torby and Red. Bobby was assigned the difficult task of knocking on doors in East Cambridge, another stronghold of his leading opponent. But Jack was most heartened to see Lem.

Lem arrived at Jack's apartment one evening while he was enjoying a favorite meal of tomato soup and beer after a busy day of campaigning. Lem said he could only work a week because he'd soon be attending Harvard Business School.

"Great, you can grab that other bed. Promise you won't snore?"

After two weeks, Lem was still around. "You still here, Lemmer? I thought you were wanted at Harvard."

Lem shifted on his feet, slightly embarrassed. "I guess Harvard can wait until the fall. I'm having too much fun."

Jack remembered when Lem, who was a year older, had stayed an extra year at Choate so they could graduate together.

"Good. Now if I lose, I won't be able to blame my defeat on your abandoning the campaign."

Jack recruited young, interesting people to his campaign. He wanted to stay as far away as possible from old-time Boston politicians. When he met somebody who impressed him, Jack said, "Get me some people who haven't been involved in politics. Fellows like yourself, around your age and just out of the service. Call me when you get eight or ten of them, and we'll have a meeting."

Several of Jack's ten opponents were formidable. Chief among them was former state legislator Mike Neville, who had the backing of the Massachusetts governor and many experienced lawmakers in Cambridge and Somerville. Cotter had strong connections in many wards in the district and was an excellent campaigner, Powers told him.

Since his campaign was financed by his father, Jack had more money than the rest, but that was no guarantee of victory. The only way to win was to outwork the opposition.

"Let's go, Jack! They're waiting for you!" shouted Dave from the living room at the Bellevue. Dave had arrived at 6:30 a.m. to get him up.

"Sure they are," Jack replied, bleary-eyed. "They can't wait to shake hands with a millionaire's son before they go to work. That will certainly make their day."

Not long after, they were at the Charlestown Navy Yard gate. For an hour, he shook hands and repeated, "I'm Jack Kennedy, and I'm running for Congress."

The responses were mostly cordial, although one guy said, "I can't support you."

"Why not?" Jack said.

"Because you're a god-damned carpetbagger!"

Jack and Dave got breakfast after the event and discussed the campaign plans for the rest of the morning.

"I suggest we walk up Bunker Hill Street and knock on every door in the neighborhood. These are all three-deckers, Jack. You'll have the opportunity to talk to the Dohertys on the first floor, the O'Briens on the second floor, and the Murphys on the third."

"By that time, I'll be sick of the Irish!" Jack said.

The housewives who opened up their doors were surprised to see a politician first thing in the morning, but Jack thought he saw their eyes brighten when they got a glimpse of his face.

About mid-day, he and Dave took a break to lunch on grinder sandwiches.

"I think those Irish mothers love you, Jack. I can picture them telling their sons tonight that Jack Kennedy was here today, and the family should vote for him. As you know, in an Irish home, the mother's word is law. The son doesn't argue with his mother."

After lunch, Jack and Dave again hit the road. They stopped in barber shops, candy and variety stores, fire stations, and police stations. Even a few taverns. It had been a busy day, but it was only just beginning. They went back to the Navy Yard at four o'clock, this time waiting outside a different gate for the departing workers.

"What do we have for tonight?" Jack asked after they got back to the Bellevue. He leaned back in the rocking chair in front of the fireplace. On the mantel was a double picture frame of his mother and father.

"We've got a full evening of house parties," said Dave. "Four of them. Should keep you busy and out of trouble. The first one is at Ronnie Murphy's house. She's a great gal." His campaign team had aggressively approached young women, schoolteachers, telephone operators, and nurses and asked them to host a party and to invite their friends to meet the candidate.

Jack arrived at 296 Bunker Hill Street shortly after 7:30 p.m. The house was packed with about seventy women standing, sitting, or splayed cross-legged on the floor. Jack waved reservedly and the room quieted.

"Thank you for coming out tonight. I'm Jack Kennedy, and I'm running for Congress." He ended the evening asking for their vote and help. "We always need good people to help out at our Charlestown headquarters." He could see the women's rapt attention and welcomed the approval. After greeting each attendee, it was on to the next party at eight, and two more after that.

"That was a helluva day," said Jack as they drove back to the hotel. "I think we made a lot of progress. The voters are getting to know me whether they want to or not," he added wryly.

His room at the Bellevue was crowded with campaign operatives. His grandfather wandered down. As usual, Honey Fitz belted out the barber shop song "Sweet Adeline."

"Veterans are sure to be in your column, Jack," said a staffer. "We've got to push the war hero angle. Can't miss."

Jack was hesitant. It still made him uncomfortable. His feelings about the PT-109 saga had not been completely resolved. He had so far resisted his father's pressure to reprint the condensed version of Hersey's article that appeared in *Reader's Digest*.

"I don't know if I want to go that route. Turning a sunk PT boat into a campaign advantage," Jack said, during a lunch with his father at Boston's Parker House.

"You're a war hero," he said, pounding the table. "That's going to be important if you want to win this election. You do want to win, don't you, Jack?"

To win, Jack realized he had to use every advantage available to him. "Well, all right. I'll expand on that in my speeches," he said, and agreed to a reprint of the story. "I hope the hundred thousand people who find it in their mailboxes will read it."

In streetcar and subway advertising, the campaign highlighted his appeal to veterans, adding a picture of one to separate placards that showed a housewife, a dockworker, and an executive, proclaiming "Why I'm for Jack Kennedy."

With the campaign in full gear, Jack felt generally pleased with how things were going. Then one day, the staffer who'd walked in on him with Dowd's secretary knocked on his half-closed door.

"Jack, I've got to talk with you. Privately."

"Come into my office."

"Remember the girl you were with when I walked in a couple of months ago?"

Jack nodded.

"She's friends with my wife. She told my wife something you'd rather not hear."

"What's that?"

"She's in trouble."

"Oh, shit. Is she sure it's mine?"

"Yes. Said you were the only one she's been with."

"I don't know if I should take that as a compliment." He couldn't have any complications. Arrangements would have to be made. "Send in Dave Powers, will you?"

When Dave came in, Jack said, "Dave, we've got a problem."

"What is it? What can I do?"

"This is a different sort of problem. You know John Dowd's secretary?"

"Yeah, she's quite a looker."

"Yeah, she is," agreed Jack. "Anyway, she's in a bit of trouble." Jack stared intently at Dave.

"Oh."

"I think you're the guy who could help her get out of that trouble."

"I don't know. Is she Catholic?" Jack shrugged.

"If she's not Catholic and she's all right with this, maybe I could help."

"Good. So, you know people or could find somebody to help her out?"

"Yeah, I guess I do, though as a Catholic, I'm ashamed to admit it."

"Can you take care of it as quickly as possible, Dave? And let her know we'll help her out afterwards."

"Okay, Jack."

"Great," Jack said, standing up. "Knew I could count on you."

Jack and Dave arrived at the Sheraton Commander Hotel in Cambridge, just outside Harvard Square. Building on its successful house parties, the campaign was staging a tea reception for women voters. It was a new kind of politics, and many of the older pols said it would be a waste of time and money. Voters, it was believed, wouldn't get dressed up on a Sunday night just to meet a candidate. Jack wasn't sure it would work either, but it was worth a try.

His sister Eunice had taken charge of the event and corralled twenty-five volunteer secretaries to hand-address thousands of engraved invitations to meet the candidate at a formal reception.

Jack stood with his parents and greeted the attendees. His father was in white tie and tails, and his mother sported a new dress from Paris. While his mother had eagerly attended several of his events, particularly his Gold Star and women-centered events, his father had stayed in the background. Instead, he made calls to the press and harangued campaign managers about every detail.

"Jack, will you look at this?" beamed his father, pointing at the line that snaked around the block. An estimated 1,500 women, some in rented ball gowns, had sent in RSVPs. "It seems you got a way with the ladies." So his wife couldn't hear him, he leaned closer and whispered, "I guess you take after me," before he resumed greeting attendees. "Welcome, don't you look nice.? Thank you for coming."

There was a bevy of beautiful women in the room, and Dave noticed Jack looking at one in particular, a brunette showing a startling amount of cleavage.

"Like her, Jack?"

"Well, who wouldn't, Dave? Would you mind seeing if she would be interested in meeting the candidate later to discuss the issues?"

"I'd be happy to. And hopefully she will be too."

Smiling broadly, Jack walked to the podium. "I'd like to express my appreciation to all of you for coming out today . . ."

Afterward, Dave intercepted the woman and arrangements were made for an assignation.

The event was a resounding success and garnered widespread press. So much so that the campaign decided to organize informal tea parties geared exclusively for women—both young and old. Jack understood he had an advantage with women voters, so he might as well use it.

In the events at American Legion Halls, armories, and in ward rooms, Jack felt more confident in meeting the challenges head on. In Charlestown one night, a heckler tried to raise Jack's ire, bringing up his father's wealth.

"I don't have to apologize for my father or any of the Kennedys," Jack said, parrying the attention away. "I'm running for Congress. Let's stick to that. If you want to talk to me about my family, I'll talk with you outside."

His opponents continually tried to use his wealth as a campaign issue. As he entered a hall one night, Neville pointed to Jack and said, "Here comes the opposition." The crowd turned to see Jack walking in. "Maybe he's going to talk to you about money and how to manage a bank." Neville had criticized the Kennedy strategy as "buy them out or blast them out."

"I'm not going to talk about banking, Mike," responded Jack with a smile. "I'm going to talk about you."

Along with the crowd, even Neville laughed.

With the primary only days away, Jack discussed his purported lead. "I don't know if I trust the polls," said Jack to his driver Bob Morey on the way to a campaign event in East Boston. Two polls showed Jack with a substantial lead. Coming out of the hall after the event, he noticed a group of Sicilians congregating in Maverick Square. Spring was on its way, but there was still icy slush on the streets. The men had turned up their coat collars, and their hands were in their pockets.

Jack grinned and said to Morey, "Those guys look like potential Kennedy voters. Think I'll go over and say hello."

He was met with stony stares, but after he'd met each one, shaken their hands, and exchanged small talk, many of them were smiling.

As they were driving away, Jack saw a car with a Kennedy bumper sticker on the back window. "Turn around and follow him," he ordered. Several miles later, they pulled up alongside the car at a traffic light. Jack rolled down his window and said, "I want to thank you for having my bumper sticker."

"It's an honor, Mr. Kennedy," the stunned man said.

"And don't forget to vote," said Jack before they drove off.

A few miles later, Jack saw one of his campaign signs in a window and told Morey to stop. Jack scampered up the steps, rang the doorbell, and thanked the store owner for his backing. When he returned to the car, Jack was ebullient. "I think we're on our way."

Then suddenly, Jack crumpled in the back seat, exhausted from months of nonstop campaigning. "Dave, do me a favor. Make sure the place is empty when I get back. I need to rest."

His apartment often became a make-shift campaign headquarters late at night when various staffers jammed into the living room and bedroom, smoking cigars and jawing away. Occasionally, they were still there in the morning—smoking and drinking. Not tonight.

Morey stopped at a phone booth. He returned to the car and said, "You're all set, Jack. It will be a quiet evening at the Bellevue. Even Honey Fitz has been told to leave you alone."

When they got back, Jack immediately removed his back brace and took a long sitz bath. "God damn back is killing me," he said aloud.

His skin was still a shade of yellow from the atabrine he'd taken for malaria. For the remainder of the campaign, he took several baths each day, along with daily back rubs from a local boxing trainer. He had to get through the rest of the campaign, but he didn't want to die trying.

"Jack?" Lem, who had been working fifteen-hour days, came into the apartment. He didn't have great political skills, but Jack didn't care. Most importantly, he provided unequivocal support and friendship.

"Everything all right, Jack?!" shouted Lem through the bathroom door.

"I'm good. Well, not good, but okay."

After Jack came out of the bathroom, he said, "Lem, I think we're in good shape." He slumped slightly. "Let's call it a night." He went directly to bed. He'd done everything he could, for this day, at least.

Chapter 39

Winter was now in the rearview mirror, the temperature having turned summerlike. "Jack, I think you should wear a hat," warned Dave. "It's going to be a hot one out there. And humid."

"I'll be all right." Jack preferred not to wear formal hats. They sat high on his head, and he thought they made him look clownish.

It was June 17, Bunker Hill Day, the day before the primary and a major holiday in Boston. Jack would be part of a parade through Charlestown commemorating the Revolutionary War battle there. This was the campaign's final event, and for it the Kennedy campaign had gone all out, taking nothing for granted. Dave and his volunteers had secured Kennedy banners on every other house along the parade route.

Two campaign workers carried a massive twenty-foot wide, five-foot high banner proclaiming "John F. Kennedy for Congress." Jack walked the parade route, nodding and giving an abbreviated half-wave to the crowd. Without losing stride, he accepted a bouquet of flowers from a woman who ran out into the street. Looking back, Jack saw a large flock of his volunteers, more than one hundred of them, all dressed in white shirts. Small rows of the volunteers stretched out the formation so he couldn't see the end.

Jack wiped sweat from his brow. It didn't usually get this hot in Boston in the middle of June, but today was a scorcher. After passing the reviewing stand, Jack felt faint and was tempted to peel off into the crowd. He held off, desperately wanting to finish the route. Then his smile froze, and he began to sag. The end of the parade route was only a few hundred yards away, but he was staggering like a runner at the end of the Boston Marathon. His vision blurred and his legs buckled, his hat falling off his head and dropping to the ground. Campaign workers behind him raced to his aid, locking arms and carrying him away.

Jack had no idea where he was.

State Senator Robert Lee saw the frail candidate crumple. "Follow me! Bring him to my house!" Lee lived nearby, just opposite the reviewing stand.

Jack was laid on the couch, his arms splayed, his eyes closed. He was made as comfortable as possible as cold damp cloths were applied to his forehead.

Lee said, "Jack, can you hear me?"

Jack didn't answer.

Lee dashed to the phone and called the senior Kennedy, who arranged for a doctor to come. Then Lee said to the others, "I'm worried. He's turning yellow and blue. He looks like a man who probably had a heart attack."

There was complete silence in the room as all eyes stared at the gaunt, semi-conscious figure on the couch.

"Do you think he'll be all right?" somebody said.

Nobody answered.

By the time the doctor arrived, Jack had partly revived. His eyes were open, but he was in another world. All he could make out was a blur of figures in front of him.

The doctor checked his pulse and performed a rudimentary examination. "This fellah looks pretty exhausted and fatigued. Frail too."

For several hours, Jack lay on the couch. He gradually regained his senses and before finally sitting up, became aware of smiling faces hovering near him. Miraculously, he seemed to have recovered.

"I guess you were right, Dave. I should have worn a hat—although if I had, it might have cost me votes."

Jack was transported back to his apartment and spent the rest of the day recuperating, but that night he made a final push. He attended the American Legion, Veteran of Foreign Wars, and Amvets open houses, and closed the evening campaigning by dancing at the Armory.

On the day of voting, Jack was accompanied to the polls by his grandparents, the Fitzgeralds. Yesterday's steamer had transformed into steady rain.

"Jack," his grandfather said, grabbing him by the shoulders, "this could be the start of something."

That night, Jack slipped out and took in a movie with Lem. There was nothing else he could do—the electorate was either going to go for him or somebody else. Anyway, he needed a good laugh and the zany Marx Brothers movie *A Night in Casablanca,* he hoped, would provide that. He found a seat where nobody was sitting in front of him so he could put his legs up. Better for his back.

Set just after World War II, the plot had the Marx Brothers running circles around former Nazis who were trying to recover a cache of stolen treasure. Jack was amused at the depiction of the befuddled Nazis and laughed out loud at their antics. He thoroughly enjoyed the movie, particularly Groucho's unique mannerisms and witty double-entendres.

On the way out, he said, "If I lose, maybe I'll act like Groucho," and then he imitated the comedian's trademark cigar flick and raised eyebrows. "It won't matter. Nobody remembers what the guy who lost says, right, Moines?"

Lem gave him a withering look. "Let me just say, I really don't want to see your Groucho imitation tonight. It's not very good."

"All right, you win. Now, let's drop by the campaign offices. I want to thank everyone for all their work."

It wasn't until after midnight that Jack made it back to his Boston

BECOMING JFK

headquarters. By then, the returns were in. The final totals were 22,183 for Jack to Neville's 11,341. He'd won about 42 percent of the vote—impressive in a ten-person race.

Surrounded by family and friends, Jack remained modest about his victory, though his grandfather was anything but. The ever-animated Honey Fitz climbed onto a table and danced a jig, eliciting laughter and applause. Predictably, the strains of "Sweet Adeline" soon followed.

"Of course, I am a happy man tonight," Honey Fitz declared, beaming at the crowd. "John F. Kennedy has brains, industry, and above all, character. He will make a great representative for the Eleventh Congressional District."

The applause roared, and then a call rang out from the back of the room: "All the way!" Someone else picked it up, then another, until the chant swept through the room. "All the way! All the way!"

When the fervor finally subsided, a voice punctuated the moment with a bold addition: "All the way with JFK!" The room erupted again, and even his parents, standing at his side, joined in the chant, their smiles wide and proud.

Jack let his gaze wander over the jubilant crowd—the thrusting fists, the beaming faces, the boundless energy that seemed to promise anything was possible. A quiet thought surfaced amid the noise: *If they believe it, maybe I can too.* He didn't say it out loud, but he allowed himself to wonder. And as the voices rang in his ears, he knew one thing for sure—he was just getting started.

A SUMMING UP

In examining the life and times of John F. Kennedy as portrayed in *Becoming JFK: John F. Kennedy's Early Path to Leadership*, the narrative reveals an extraordinary confluence of privilege, adversity, and character that forged one of the most iconic figures of the twentieth century. This account is not a conventional biography but an exploration of the crucible in which JFK—the second son, the reluctant leader, the eventual president—was formed. These early years were not merely a prelude to greatness; they were the essential proving ground for the resilience, charm, and complexity that would define his legacy.

At its core, JFK's early life is a study in contrasts. He was a young man born into ex traordinary privilege, the scion of a wealthy and ambitious family whose patriarch, Joseph P. Kennedy, demanded excellence and victory at every turn. Yet, for all his advantages, Jack—as he was known to his family and friends—faced a litany of challenges that tested him in ways that wealth and status could not shield. Chronic health issues plagued him from a young age, leaving him often bedridden and isolated. These physical frailties, however, became a source of quiet strength, fostering an inner resilience that belied his outward charm and nonchalance.

This tension between external ease and internal struggle is a recurring theme in JFK's formative years. The competitive dynamic with his elder brother, Joe Jr., looms large throughout the narrative. Joe Jr. was the golden child, the one groomed for greatness, while Jack was often relegated to the role of the rebellious younger brother. Yet, as events unfolded, it became clear that Jack possessed a depth of character and a capacity for growth that set him apart. Whether it was his mischievous exploits at Choate or his early failures in sailing competitions, Jack's setbacks became opportunities for reflection and adaptation. He learned, over time, to channel his frustrations and disappointments into a quiet determination to carve his own path.

The narrative illustrates how Jack's experiences—from his struggles at school to his adventures on the family sailboat Victura—shaped his worldview and emerging leadership style. Sailing, in particular, serves as a poignant metaphor for Jack's life. On the water, he was in his element, navigating unpredictable winds and tides with a combination of skill, intuition, and courage. These qualities would later define his approach to politics and public service: a willingness to take calculated risks, an ability to adapt to changing circumstances, and an unshakable belief in the possibility of triumph even in the face of adversity.

Jack's travels in Europe during his youth were equally formative. Witnessing firsthand the tensions and contradictions of a continent on the brink of war deepened his understanding of international affairs and shaped his global outlook. From observing the rise of fascism in Germany to studying the vulnerabilities of Britain, these experiences provided him with a keen sense of the stakes involved in global leadership. These travels were not mere sightseeing tours but opportunities for critical observation, reflection, and the development of a worldview that would later inform his foreign policy decisions.

Jack's work under his father, particularly as a political aide and observer, offered a different kind of education. Joseph Kennedy's tenure as U.S. Ambassador to the United Kingdom exposed Jack to the intricacies of diplomacy and the pressures of public service. While his father's controversial views and actions during this time often placed the family in difficult positions, Jack's ability to navigate these challenges with discretion and tact demonstrated an early maturity and political acumen. These experiences also reinforced his understanding of the importance of perception, public opinion, and strategic decision-making—qualities that would define his political career.

Jack's early foray into writing, culminating in the publication of *Why England Slept*, further revealed his intellectual curiosity and ability to synthesize complex ideas into accessible narratives. The book, which analyzed Britain's lack of preparedness for World War II, showcased Jack's analytical skills and his capacity to engage with weighty political and historical questions. This work marked the beginning of his ability to communicate effectively on the global stage, a skill that would prove invaluable during his presidency.

The most dramatic and transformative chapter of Jack's early life was his service in the U.S. Navy during World War II. As the commander of PT-109, Jack's leadership and bravery were tested under the most extreme conditions. The harrowing experience of his boat's sinking and his efforts to save his crew demonstrated not only his physical courage but also his unwavering commitment to those under his command. This episode became emblematic of Jack's character: resourceful, resilient, and deeply loyal. It also provided him with a reservoir of credibility and authenticity that would later resonate with voters during his political campaigns.

Yet, it is not only Jack's successes that define his story; it is also his failures, vulnerabilities, and contradictions. His romantic entanglements, his brushes with authority, and his moments of self-doubt paint a portrait of a young man who was far from perfect but who was, in his imperfections, profoundly human. These qualities made him relatable to those around him and, later, to a nation. Jack's ability to connect with people—to make them feel seen and heard—was not a skill he learned in books; it was a natural extension of his personality, honed through years of navigating the complexities of his family, his friendships, and his own ambitions.

BECOMING JFK

As the narrative progresses, Jack steps out from under the shadow of his domineering father and his larger-than-life brother. The tragedy of Joe Jr.'s death in World War II was a turning point, thrusting Jack into a role he had neither sought nor prepared for. In taking up the mantle of the family's ambitions, Jack did not simply mimic the path laid out for his brother; he redefined it. He brought to the role of leader a sense of pragmatism and humility that was uniquely his own. These traits, combined with his innate curiosity and wit, allowed him to connect with people across social and political divides.

The most striking aspect of Jack's early years is his ability to learn from his experiences and grow in the face of adversity. Time and again, he faced situations that could have broken a lesser man: debilitating illnesses, academic struggles, and the relentless expectations of a father who demanded nothing less than perfection. Yet, rather than succumbing to these pressures, Jack used them as catalysts for self-improvement. He developed a remarkable capacity for introspection, for turning his failures into stepping stones and his challenges into opportunities.

By the time Jack entered the political arena, he was no longer the aimless younger brother or the mischievous schoolboy. He had become a man shaped by the trials and triumphs of his youth, a man who understood that leadership was not about the absence of flaws but about the ability to rise above them. This understanding would serve him well in the years to come, as he navigated the turbulent waters of mid-twentieth-century politics and led the nation through some of its most challenging moments.

Becoming JFK is, ultimately, a story of transformation. It reveals how a boy who was often underestimated and overlooked grew into a leader who inspired millions. It shows how the pressures of family, the trials of illness, and the lessons of failure forged a character of extraordinary depth and resilience. And it illustrates how John F. Kennedy's early years laid the foundation for a legacy that continues to resonate to this day.

The trajectory of JFK's life, as explored in this narrative, underscores a profound truth: leadership is not born in moments of triumph but forged in moments of trial. The seeds of his later achievements—from his stirring inaugural address to his leadership during the Cuban Missile Crisis—can be traced back to these formative experiences. The lessons of his youth—humility, adaptability, and resilience—became the hallmarks of his presidency. To understand the man, one must first understand the boy, and in telling his story, this narrative offers a window not only into the origins of a leader but also into the enduring essence of his legacy.

APPENDIX A: LIST OF LOCATIONS

A Life Defined by the World He Touched

By the time he was just 29 years old, John F. Kennedy had traversed more of the globe than most people do in a lifetime. These travels were not merely geographical—they shaped his perspective, informed his values, and set the stage for his enduring legacy. From the bustling cities of Europe to the remote islands of the South Pacific, JFK's journeys reflect a life of curiosity, ambition, and connection.

The following list of locations charts the places JFK visited or lived during the transformative years of his youth, from his days as a student and budding journalist to his heroic service in World War II and his campaign for Congress. Each entry offers a glimpse into the world that shaped one of America's most iconic leaders, capturing the breadth of his experiences and the depth of his engagement with history, culture, and humanity.

A
- Aachen, Germany
- Addis Ababa [town in Ethiopia]
- Algeria (country in North Africa)
- Amsterdam, Netherlands
- Antibes, France
- Athens, Greece
- Austria (country in Central Europe)

B
- Baltimore, Maryland, USA
- Beauvais, France
- Beirut, Lebanon
- Berlin, Germany
- Biarritz, France
- Boston, Massachusetts, USA

- Boulogne, France
- Bremen, Germany
- Bremerhaven, Germany
- Bronxville, New York, USA
- Bucharest, Romania

C

- Cairo, Egypt
- Calais, France
- Cambridge, Massachusetts, USA
- Cannes, France
- Cape Cod, Massachusetts, USA
- Carmel-by-the-Sea, California, USA
- Castle Hot Springs, Arizona, USA
- Charleston, South Carolina, USA
- Chelsea, Massachusetts, USA
- Choiseul Island, Solomon Islands
- Cohasset, Massachusetts, USA
- Cologne, North Rhine-Westphalia, Germany
- Crimea, Black Sea region, disputed territory between Ukraine and Russia

D

- Damascus, Syria
- Danzig, Poland
- Denmark (country in Scandinavia)
- Dublin, Ireland

E

- Edgartown, Massachusetts, USA
- Egypt (country in North Africa)
- El Alamein, Matrouh Governorate, Egypt
- Espiritu Santo, Vanuatu (South Pacific)
- Estonia (Baltic state in Northern Europe)

F

- Frankfurt, Hesse, Germany

G

- Gdańsk [city in Poland]

- Genoa, Liguria, Italy
- Giza, Cairo, Egypt
- Guadalcanal, Solomon Islands
- Guernica [city in Spain]

H
- Holy Land (region of historical and religious significance in the Middle East)
- Hungary (country in Central Europe)
- Hyannis Port, Massachusetts, USA

I
- Innsbruck, Tyrol, Austria
- Irun, Spain
- Istanbul, Turkey
- Italy (country in Southern Europe)
- Iwo Jima, Ogasawara Islands, Japan

J
- Jacksonville, Florida, USA
- Jerusalem, Israel

K
- Kiev (Kyiv), Ukraine
- Kraków, Poland

L
- Latvia (Baltic state in Northern Europe)
- Le Havre, France
- Leningrad (now Saint Petersburg), Russia
- Libya (country in North Africa)
- Lithuania (Baltic state in Northern Europe)
- Little Rock, Arkansas, USA
- London, England
- Los Angeles, California, USA

M
- Martha's Vineyard, Massachusetts, USA
- Melville, Long Island, New York, USA
- Milan, Italy
- Moli Island, Solomon Islands

- Montevideo, Uruguay
- Morocco (North African country)
- Moscow, Russia
- Munich, Bavaria, Germany

N
- Naru Island, Solomon Islands
- New Georgia, Solomon Islands
- Newport, Rhode Island, USA
- Nogales, Mexico
- North Africa (region encompassing countries like Egypt, Libya, and Morocco)
- Norway (Scandinavian country)
- Nuremberg, Germany

O
- Olasana [island in the South Pacific]

P
- Palestine (region in the Middle East)
- Palo Alto, California, USA
- Pearl Harbor, Honolulu, Hawaii, USA
- Peru (country in South America)
- Philippines (country in Southeast Asia)
- Plum Pudding Island, Solomon Islands (now Kennedy Island)
- Poland (country in Central Europe)
- Potsdam, Brandenburg, Germany
- Prague, Czech Republic

R
- Rendova Island, Solomon Islands
- Rio de Janeiro, Brazil
- Riverside, California, USA
- Rochester, Minnesota, USA
- Romania (country in Eastern Europe)
- Rome, Italy
- Russell Islands, Solomon Islands
- Russia (country in Eastern Europe and Northern Asia)

S
- Saint-Jean-de-Luz, France
- San Francisco, California, USA
- Santiago, Chile
- South Holland, Netherlands
- Squantum, Quincy, Massachusetts, USA
- Stalingrad (now Volgograd), Russia
- Stein am Rhein, Switzerland
- Suez, Egypt
- Switzerland (country in Central Europe)

T
- Tulagi, Solomon Islands
- Tunisia (country in North Africa)

U
- Unter den Linden, Berlin, Germany

V
- Valparaiso, Chile
- Vienna, Austria
- Villa Plantation, Martinique

W
- Warsaw, Poland
- Wyntoon, McCloud, California, USA

SOURCE NOTES

The following abbreviations are used:

JFKL-John F. Kennedy Presidential Library, Boston, Massachusetts.

PUL-Princeton University Library, Princeton, New Jersey.

Chapter 1

Jack smiled at the memory, Julius Fanta, *Sailing with President Kennedy* (New York: Sea Lore, 1968), 22-26.

Their father had hired the man, Leo Damore, *The Cape Cod Years of John Fitzgerald Kennedy* (Englewood Cliffs, NJ: Prentice-Hall, 1967), 39.

El Cid had finished ahead of the *Victura*, "The Yachts, Their Names, Skippers, Numbers, Classes," *Martha's Vineyard Gazette,* July 30, 1935.

Never in contention, ibid.

Chapter 2

"And the Dukes County Jail," Damore, The Cape Cod Years of John Fitzgerald Kennedy, 40.

Gloomily, he remembered scribbling, JFKL.

It didn't have the results, "Regatta Entry List of 188 Second Day, Breaks the Record," Martha's Vineyard Gazette, July 23, 1935.

Perhaps that shift had begun, Nigel Hamilton, *JFK: Reckless Youth (*New York: Random House, 1992), 130.

Chapter 3

Joe was revered by the family, Ilene Cooper. *JACK: The Early Years of John F. Kennedy.* (New York: Dutton Children's Books, 2003), 24.

After docking in Hyannis Port, ibid., 68.

Acknowledging the other time Joe had been in lockup, Hank Searls, *The Lost Prince: Young Joe, The Forgotten Kennedy* (New York: World Publishing, 1969), 93.

Milk, JFKL.

He was at St. Francis Xavier Church, Kate Storey, *White House By The Sea: A Century of the Kennedys at Hyannis Port* (New York: Scribner, 2023), 13.

Chapter 4

Jack joined his friends, PUL.

But it wasn't long before his skin yellowed, Hamilton, *JFK: Reckless Youth,* 146-147.

Jack withdrew, ibid., 147.

They hadn't seen anything but desert, ibid., 155-6.

He titled his letter, ibid.,156.

Chapter 5

He recalled Gloria Swanson, Storey, *White House By The Sea: A Century of the Kennedys at Hyannis Port*, 20.

"I don't know why it is," Hamilton, *JFK: Reckless Youth*, 156.

Jack's eyes widened, ibid., 157.

"She is the best-looking thing," ibid., 157.

Chapter 6

"Exam tomorrow," Hamilton, *JFK: Reckless Youth,* 170.

He garnered Cs, ibid., 176.

Demoted, Hamilton, ibid., 166.

Jack was especially excited, Peter Britell, "Kennedy at Harvard: From Average Athlete To Political Theorist in Four Years*," Harvard Crimson,* November 4, 1960, accessed October 23, 2024, thecrimson.com

"Ambitious, spoiled, possessed," Hamilton, *JFK: Reckless Youth* 169.

Chapter 7

During Christmas creak, Jack's father advised him, Frederick Logevall, *JFK: Coming of Age in the American Century, 1917-1956* (New York: Random House, 2020), 139.

After parking their car, Hamilton, *JFK: Reckless Youth,* 179.

In Paris, Jack had used, ibid., 180.

"The bull doesn't have a chance," JFKL.

"They thought the funniest sight," ibid.

"Shows that you can be easily," ibid.

When they arrived in Rome, ibid.

Ever curious to chat, ibid.

"It was none too good," ibid.

When the Germans' arms, ibid.

But as they neared the door, ibid.

They decided on *Swing High, Swing Low*, ibid.

CHAPTER 8

"If Torby can't get in," Hamilton, *JFK: Reckless Youth,* 207.

He closed his eyes, ibid., 208.

The Spee offered conveniences, ibid., 208.

Jack thought he'd stop, ibid., 210.

"The Yale meet," ibid., 219.

Jack got in the pool briefly, ibid., 219.

Instead, the award went to, ibid., 229.

CHAPTER 9

The Kennedys headquartered at the expansive, Logevall, *JFK: Coming of Age in the American Century, 1917-1956,* 177.

It wasn't uncommon for Jack to ask others, *The Kennedy Wealth,* American Experience, pbs.org/wgbh/americanexperience/features/kennedy-wealth/3:~:text=As%, accessed November 18, 2024.

"It is my father's view," Hamilton, *JFK: Reckless Youth,* 237.

They danced a slow rhumba, Cari Beauchamp, "It Happened at the Hotel Du Cap,"

Vanity Fair. March, 2009.

The next day he and Lem attended, ibid., 248.

Chapter 10

Once again, he found himself at the Mayo Clinic, Hamilton, *JFK: Reckless Youth,* 253.

"It's called DOCA," Robert Dallek, "The Medical Ordeals of JFK," *The Atlantic*. December, 2002.

Jack wore the required white tie, Hamilton, *JFK: Reckless Youth,* 255.

Before beginning his journey, Jack attended the coronation of, ibid., 256-257.

He stayed a few days in in Paris, Logevall, *JFK: Coming of Age in the American Century, 1917-1956*, 207.

Chapter 11

In his room, he reached into his trunk, John Gunther, *Inside Europe: Again Completely Revised*. (New York: Harper & Brothers, 1937), 180.

Jack next visited, Robert Dallek, *An Unfinished Life: John F. Kennedy, 1917-1963* (New York: Back Bay Books, 2003), 57, 59.

There was plenty of heiling, Hamilton, *JFK: Reckless Youth,* 262.

"Leave tomorrow for Russia," ibid., 263.

Chapter 12

Jack shuddered and trembled, Logevall, *JFK: Coming of Age in the American Century, 1917-1956*, 201.

He was shocked that, "Historian offers first deep dive into secret German-Soviet alliance that laid groundwork for WWII," *Notre Dame News*, 14 July 2021,

https://news.nd.edu/news/historian-offers-first-deep-dive-into-secret-german-soviet-alliance-that-laid-groundwork-for-wwii/.

In his subsequent travels, Jack visited Leningrad, Logevall, *JFK: Coming of Age in the American Century, 1917-1956*, 212.

Chapter 13

He learned during the voyage from *Inside Europe*, Gunther, *Inside Europe: Again Completely Revised*, 414.

Before that, he'd toured Hungary, Hamilton, *JFK: Reckless Youth,* 264.

Chapter 14

"I see no hope," Hamilton, *JFK: Reckless Youth*, 266.

On June 8, his final evening in Jerusalem, ibid., 266.

Later that week, Jack hired a guide, "John F. Kennedy and one of his sisters ride camels in Egypt in 1939," Getty Images, Corbus Historical, 1 January 1939, gettyimages.com/detail/news-photo/john-f-kennedy-and-one-of-his-sisters-ride-camels-in-egypt-news-photo/615299346.

Chapter 15

On June 27, Hamilton, *JFK: Reckless Youth*, 268.

"The problem is a small group," JFKL.

His father had called them, Hamilton, *JFK: Reckless Youth*, 269.

When White arrived, ibid., 269.

When White slowed down, Logevall, *JFK: Coming of Age in the American Century, 1917-1956*, 217.

Chapter 16

The car was veering, Hamilton, *JFK: Reckless Youth*, 270.

They danced a slow rhumba, Cari Beauchamp, "It Happened at the Hotel Du Cap,"

Vanity Fair. March, 2009.

"Marlene Dietrich's 1930's home movies with John F. Kennedy and Douglas Fairbanks Jr." *YouTube*, uploaded by Spiffykitchen, 10, Nov. 2013, https://www.youtube.com/watch?v=XCeGof3OkV4.

On his way back, Jack ran in to Pell and bragged, William Doyle, *PT 109: An American Epic of War, Survival, and The Destiny of John F. Kennedy* (New York: William Morrow, 2015), 19.

Soon, Jack had his documents, Hamilton, *JFK: Reckless Youth*, 271.

He and Joe were staying, Logevall, *JFK: Coming of Age in the American Century, 1917-1956*, 219.

Jack went back to his room and took out his Zeiss, Hamilton, *JFK: Reckless Youth*, 271.

Inside, Kirk pressed the envelope into his hand, ibid., 272.

Before dawn the next morning, Logevall, *JFK: Coming of Age in the American Century, 1917-1956*, 225.

Jack flew to Glasgow, Hamilton, *JFK: Reckless Youth,* 285.

"It is much better," Logevall, *JFK: Coming of Age in the American Century, 1917-1956,* 226.

"And we get nothing," Hamilton, *JFK: Reckless Youth,* 284.

Among his recommendations, ibid., 285.

Chapter 17

"Send immediately pamphlets," Hamilton, *JFK: Reckless Youth,* 307.

He read the ad, ibid., 320.

Krock directed an agent, Logevall, *JFK: Coming of Age in the American Century, 1917-1956,* 255.

Roosevelt had sent a warm post, Hamilton, *JFK: Reckless Youth,* 336.

But he'd done a curious thing, Logevall, *JFK: Coming of Age in the American Century, 1917-1956,* 268.

Chapter 18

In late August, Jack checked into the Mayo Clinic, Hamilton, *JFK: Reckless Youth,* 342.

He slipped out and found a seminar on contemporary world politics, ibid., 355.

After reading the interview, ibid., 356.

"That's the challenge," ibid., 358.

He decided to take a different approach, ibid., 351.

Flip got to her feet, ibid., 382-383.

The eighteenth blue capsule, ibid., 360-361.

"They will never take me into the army," JFKL.

The fun and games of his West Coast trip, Hamilton, *JFK: Reckless Youth,* 379.

"You know this guy here," ibid., 382.

"When will that outline on that appeasement article," ibid., 383.

"You are an appeaser," ibid., 392.

Chapter 19

Jack sagged, dismayed that his success, Logevall, *JFK: Coming of Age in the American Century, 1917-1956*, 271.

Jack hurriedly sent off a letter, Hamilton, *JFK: Reckless Youth*, 401.

Jack flew to Montevideo, ibid., 404.

Joe, who had argued vehemently, Hamilton, *JFK: Reckless Youth*, 290.

A few days after Joe returned to his base, Doyle, *An American Epic of War, Survival, and The Destiny of John F. Kennedy*, 21.

Chapter 20

Desiring that Jack join him in Naval Intelligence, Logevall, *JFK: Coming of Age in the American Century, 1917-1956*, 292.

The discussion was lively, ibid., 297-298.

Kick hosted her own party, Hamilton, *JFK: Reckless Youth*, 421.

"I told Mother it's not what we want done for Rosie," Elizabeth Koehler-Pentacoff, *The Missing Kennedy: Rosemary Kennedy and the Secret Bonds of Four Women* (Baltimore: Bancroft, 2015), 50.

"To you I need not pretend," JFKL.

Looking to promote Hitler, Goebbels arranged an interview, Hamilton, *JFK: Reckless Youth*, 431, 432.

"I raised my arm and said 'Heil Hitler,'" Hamilton, *JFK: Reckless Youth*, 431.

"I frisked him," Geoffrey Gray, "Dear Inga, Love, Jack," *Alta*. July, 2002.

'To Inga Arvad, in friendly memory,' Scott Farris, *Inga: Kennedy's Great Love, Hitler's Perfect Beauty, and J. Edgar Hoover's Prime Suspect* (Guilford, CT: Lyons Press, 2016), 148.

"One liked him immediately," Logevall, *JFK: Coming of Age in the American Century, 1917-1956*, 305.

On her last trip, Hamilton, *JFK: Reckless Youth*, 432.

Chapter 21

"I am convinced must be an FBI agent," Hamilton, *JFK: Reckless Youth*, 433.

"She's already married," ibid., 440.

It was equipped, ibid., 432.

Underneath the picture, the caption said, Farris, *Inga: Kennedy's Great Love, Hitler's Perfect Beauty, and J. Edgar Hoover's Prime Suspect,* 145.

He telegrammed from New York, ibid., 435.

"One of ex-Ambassador Kennedy's eligible sons," Logevall, *JFK: Coming of Age in the American Century, 1917-1956,* 307.

"They shagged my ass," Hamilton, *JFK: Reckless Youth,* 439.

Chapter 22

"Why don't you come here?" Hamilton, *JFK: Reckless Youth,* 449.

Jack balked at the admission price, Farris, *Inga: Kennedy's Great Love, Hitler's Perfect Beauty, and J. Edgar Hoover's Prime Suspect,* 227.

"I thought I might become pregnant," ibid., 255.

"I heard you had a big orgy," Hamilton, *JFK: Reckless Youth,* 449.

Disturbed about the day's events, ibid., 460.

Jack and Inga spent most of the next day in bed, ibid., 453.

The same day they'd made love, ibid., 457.

Jack arranged for leave, ibid., 474.

A few days later, ibid., 478.

He was afraid of getting soft, ibid., 486.

For What We Fight, JFKL.

Chapter 23

"Have you heard," he kidded Rosen, who was Jewish, Logevall, *JFK: Coming of Age in the American Century, 1917-1956,* 324-5.

Jack walked in to the Quonset hut and announced, "I got shafted," Doyle, *PT 109: An American Epic of War, Survival, and The Destiny of John F. Kennedy,* 33.

Jack decided to go around the chain of command, Hamilton, *JFK: Reckless Youth,* 522.

Jack completed the minimal training session, ibid., 514.

The squadron was off the coast of Virginia, Michael O'Brien, *John F. Kennedy: A Biography* (New York: St. Martin's Press, 2005), 131.

Jack spent three days in bed, ibid., 131.

Chapter 24

But his reverie was interrupted, Logevall, *JFK: Coming of Age in the American Century, 1917-1956*, 327.

The transport listed and the stern lifted, Hamilton, *JFK: Reckless Youth*, 530.

Jack ran to the stern and began passing shells, Doyle, *PT 109: An American Epic of War, Survival, and The Destiny of John F. Kennedy*, 36, 38.

A Japanese pilot's parachute, ibid., 531.

He learned later that it had been the largest Japanese air attack, John Domagalski, "JFK's First Brush With Death," *World War II History*. February, 2016.

Chapter 25

It was PT boat headquarters for the Pacific, Hamilton, *JFK: Reckless Youth*, 532.

Although it was the dry season, Doyle, *PT 109: An American Epic of War, Survival, and The Destiny of John F. Kennedy*, 43.

"All they want is a pipe," Hamilton, *JFK: Reckless Youth*, 541.

"It is the end of my greatly illusioned dream," Farris, *Inga: Kennedy's Great Love, Hitler's Perfect Beauty, and J. Edgar Hoover's Prime Suspect*, 299.

Jack scrambled aboard and into the cockpit, Hamilton, *JFK: Reckless Youth*, 533.

He became adept at maneuvering, ibid., 539.

Jack learned basic pidgin English, ibid., 541.

Chapter 26

He clenched the wooden steering wheel, Hamilton, *JFK: Reckless Youth*, 547.

He worried he might be relieved of his command, Hamilton, *JFK: Reckless Youth*, 547.

A Japanese floatplane, ibid., 553.

In mid-July, Jack learned he'd been reassigned, ibid., 550.

The floatplane dropped its payload, ibid., 553.

"I won't be around much longer," Doyle, *PT 109: An American Epic of War, Survival, and The Destiny of John F. Kennedy*, 64.

Chapter 27

Jack wanted more firepower, Hamilton, *JFK: Reckless Youth*, 554.

Jack had no luck, Doyle, *PT 109: An American Epic of War, Survival, and The Destiny of John F. Kennedy*, 66-67.

"Dive bombers!" ibid., 69-70.

"It looks like the enemy means business," ibid., 71.

"I won't be going home," ibid., 78.

At midnight, Jack received a report, ibid., 86.

Thinking it would be advantageous, ibid., 91.

Chapter 28

"Ship at two o'clock," Doyle, *PT 109: An American Epic of War, Survival, and The Destiny of John F. Kennedy*, 93.

His instinct was to attack, ibid., 93-94.

It pierced the boat, ibid., 95.

"Who's aboard?" ibid., 108.

"For a guy from Boston," ibid., 109.

"I will not allow you to die!" ibid., 111.

"There's nothing in the book about a situation like this," ibid., 114.

"We will swim to that small island," ibid., 115.

"Only the good die young," ibid., 116.

Chapter 29

The eleven men peered through the bushes, Doyle, *PT 109: An American Epic of War, Survival, and The Destiny of John F. Kennedy*, 120.

At first sustenance seemed plentiful, ibid., 137.

But the current had become his foe, ibid., 135.

"Here's Kirksey!" ibid., 136.

"Barney, you try it tonight," ibid., 137.

"We're going to that small one," ibid., 141.

They were astonished to see, ibid., 142.

Chapter 30

"We're saved," Hamilton, *JFK: Reckless Youth*, 590.

"Hello, I'm Kennedy," ibid., 594.

When Liebenow shot four rounds, ibid., 599.

"No thanks, I just had a coconut," 599.

Although a watch had been set, Doyle, *PT 109: An American Epic of War, Survival, and The Destiny of John F. Kennedy*, 169.

"Lieb, to tell you the truth," ibid., 170.

Chapter 31

"At least one of the other boats had seen the explosion," Hamilton, *JFK: Reckless Youth*, 606.

"I thought, my God, I owe Joe Kernell," ibid., 606.

One of them was, ibid., 577.

On August 21, the five-page report, Doyle, *PT 109: An American Epic of War, Survival, and The Destiny of John F. Kennedy*, 290.

"Jack Kennedy believes that the reason," O'Brien, *John F. Kennedy: A Biography*, 59.

Chapter 32

"Why the hell are we out here?" Doyle, *PT 109: An American Epic of War, Survival, and The Destiny of John F. Kennedy*, 184.

"What kind of guy are you," Hamilton, *JFK: Reckless Youth*, 610.

He volunteered for dangerous missions, O'Brien, *John F. Kennedy: A Biography*, 163.

"Let's go get them!" ibid., 188.

"We'll find a place for him," ibid., 190.

After the conflict, Jack hatched his own plan, ibid., 190.

"If there is ever anything I can do for you," ibid., 193.

CHAPTER 33

"Tells Story of PT Epic," Hamilton, *JFK: Reckless Youth,* 638.

He didn't know what he was doing here, Logevall, *JFK: Coming of Age in the American Century, 1917-1956,* 365.

The foursome at New York City's Café Society, ibid., 366.

"I've read accounts," Hamilton, *JFK: Reckless Youth,* 643.

He'd also scheduled his interview, ibid., 644.

"At about ten o'clock, the hulk heaved," John Hersey, *The New Yorker,* June 10, 1944.

Although no ruptured or herniated discs, Logevall, *JFK: Coming of Age in the American Century, 1917-1956,* 369.

They slipped out of the hospital, Hamilton, *JFK: Reckless Youth,* 657.

CHAPTER 34

"I understood that we had," Hamilton, *JFK: Reckless Youth,* 659.

"Where the hell were you," ibid., 659.

"Joe wouldn't want us to sit here crying," Logevall, *JFK: Coming of Age in the American Century, 1917-1956,* 377.

Once, when they were young, Dallek, *An Unfinished Life: John F. Kennedy, 1917-1963,* 54.

A few days later, ibid., 663.

She was shocked at how gaunt, ibid., 663.

CHAPTER 35

Since then, he'd been convicted, Hamilton, *JFK: Reckless Youth,* 674.

"I can feel Pappy's eyes," Logevall, *JFK: Coming of Age in the American*

Century, 1917-1956, 381.

"As I may have told you," Hamilton, *JFK: Reckless Youth,* 674.

But he'd mistakenly opened, Logevall, *JFK: Coming of Age in the American Century, 1917-1956,* 391.

"I just can't understand it," Hamilton, *JFK: Reckless Youth,* 693.

Once again, as he had with Inga, ibid., 684.

Chapter 36

At the behest of Jack's father, Hamilton, *JFK: Reckless Youth,* 687.

Above it was his picture, ibid., 695.

"There is an impression, ibid., 696.

After hanging up, Jack said, ibid., 689.

When their dance ended, ibid., 693.

"Everyone thinks you're doing a fine job," ibid., 704.

Inside each was a copy, ibid., 704.

"It was the best we can get," ibid., 171.

Chapter 37

In his dispatch, Jack noted the differences, Hamilton, *JFK: Reckless Youth,* 716.

Jack joined Forrestal on his C-54 plane on July 28, John Kennedy, *Prelude to Leadership: The European Diary of John F. Kennedy* (Washington D.C.. Regnery Publishing, 1995), 126.

After landing in Berlin, Logevall, *JFK: Coming of Age in the American Century, 1917-1956,* 401.

Jack got out of the car, Hamilton, *JFK: Reckless Youth,* 719.

As they walked, Jack noticed, Kennedy, *Prelude to Leadership: The European Diary of John F. Kennedy,* 110.

"I waved a bottle of wine," ibid., 110.

Before Jack left Berlin, ibid., 107.

They drove up to the Eagle's Nest, ibid., 126.

"Hitler will emerge," ibid., 74.

Jack spent the next couple of days, Hamilton, *JFK: Reckless Youth,* 722.

Chapter 38

The writer said my voice," Hamilton, *JFK: Reckless Youth,* 729.

On a bone-chilling, late January evening, Kenneth O'Donnell, *Johnny, We Hardly Knew Ye: Memories of John Fitzgerald Kennedy.* (Boston: Little Brown, 1972), 55.

They talked further and, as he was leaving," ibid., 59.

Dave had arrived at 6:30 a.m. to get him up, Seth Ridinger, "John F. Kennedy: Public Perception and Campaign Strategy in 1946," *Historical Journal of Massachusetts,* Summer 2013.

After two weeks, Lem was still around, David Pitts, *Jack and Lem: John F. Kennedy and Lem Billings: The Untold Story of an Extraordinary Friendship* (Boston: Da Capo, 2009), 120.

"Call me when you get eight or ten," O'Donnell, *Johnny, We Hardly Knew Ye: Memories of John Fitzgerald Kennedy*, 62.

Jack arrived at 296 Bunker Hill Street, ibid., 71.

Then one day, the staffer who'd walked in on him, Hamilton, *JFK: Reckless Youth,* 737.

For the remainder of the campaign, ibid., 768.

Chapter 39

This was the final event, and the Kennedy campaign had gone all out, O'Donnell, *Johnny, We Hardly Knew Ye: Memories of John Fitzgerald Kennedy*, 78.

"He looks like a man," Hamilton, *JFK: Reckless Youth,* 769.

He attended the American Legion, O'Donnell, *Johnny, We Hardly Knew Ye: Memories of John Fitzgerald Kennedy*, 78.

The zany Marx Brothers, O'Brien, *John F. Kennedy: A Biography,* 204.

BIBLIOGRAPHY

BOOKS

Blair, Joan, and Clay Blair Jr. *The Search for JFK*. New York: G.P. Putnam's Sons, 1976.

Blumenthal, Ralph. *Stork Club: America's Most Famous Nightspot and the Lost World of Café Society*. Boston: Little, Brown, 2000.

Cooper, Ilene. *JACK: The Early Years of John F. Kennedy*. New York: Dutton Children's Books, 2003.

Dallek, Robert. *An Unfinished Life: John F. Kennedy, 1917-1963*. New York: Back Bay Books. 2003.

Damore, Leo. *The Cape Cod Years of John Fitzgerald Kennedy*. Englewood Cliffs, NJ: Prentice-Hall, 1967.

Donovan, Robert J. *PT 109: John F. Kennedy in World War II*. New York: McGraw-Hill, 1961.

Doyle, William T. *PT 109: An American Epic of War, Survival, and the Destiny of John F. Kennedy*. New York: William Morrow, 2015.

Fanta, Julius J. *Sailing with President Kenned*. New York: Sea Lore, 1968.

Farris, Scott. *Kennedy's Great Love, Hitler's Perfect Beauty, and J. Edgar Hoover's Prime Suspect*. Guilford, CT: Lyons Press, 2016.

Goodwin, Doris Kearns. *The Fitzgeralds and the Kennedys: An American Saga*. New York: Simon and Schuster, 1987.

Graham, James W. *Victura: The Kennedys, a Sailboat, and the Sea*. Lebanon, NH: ForEdge, 2014.

Gunther, John. *Inside Europe: Again Completely Revised*. New York: Harper & Brothers, 1937.

Hamilton, Nigel. *JFK: Reckless Youth*. New York: Random House, 1992.

Kennedy, John F. *Prelude to Leadership: The Post-War Diary of John F. Kennedy*, Edited by Deirdre Henderson. Washington DC: Regenery, 1997.

Why England Slept. New York: Wilfred Funk, 1940.

Koehler-Pentacoff, Elizabeth. *The Missing Kennedy: Rosemary Kennedy and the Secret Bonds of Four Women*. Baltimore: Bancroft, 2015.

Larson, Erik. *In the Garden of Beasts: Love, Terror, and an American Family in Hitler's Berlin*. New York: Crown, 2011.

Larson, Kate Clifford. *Rosemary: The Hidden Kennedy Daughter*. Boston: Mariner. 2015.

Leamer, Laurence. *The Kennedy Men: 1901-1963*. New York: William Morrow, 2001.

Logevall, Frederik. *JFK: Coming of Age in the American Century, 1917-1956*. New York: Random House, 2020.

Michaelis, David. *The Best of Friends*. New York: William Morrow, 1983.

Michener, James A. *Tales of the South Pacific*. New York: Random House, 1946.

Nasaw, David. *The Patriarch: The Remarkable Life and Turbulent Times of Joseph P. Kennedy*. New York: Penguin Press, 2012.

O'Brien, Michael. *John F. Kennedy: A Biography*. New York: St. Martin's Press, 2005.

O'Donnell, Kenneth P, and David F. Powers. *Johnny, We Hardly Knew Ye: Memories of John Fitzgerald Kennedy*. Boston: Little Brown, 1972.

Parmet, Herbert S. *Jack: The Struggles of John F. Kennedy*. New York: Dial Press, 1980.

Perret, Geoffrey. *Jack: A Life Like No Other*. New York: Random House, 2001.

Pitts, David. *Jack and Lem: John F. Kennedy and Lem Billings: The Untold Story of an Extraordinary Friendship*. Boston: Da Capo, 2009.

Renehan, Edward., Jr. *The Kennedys at War*. New York: Doubleday, 2002.

Sandford, Christopher. *Union Jack: John F. Kennedy's Special Relationship with Great Britain*. Lebanon, NH: ForEdge, 2017.

Searls, Hank. *The Lost Prince: Young Joe, The Forgotten Kennedy*. New York: World, 1969.

Smith, Jean Kennedy. *The Nine of Us: Growing Up Kennedy*. New York: Harper, 2016.

Stack, Robert Stack. *Straight Shooting*. New York: Macmillan, 1980.

Storey, Kate. *White House By The Sea: A Century of the Kennedys at Hyannis Port*. New York: Scribner, 2023.

Swift, Will. *The Kennedy Amidst the Gathering Storm: A Thousand Days in London*, 1938-1940. Washington DC: Smithsonian, 2008.

White, William. *They Were Expendable*. New York: Harcourt, Brace, 1942.

VIDEOS

JFK: Reckless Youth, Echo Bridge Home Entertainment (2010)

They Were Expendable, MGM (1945)

This is the House that Jack Built, PBS (2017)

RESEARCH COLLLECTIONS

Choate School Archives, Choate Rosemary Hall, Wallingford, Connecticut

Harvard University Archives, Harvard University, Cambridge, Massachusetts

John F. Kennedy Presidential Library, Boston, Massachusetts

Princeton University Library, Princeton, New Jersey

UC Berkeley Library, Berkeley, California

Westfield State University Archives, Westfield, Massachusetts

NEWSPAPERS and MAGAZINES

Alta

Boston Globe

Boston Post

Chicago Sun Times

Harvard Crimson

Life Magazine

New York Times

San Francisco Chronicle

The New Yorker

Vineyard Gazette

Washington Times Herald

World War II History

INDEX

Aaron Ward, 222, 223
Albert, Ray
   on Blackett Strait operation, 250
   drinks everyone's water, 273–274
   Jack asks Ross and Thom to watch, 266
   morale and, 231, 270
   morning after crash, 260
   at Plum Pudding Island, 263–264
   on swimming to small island, 261, 263
Amagiri, 252, 256, 285
Amsterdam visit (1937), 68–69
"Appeasement at Munich: The Inevitable Result of the Slowness of Conversion of the British Democracy from a Disarmament to a Rearmament Policy," 144
Arabs, Palestinian, 115–116
Arashi, 252
Armenians, Turkey's mass slaughter of, 113
Arvad, Inga
   Charleston visits by, 200–203, 205
   FBI phone taps and bugs of, 190
   on her husband coming to Washington, 192–193
   Hitler interview article, 186–187
   interviews Jack after return from Pacific, 299–300
   on Jack's character, 199
   Jack's relationship with, 179–186, 195–196
   Kick introduces Jack to, 174–175
   letters by, 199, 205, 208–210
   Naval Intelligence suspicions of, 193–194
As We Remember Joe (Jack Kennedy), 331
atabrine, for malaria, 294, 362
Atatürk, Kemal, 109
Athenia, 136–139, 199
Athens, senior thesis research in, 118

Atlas, Charles, strength and health program, 209–210
Atlee, Clement, 337
atomic bomb, 346

---

barge-men (local scouts), 272, 273
Baruch, Bernard, 174
A Bell for Adano (Hersey), 303–304
Bemelmans, Ludwig, 321
Bennett, Constance, 41–42
Berlin, 132–134, 337–340, 343
Billings, LeMoyne "Lem"
   in Amsterdam, 68–69
   in Britain, 69–70
   at Choate, 182
   in France, 53–57
   in Germany, 60–68
   in Italy, 57–60
   Jack hints at running for public office to, 318
   Jack on publishing his thesis, 147
   Jack's bid for Congress and, 354, 362, 365
   Jack's concern about war and, 306
   Jack's return from England and, 87
   at Princeton, 5, 33
   Stork Club, New York and, 76–77, 78
   touch football with Jack in DC and, 190–191
Billingsley, Sherman, 78, 79
Biuku (Pacific-Islander scout), 273, 274, 287
Blok, Nils, 206
Bohlen, Charles "Chip," 101–103, 106–107, 328–329
Boston Globe, 300
Boston Herald, 88
Brantingham, Hank, 248–249, 251, 281
Bremen, 87

Breton, 295
Britain, 69–70, 330. *see also* London
British White Paper on Palestine, 115, 117
Brooke, Basil, 335
brownshirts, attack by, 125–126
Bucharest, Romania, senior thesis research in, 118
bullfights, 56–57
Bunker Hill Day parade, 363–364

Cannon, Frances Ann, 168, 303–304
Cape Cod Times, 349
Castle Hot Springs, Arizona, 318–319
Cave Canum, 9
Cawley, Olive, 312
Chamberlain, Neville, 85, 99, 121–122, 136, 141–142
Charleston, South Carolina, 199, 200–202, 209, 210–211
Chelsea, Massachusetts, naval hospital, 210
Chicago Herald-American, 325–328, 329–330
Choate, 4–5, 8, 35
Choiseul Island, 290, 291–292, 293–294
Christiansen, Glen, 292, 294
Churchill, Winston, 136, 146, 330, 333–334
Cluster, Alvin
 on Allies' strategy, 231
 Jack venting after rescue to, 281–282
 on Jack's plan for Choisuel, 293
 on medal for Jack, 287–288
 orders Jack to Tulagi hospital, 294
 on PT boats conversions to gun boats, 289
 on PT-109 plowing into the dock, 235
 as PT-109 squadron commander, 228–229
Cohasset Golf Club, Massachusetts, 5
Congressional campaign
 Eleventh District analysis, 349–350
 final events in, 365
 friends and young people staffing, 354–355
 heat on Bunker Hill Day parade, 363–364
 meeting his constituents, 355–356, 359–361
 opponents in, 355
 Powers and, 350–352
 primary day, 365–366
 PT-109, veterans and, 357–358
 speeches for, 352–353
 unwanted pregnancy and, 358–359
Cooper, Gary, 320, 322
Corio, Ann, 45, 46
Costello, Frank, 78
Cotter, John, 351, 355
Curley, James Michael, 45–46, 317

Damascus, Lebanon, senior thesis research in, 118
Danzig (Free Polish City), 96
de Havilland, Olivia, 320–322
de Valera, Eamon, 335
Dean, Dizzy, 50
Dexter, Thomas A., 18–21, 22–23
Dietrich, Marlene, 86–87, 127–130
DOCA (Desoxycorticosterone acetate), 91–92
Dowd, John, 353
Dublin, Ireland, 334–336

Earhart, Amelia, 138
Eastern Europe, senior thesis research in, 109
Eden, Anthony, 328
Edgartown Regatta
 arrests due to party, 18–20
 Joe, Sr.'s anger after party, 28–29
 party after, 13–18
 races, 5–8, 9–11
 reflecting on arrest, 20–22
Edgartown Yacht Club, 7, 23

Edison, the Man (film), 161
Egypt senior thesis research in, 118–119
Eisenhower, Dwight, 343
El Cid, 9
Eleventh Congressional District, Massachusetts. *see* Congressional campaign
Elizabeth, Princess of England, 92
Elizabeth, Queen of England, 85, 92
Eroni (Pacific-Islander scout), 273, 274–275, 287
Ethiopia, Italian conquest of, 58
Europe. *see also specific countries*
    war in, 221
Evans, Reginald, 277–278

———————————

Farley, James A., 148–149
Fascist Nationalists, in Spain, 55
Fay, Paul "Red," 295, 318, 328, 354
FBI (Federal Bureau of Investigation), 182, 185, 190, 196–197, 202
Fejos, Paul, 176, 192, 193, 194
Ferguson Passage, Solomon Islands
    finding food and, 269
    Hersey on location of, 305
    Naru Island and, 271
    PT-109 crew pass through, 251
    swimming for help and, 266, 267–268, 270
Fish, Bert, 118
Fitzgerald, John "Honey Fitz"
    cigarette girl affair rumor, 46
    Eleventh Congressional District and, 350, 352
    Jack's bid for Congress and, 357, 362
    primary day and, 365, 366
    sea duty for Jack and, 215–216
    football at Harvard, 45, 47, 48–49, 74–76
For What We Fight (speech), 211
Forrestal, James, 307, 336–339, 343–345, 346

400 Club, London, 135
France, Jack and Lem's 1937 visit to, 53–57
Francis I, king of France, 51–52
Franco, Generalissimo, 55, 57
Frisch, Frankie, 50

———————————

Gardiner, Gertrude, 152
Gdańsk, Poland, senior thesis research in, 97–99
George VI, king of England, 85, 92
Germany. *see also* Hitler, Adolf
    invades Poland, 135
    Jack's postwar tour of, 336–341
    pact of steel with Italy, 118
    senior thesis research in, 60–68
    war against Russia and North Africa and, 221
Gizo Island, Solomon Islands, 248, 259, 265, 267
Goebbels, Joseph, 124, 125, 133, 182, 183, 184
Gold Star Mothers, Chestertown, Massachusetts, 351–352
Göring, Hermann, 182–183, 345
Grand Bazaar, Istanbul, 109–110
Gray, David, 336
Graziani, Rodolfo, 58
Greiser, Arthur, 98
Gromyko, Andrei, 329
Guadalcanal, Jack's orders to, 222
Guernica, Spain, Luftwaffe bombing of, 55
Gunboat 1, 290, 293, 303
Gunther, John, 95, 100

———————————

Hagikaze, 252
Harlow, Dick, 48–49, 75
Harriman, Averill, 326–327, 328–329
Harris, Bucky
    Kirksey's morale and, 251
    machine guns and, 228

PT-109 crew and, 227
shooting at Japanese airplanes, 246–247
warship crash into PT-109 and, 257, 259, 266

Harvard University. *see also* senior thesis, for Harvard
  academic record, 47
  acceptance to, 5
  anti-Catholic prejudice at, 5
  football, 45, 47, 48–49, 74–76
  Freshman Smoker, 34, 49–50
  graduation, 145
  Jack visiting Joe at, 33–34
  Joe, Jr.'s graduation from, 81
  late return to senior year, 141
  Spee Club, 73–75
  swim team, 79–80
  war relief fund appeal, 144–145

Haverty, Oklahoma Pete, 36–37

Hayworth, Rita, 326

health issues. *see also* Mayo Clinic; pellets, adrenal extract
  acute gastroenteritis, 217
  allergy to German dog, 67–68
  atabrine, for malaria, 294, 362
  back, 205, 210
  back, sea duty training and, 213
  back, stomach, gonorrhea, 151
  back surgery and recovery, 308–309
  car wreck in France with Torby, 127
  difficulty diagnosing, 33
  gonorrhea, 42
  gut pain, 9
  gut pain and weight loss, 89–92
  hot springs in Arizona and, 318–319
  malaria and colitis, 294
  malaria flare, 346
  post-traumatic stress, 303

stomach and back, 305–307
swim team at Harvard and, 79–80
Tulagi hospital assessment, 295

Hearst, William Randolph, 160
Heinz (hitchhiker), 60–61, 132
Hemingway, Ernest, 78
Henie, Lief, 77
Henie, Sonja, 77–78, 322–323
Hersey, John, 167–168, 235, 303–308
Himmler, Heinrich, 187
Hiroshima, atomic bombing of, 346
Hitler, Adolf
  Arvad and, 182, 183–185, 187
  British Consul General in Gdańsk on placating, 98–99
  Diane Mitford's wedding and, 133
  Eagle's Nest mountain retreat, 344, 345
  German hitchhikers on, 60
  Jack asks Lindbergh about, 94
  Jacks asks his dad about Jews under, 93
  Nazi-Soviet Non-aggression Pact and, 134
  opposition to Communism by, 102–103
  on Poland returning Danzig to Germany, 121
  Reich Chancellery in Berlin of, 337–338
  Sonja Henie and, 322–323
  Sudetenland occupation and, 86

Hofbräuhaus, Munich, 62–63, 124
Hollywood, 39, 157–159, 161–162, 320
homosexuality, 68–69
hookah-smoking, in Turkey, 111–113
Hoover, J. Edgar, 78, 182
Hopper, Bruce, 141–142
Horton, Rip, 5, 33, 76–77, 78
Hotel Du Cap (southern France), 86–87
Huidekoper, Page, 193
Huston, Walter, 320
Hyannis Port, Kennedy home at, 27–28

Hyannis Port Yacht Club, 3, 313
Hyannis Rotary Club, 349

Iles, Johnny, 225–226, 230
I'm for Roosevelt, 145
Imhoff, Susan, 155
Inside Europe (Gunther), 95, 100, 109
Institute of World Affairs, 164
International Exposition, Paris (1937), 55
Istanbul, senior thesis research in, 109–113
Italy, 57–60, 118

James, Henry, 153–154, 161–163
Japan
    aerial attacks on PT boats, 235–236, 246–247
    increased aggression by, 169
    MacMurray on domination in China by, 111
    Pearl Harbor attack by, 191
Jay Six Ranch, Arizona, 35–36, 39–40
Jerusalem, Palestine, 115, 117
Jews, 93, 98, 116, 117–118, 213–214
Johann (hitchhiker), 60–61
Johnston, William, 255, 260, 262, 265–266, 270

Kelly, Commander, 279
Kennan, George, 130 131
Kennedy, Bobby, 28, 171–172, 306, 330, 349, 354
Kennedy, Eunice, 30–31, 168, 171, 172, 178, 359
Kennedy, Jack. *see also* Congressional campaign; Edgartown Regatta; health issues; PT-109; senior thesis, for Harvard; women
    in Amsterdam, 68–69
    Athenia survivors and, 136–139
    in Britain, 69–70
    British war against Germany and, 135–136
    in Cannes, 128–130

car wreck in France, 127
Choate athletics and, 35
chooses new assignment after PT-109 disaster, 288
Churchill's re-election campaign and, 333–334
competition with Joe, Jr., 24, 93, 149–150, 169–171, 218
confession after jail time, 31–32
Edgartown Regatta races and, 5–8, 9–11
on European peace, 70–71
football at Harvard and, 47, 48–49, 74–76
in France, 53–57
on Francis I of France, 51–52
in Germany, 60–68
Harvard's Freshman Smoker and, 49–51
Hersey interview on PT-109 incident, 305–306
on Hitler, 345–346
Hollywood parties, 161–163
home from war and depressed, 301
at Howard Athenaeum, Boston, 45–46
interviewing to write about Joe, 315–316
in Italy, 57–60
at Jay Six Ranch, 35–36
Jim Crow South and, 204
Joe, Jr.'s death and, 312–314
Joe, Sr. as British ambassador and, 85, 86–87
Joe, Sr. on jail time, 29
Joe, Sr. and, 3–4
Lani and, 230–231
on *Leave it to Me!* 88
LST 449 attacked and, 222–224
medal ceremony, 307
messy habits, 74–75
on Mexican bordello, 38–39
midshipman training, 213, 214–215
military draft and, 159

in Munich, 122–126
party after Regatta races, 13–18
on political career decision, 327–328
prewar British embassy work of, 121–122
PT boat at Martha's Vineyard and, 171–172
reads "Survival" to a nurse, 307–308
reflecting on Regatta party arrest, 20–22
religion, Pacific War and, 238–239
return to Hyannis Port after jail time, 28–31
returns to states after thesis research (1938), 139–140
on Rosemary in convent school, 178–179
senior thesis research abroad, 89, 95
speech as inspiration by, 211
speeches, effectiveness of, 332
Stork Club, New York and, 76–79
takes charge after Vineyard jail time, 23–25
touch football with Lem in DC and, 190–191
at Tulagi in the Solomons, 225–226, 281–282, 295
on Warfield and morale, 248
wealth of, 85–86
world affairs debates in Pacific War and, 289

Kennedy, Jean, 28, 313

Kennedy, Joe, Sr.
anger at Joe for drunken party, 28–29
asks Jack to be his eyes and ears in Europe, 92–93
asks Jack to ghostwrite for him, 160–161
as British ambassador, 85, 86, 91, 121–122
on democracy as finished, 142
on Edgartown Regatta races, 3–4, 29–30
enrolls Rosemary in convent school, 178
heat on Bunker Hill Day parade and, 364
on Hitler and Poland, 121
honorary Harvard degree and, 81
on Jack and Inga, 192, 205–207
on Jack and Sonja Henie, 322
Jack finds substitute writer for, 167–169
Jack on rejecting appeasement by, 164–165
on Jack running for Curley's Congressional seat, 317–318
Jack's bid for Congress and, 357, 359
Jack's book's sales and, 167
Jack's campaign speeches and, 352–353
Jack's medal ceremony and, 307
Jack's research in Prague and, 130–131
on Jack's wasting physique, 34–35
on Jack's work in San Francisco, 331–332
Joe, Jr.'s death and, 313, 314, 315
Kennedy creed on winning and, 3–5, 10
Kirk has Jack deliver letter to, 134–135
Los Angeles movie business and, 39
military assignments for his sons and, 217–218
named ambassador to London, 77
on PT-109 incident publicity, 304
sends Jack to aid *Athenia* survivors, 136–138
on U.S. neutrality regarding Europe, 70
visits Jack in San Francisco, 159–160
on war precursors, 122
on *Why England Slept*, 148

Kennedy, Joseph, Jr.
arrest due to Regatta party, 18–20
British declaration of war against Germany and, 135–136
death in bombing mission explosion, 311, 315
as Democratic Convention delegate (1940), 148–149
Edgartown Regatta races and, 5–8, 9–11
father's anger after Regatta party, 28–29
Harvard graduation, 81
at Harvard Law School, 143–144
on Harvard social life, 33–34
as his dad's eyes and ears in Europe, 93
on Jack as 'a smoothie,' 27

Jack in Berlin and, 132–133
Jack's competition with, 24, 93, 149–150, 169–171, 218
Jack's concern about war and, 306
Joe, Sr. as British ambassador and, 85, 86
Joe, Sr.'s expectations of, 3–4
in London, 70
on Rosemary in convent school, 178
volunteers for military service, 169–170

Kennedy, Kathleen "Kick"
British war against Germany and, 135–136
Churchill's re-election campaign and, 333
comforts Jack after *Athenia* survivors mission, 139
F Street Club party hosted by, 174–175
Henry James and, 153–155
on Inga suspected of spying, 192–193
on Jack 's admission of being jailed, 31
Joe, Jr.'s death and, 314–315
on Rosemary in convent school, 178–179
Torby's courtship of, 122
Washington Times-Herald job and, 174

Kennedy, Patricia, 28
Kennedy, P.J., 350
Kennedy, Rose, 30, 300–301, 312–313, 359
Kennedy, Rosemary, 30–31, 177–178
Kennedy, Ted, 30, 150, 301, 302–303, 313
Kernell, Joe, 281–282
Kiley, Jean, 9, 13–14
Kiley family, Edgartown Regatta races and, 9–10
King David Hotel, Jerusalem, senior thesis research in, 115–116
Kirk, Alan, 173
Kirk, Alex, 133–134
Kirksey, Andrew Jackson
Blackett Strait operation and, 251
crew mistake Jack for, 268–269
Jack's flashbacks of, 281, 301

PT-109 crew and, 227, 242–243
shooting at Japanese airplanes, 246–247
warship crash into PT-109 and, 257
Kolombangara Island, Solomon Islands, 248, 252
Komu Island, Solomon Islands, 277
Kristallnacht, 124
Krock, Arthur, 145, 146–147, 167, 175, 328

Lani (Melanesian youth), 230
Lannan, Pat, 319–320, 333, 346
Larson, Bryant, 226, 227
Laski, Joseph, 33, 70
League of Nations, 144
Lee, Robert, 364
Lem. *see* Billings, LeMoyne "Lem"
Lend-Lease, 165
"Let's Try an Experiment in Peace" (Jack Kennedy), 346
Liebenow, Bud, 239–240, 248–250, 278–279
Life magazine, 235
life raft. *see also* PT-109
anti-tank gun replaces, 245
construction of, 261
leaving Plum Pudding, 270
Lennie on survivors riding, 262, 263–264
on PT-109, 229
White's interrogation on, 285–286
Lindbergh, Charles, 93–94, 160
local scouts (barge-men), 272, 273
Lombard, Carole, 65
London, 135, 159–160
embassy in, 92, 121–122
London School of Economics, 33
Love at First Flight (Spalding), 300
Lowrey, John, 248–249, 252, 253
LST 449 (transport vessel), attack on, 222–224

MacArthur, Douglas, 282
MacMurray, John, 110–111
Maguire, John
    crew for PT-59 and, 289–290
    just before collision, 285
    mistakes Jack for Kirksey, 268–269
    PT-109 crew and, 227
    warship bearing down and, 255
    warship crash into PT-109 and, 256, 257
Marie (stenographer), 143
Marney, William, 246–247, 255, 257, 281, 301
Martha's Vineyard, 13–15, 171–172
Marx Brothers, 365
Massachusetts State House, first speech before, 332
Mauer, Edman
    crew for PT-59 and, 289–290
    on morning-after-crash assessment, 260
    PT-109 crew and, 227–228
    raft to small island and, 262
    search for crash survivors, 257
    warship crash into PT-109 and, 255
Mayo Clinic. *see also* health issues
    after Jack's return from Pacific War, 300
    Jack's back and, 325
    Jack's back and stomach pain, 210
    Jack's gut pain and weight loss and, 89–92
    Jack's gut pain and, 9
    Lem's sexual favor and, 68–69
    various ailments, 151
McDonald, Torbert "Torby"
    car wreck in France and, 127
    football at Harvard and, 45, 47, 76
    in Germany, 122–126
    at Howard Athenaeum, Boston, 46
    Jack and, 51
    Jack's ad for typist and, 142–143
    Jack's bid for Congress and, 354
    Jack's messy habits and, 74–75
    Spee Club, Harvard and, 73–74
    visits Jack in Boston hospital, 308–309
    welcomes Jack to Harvard senior year, 141
McMahon, Pappy
    burns of, 265
    Jack towing, to small island, 261–263
    Japanese aerial attacks and, 241
    morale on PT-109 and, 231
    morning after crash, 259, 260
    on Olasana, natives assist, 277
    warship crash into PT-109 and, 257–258
Melanesians, on Tulagi in the Solomons, 225–226, 230, 237–238
Melville, Rhode Island, midshipman training school at, 213–216
Metropol Hotel, Moscow, 101–103
Mitford, Diane, 133
Mitford, Unity, 133
Molotov, Vyacheslav, 326, 327, 329
Moore, Eddie, 47
Morey, Bob, 361
The Mortal Storm (film), 157–158
Mosquito Bites (newsletter), 286–287
Muckers Club, at Choate, 4
Munich, Germany, 62–65, 122–126
Munich Agreement, 96
Murphy, Ronnie, 356–357
Mussolini, Benito, 58–59, 118

———

Naru Island, Solomon Islands, 271–272, 273, 274–275
Nazi-Soviet Non-aggression Pact, 134
Neville, Mike, 355, 360–361, 366
New York Times, 149, 287
The New Yorker, 307
Niagara, 227

Niesen, Gertrude, 50

A Night in Casablanca, 365

Nogales, Arizona, Jack and Jim Wilde in, 38–39, 41

Normandy, 81

North Africa, war efforts in, 221

Northwestern University, midshipman training school at, 211, 213

Nuremberg, Germany, 65–66, 67–68

Office of Naval Intelligence, Washington, D.C., 173–174, 191, 198

O'Hara, John, 51

O'Hara, Neal, 50

Olasana Island, Solomon Islands, 270–271, 273. *see also* Naru Island, Solomon Islands

Orizaba, 139

P-40s, Australian, 292

Pacific War. *see also* Japan; PT-109
    Allies' efforts in, 221
    Jack at war bond funding event on, 304–305
    LST 449 (transport vessel), 222–224

Palestine, senior thesis research in, 115

Palm Beach, Florida, Kennedys in, 34, 167–168, 217–218, 301

Paramount, 39

paternity tests, early 1940s, 152

Patterson, Eleanor "Cissy," 174, 176–177

Pearl Harbor attack, 191

Pell, Claiborne, 127, 128

pellets, adrenal extract, 91–92, 116, 222, 249, 251

Pilgrim's Way, 222

Pius XII, Pope, 93

Plum Pudding Island, Solomon Islands, 263–264, 265

Poland
    Germany invades, 135

Nazi-Soviet Non-aggression Pact and, 134
    senior thesis research in Gdańsk, 97–99
    senior thesis research in Warsaw, 95–97

police, party after Regatta races and, 17–19, 29

Porter, Cole, 88

Potsdam Conference, 337–338

Powers, Dave
    Jack's bid for Congress and, 350–352, 354, 355, 363
    unwanted pregnancy and, 358–359

Prague, Czechoslovakia, senior thesis research in, 130–132

press, Jack's return from England (1938) and, 87–88

Price, Harriet "Flip," 155–156, 164

Princeton, 5, 25, 33, 34

Pritchett, Flo, 303–304

PT boats, 171–172, 213, 214–215, 289, 302

PT-59, 289

PT-101, 216–217

PT-109. *see also* Kennedy, Jack; life raft
    Albert drinks rest of water, 273–274
    Amagiri crashes into, 255–256
    anti-tank gun for, 245–246
    armaments, 229
    assembling the crew, 227–229
    assigned to Jack, 226
    Blackett Strait operation and, 251–252
    celebration after interrogation, 287
    crew arrives Plum Pudding Island, 263–264
    crew swimming to island, 261–263
    escaping Rendova, 247
    food aboard, 229–230
    food and prayer on Olasana Island, 270–271
    Hersey on writing about crash of, 304
    insects and disease aboard, 228
    Jack chooses island to swim to, 269–270
    Jack considers his responses to crash,

283–284

Jack interrogated by White after rescue, 284–286

Jack rescuing survivors of crash, 256–258

Jack swims for help, 266–268

Jack weeping after rescue, 281–282

Jack's bid for Congress and, 357

Jack's flashbacks of crash, 281, 301

Japanese aerial attacks on, 235–236, 240–242

Japanese at Kolombangara Island and, 248–249

Japanese warship crashes into, 255–256

local scouts on Olasana Island, 273

message on coconut for rescue, 274–275

morale aboard, 231–232, 239–240, 243

morning-after-crash assessment, 257–260

Mosquito Bites story on crash, 286–287

natives bring stove and food, 277

Olasana survivors rescued, 278–279

ordered to Rendova, 238–239

ordered to Russell Islands, 233

patrolling with one engine, 242

plows into the dock, 233–235

Ross and anti-tank gun on, 250–251

Ross and Jack canoeing from Naru, 275–276

Ross and Jack find candy and rainwater, 271–272

Ross swims for help, 269

shooting at Japanese airplanes, 246–247

Warfield chews Jack out after rescue, 282–283

PT-157, 248–249, 278–279

PT-159, 248–249

PT-162, 251

PT-166, 250

PT-169, 248–249, 252

Queen Mary, 89

---

raki (Turkish national drink), 110

Rendova Island, Solomon Islands, 238, 246–247, 279. *see also* PT-109

Rip. *see* Horton, Rip

Rochambeau, 221

Romanian princess, Jack in Moscow and, 104–106

Rommel, Erwin, 221

Roosevelt, Franklin

death of, 319–320

declares war on Japan, 191

Joe, Jr. votes at convention against, 148–149

Joe, Sr. rejecting appeasement and, 165

Joe, Sr.'s resignation and, 160

on no convoy for *Athenia* survivors, 138

on *Why England Slept*, 147–148

Rosen, Fred, 213–214

Ross, Barney

arrives at Plum Pudding Island, 264

canoeing from Naru to Olasana, 275–276

crew swimming to small island and, 262

Jack and Thom on surviving and, 266

joins PT-109, 250–251

snail on Olasana Island and, 270

swims for PT-109 crew help, 269

at Tulagi in the Solomons, 225

Royal Palm Club (Tulagi officers' club), 227

Ruppel, Louis, 325, 327

Russ, Pierre, 343

Russia. *see* Soviet Union

San Francisco, United Nations creation in, 325
Santa Lucia, 169
Schnell, Edward, 291–292
Senate of the Free City of Danzig, Gdańsk, 98
senior thesis, for Harvard
    ad for typist, 142–143
    Bucharest, Beirut, Damascus, Athens research, 119
    Egypt research, 118–119
    European research, 89, 95
    Gdańsk research, 97–99
    Istanbul research, 109–113
    Jerusalem research, 115–116
    Krock on rewriting and publishing, 145–147
    Munich research, 122–126
    Prague research, 130–132
    Soviet Union research, 101–107
    stenographers working on, 143–144
    U.S. embassy in London and, 121–122
Shawn, William, 304, 307
Shepherd, Gerald, 98–99
Shigure, 252
Skipper, 7–8, 14, 19, 21, 23, 29
Solomon Islands. *see also* Ferguson Passage; Rendova; Tulagi
    The Slot of, 236
Sonnemann, Emmy, 182–183
South America, Eunice, Rose, and Jack tour, 168, 169
Soviet Union, 55, 101–107, 134, 343, 344. *see also* Molotov, Vyacheslav; Stalin, Josef
Spain, 55, 56, 57
Spalding, Chuck, 300, 301, 320, 322, 325, 327
Spee Club, Harvard, 73–74
Speiden, Jack, 36
St. Francis Xavier Church, Hyannis, Massachusetts, 31–32

Stack, Robert, 157–159
Stalin, Josef, 100, 102–103, 106, 134, 337
Stanford Business School, 152, 164
Stanford Daily, 153, 159
steroid (DOCA), 91–92
Stettinius, Edward, 326
Suez Canal, German–Italian pact of steel and, 118
"Survival" (*New Yorker* story), 307–308
Swanson, Gloria, 39, 42
Swope, Bernard, 174

Taylor, George, 89–92, 116, 222
They Were Expendable (White), 215, 235
Thom, Leonard "Lennie"
    on Allies' strategy, 231
    on anti-tank gun, 245
    Blackett Strait operation and, 253, 255
    coconut on Olasana Island and, 270
    crew swimming to small island and, 262, 263
    Jack on surviving Plum Pudding Island and, 266
    Japanese aerial attacks and, 236–237, 247
    Johnston and Mauer and, 262
    on Kirksey's morale, 243
    Lani and, 230
    local scouts and white skin of, 273
    PT-109 crew and, 227
    PT-109 patrols and, 240
    raft to small island and, 261
    rescue from Olasana and, 278–279
    at Tulagi in the Solomons, 225–226
    warship crash into PT-109 and, 257
Tokyo Express. *see* Japan
Topping, Dan, 322
touch football, 6, 76, 190–191
Tracy, Spencer, 161–162

Treaty of Versailles, Germans and Russians and, 102

Truman, Harry, 337

Tulagi, Solomon Islands, 225–226, 237–238, 281–282, 295

Turkey, senior thesis research in, 109–113

Turner, Lana, 162–163, 326

Ulster, government of, 335–336

United Nations creation conference, 325, 326–327

United Nations Security Council, 329–330

Vella Lavella Island, Solomon Islands, 290

Victura, 3, 6–8, 9, 10, 171, 313

Walsh, David, 216

Warfield, Thomas, 240, 246, 247–249, 277–278, 281, 282–283

Warsaw, senior thesis research in, 95–97

Washington, 53, 70–71

Washington Times-Herald, 149, 174, 175, 197–198

Welles, Orson, 326

Wenner-Gren, Axel, 175, 193–194

Wessel, Horst, 125

whale steak, 73–74

Wheeler, Burton, 174

White, Byron "Whizzer," 122–126, 284–286

Why England Slept (Churchill), 146

Why England Slept (JFK), 145–148

Wilde, Jim "Smoke" or "Smoky," 35–36, 39–40

Wilfred Funk, 147

Wilson, Patricia, 334

Winchell, Walter, 78–79, 197–198

women
- burlesque stripper, 45, 46
- Dowd's secretary, 353–354, 358–359
- Flip, 155–157
- Francis I of France and, 51–52
- German hitchhiker, 60–68
- at Harvard and, 73
- for Harvard freshman football team, 47, 48
- in Hollywood, 41–43
- Inga Arvad, 174–177, 179–187, 189–190, 200–203, 205–209, 299–300
- Jack to Henry James on, 154–155
- Jack's bid for Congress and, 360
- Jack's mother's lack of physical affection and, 66
- Marlene Dietrich, 86–87
- Melanesian, on Tulagi, 237–238
- at Mexican bordello, 38–39
- Olivia de Havilland, 320–322
- Patricia Wilson, 334
- political power and, 329
- in postwar Berlin, 339–342
- Sonja Henie, 77–78, 322–323
- Stork Club waitress, 79
- that Joe had dated, 311, 312

wood plank for Jack's bed, 155, 213

The World Crisis (Churchill), 136

Yale Law School, 144, 173

Zinser, Gerard, 245, 251, 257, 260, 265

ACKNOWLEDGMENTS

In May of 2019, Maryrose Grossman, a prominent archivist at the John F. Kennedy Presidential Library and Museum, invited me to a private showing of JFK's diary and Lem Billings' scrapbook detailing their 1937 European tour. As she carefully turned the withered pages, I became captivated by JFK's remarkable insights and playful jottings, and with Billings' (mostly) remarkable photos.

That viewing set me on the path to explore what JFK's life was like before he ever ran for public office, including the eleven years between the time he graduated from prep school (Choate) until he won his first term as a congressman. During my subsequent research, I found that period to be as engrossing as any in JFK's life. For here is JFK exploring the world despite severe health problems, putting his ideas into print, finding (and losing) the love of his life, escaping death and becoming a war hero, and finally throwing his hat into the political ring.

I had much help along the way. The JFK Library in the Boston area is a treasure trove of information and I immersed myself in it, both in person and online.

The staff members of the JFK Museum in Hyannis, MA were wonderfully helpful.

Locally, the UC Berkeley Library was a valuable resource. Tour guide Becky Alexander assisted me as I investigated JFK's short but eventful stay in Charleston, SC.

I am also indebted to Bob Day and his volunteer crew at *Save the Boat* in Portland, OR. They not only gave me a tour of PT-658 but patiently answered every question I had about the workings of PT boats.

The process of bringing *Becoming JFK* to the printed page was aided by my friends Bruce Yelaska, Lucy Rudolph, Richard Stone, and Mario

Glaviano, all of whom served as sounding boards, advice-givers and, at times, therapists. My editor/coach, Robin Henry, kept me on task and helped me shape the material, and Melissa Stevens was magnificent in making sure the final product was the best it could be.

And finally, thanks to Bruce Bortz, Bancroft Press' founder and publisher, who recognized the potential for another story about young John Kennedy, contributed his own invaluable editing, and again made it into the important book I always thought it should be.

ABOUT THE AUTHOR

Scott Badler is an accomplished writer, educator, and humorist whose diverse career spans journalism, academia, and authorship. A former newspaper reporter, he has contributed extensively to prestigious publications including *The Boston Globe*, where his humor pieces earned him widespread acclaim, as well as *The Dallas Morning News* and *The Connecticut Post*. His essays often explore themes of political history, the Kennedy legacy, and sharp satire.

As an educator, Scott has shared his expertise in Humor Writing at institutions like Harvard and Emerson College. His engaging teaching style reflects his lifelong passion for storytelling and wit.

A California native born and raised in Los Angeles, Scott spent many formative years in the Greater Boston area, residing in the very district where John F. Kennedy launched his political career in 1946. This proximity deepened his fascination with the Kennedys and their impact on American history.

Scott holds a degree from San Francisco State University and a Master's in Education from Cambridge College. Currently, he resides in the San Francisco Bay Area.

He is the author of three insightful and entertaining non-fiction books: *What's So Funny About Looking for a Job?*, *Oh Brother, and Other Revelations on Family, Relatives, Pets, and Sex*, and *JFK & the Muckers of Choate* (Bancroft Press, 2022). His latest work, *Becoming JFK: John F. Kennedy's Path to Leadership*, continues his exploration of one of America's most iconic figures, delving into the experiences that shaped Kennedy's journey to greatness.